CONTENTS

FOREWORD

There is an immense literature of war, so any new entry into that formidable body of narratives, commentaries, analyses, and memories needs to be looked at carefully to see if it adds something significant to our knowledge of war and those who are drawn into it. I believe that this book meets that test and informs and touches us in ways that we will not easily forget.

It has several qualities that strike me as unusual. First, it brings us the thoughts and feelings of veterans not of one war but many wars, going as far back as any living veteran can recall, that is, back to the Spanish Civil War in which Clarence Kailin, now 93 years old, fought. It remains burned in his memory. He is one of the few remaining survivors of that war, and so listening to him is a rare opportunity for all of us. And the stories go right up to that of a veteran of the current war in Iraq.

Second, this is not a random selection. These are veterans with a point of view whose trajectories of belief had many different starting points, took many different paths, but in every case led to an abhorrence of war. We know this is not true of all veterans. Indeed, we find in the reminiscences of war veterans much nostalgia, much glorifying in military heroism, and great reluctance to believe that the wars they fought in may have been not only illegal in international law, but also unjustified in moral terms. This volume is unabashedly anti-war and does not pretend to be a cross-section of veterans' thinking. This selectivity can be defended, I believe, on the ground that anti-war feeling among veterans has not been given the attention it deserves, and that this volume is a modest attempt to correct that imbalance.

Third, the statements are accompanied by photographs, taken at two points in the veterans' lives: when they were in the military; and long after, when they were being interviewed for this book. Aside from satisfying our curiosity about how these soldiers looked then and now, the photographs enhance the stories.

I should add something else from my own point of view as a historian. The history presented to students in our schools, in their textbooks, and too often in their classrooms, has a nationalist bias. That is, it almost always glorifies the wars our nation has engaged in and certainly pays much more attention to acts of heroism on the battlefield than to the heroic acts of those in the military who deserted, rebelled, or criticized the government for carrying on the war.

For instance, the Revolutionary War is generally presented as a noble episode in which the soldiers fought with enthusiasm for the cause of independence from England. What are emphasized are the battles, fought valiantly against great odds: the battle of Bunker Hill, the crossing of the Delaware, the hardships endured bravely at Valley Forge. What is omitted from that story is the amount of desertion, resentment, and rebellion in Washington's army.

There was resentment among the ordinary soldiers as they saw their own needs being neglected while their officers lived in luxury and merchants profited from the war. In October of 1779, in an episode known as the "Fort Wilson riot," soldiers marched into Philadelphia and to the house of James Wilson, a wealthy lawyer and Revolutionary official who had opposed the democratic constitution adopted in Pennsylvania in 1776. In the year 1781 thousands of soldiers in the "Pennsylvania line," were angry at not being paid, at being ill-treated, at being kept in the war beyond their time. They mutinied, dispersed their officers, and marched on the Continental Congress in Philadelphia. They had to be mollified with promises to deal with their grievances. There were more mutinies in the next two years in the "New Jersey line" and again in the "Pennsylvania line."

The war against Mexico (1846–1848) is treated with kid gloves in the traditional histories, and what most often stands out in the minds of Americans is what preceded it, the much glorified "Battle of the Alamo," in which courageous Americans fought to the end against an attacking Mexican army in Texas. But the war itself, after the first flush of patriotism induced young men to enlist, began to lose its glow. Deaths and injuries mounted up and bloody battles accompanied the march to Mexico City. During that march there were thousands of desertions. Some soldiers, Irish immigrants fed up with the war's horrors and not convinced that the war was just (indeed, abolitionists pointed to it as a war to extend slave territory), went over to the Mexican side.

Slavery was certainly central to the Civil War, but most histories emphasize the idealism and the military heroism, and ignore the deep class resentment against the war in both the North and the South. The working class poor in the North were aware of the corpses of their fellow men piling up on the battlefields, while the rich evaded the draft and businessmen amassed fortunes. Thus, there were riots against the draft in 1863 in New York and other cities. In the South, soldiers deserted from the Confederacy in greater and greater numbers, for most of them were not slaveholders, and began to understand they were fighting for the Southern plantation elite. Their own families back home were going hungry, as the planters grew cotton instead of food, because cotton brought great profits.

The Spanish-American War of 1898 was short but hardly the "splendid little war" that U.S. Secretary of War John Hay called it. Some veterans of that war might relish the quick victory. Others, however, might remember that over 5,000 of their comrades died in that war, not from battle wounds, but of sickness resulting from the tainted beef supplied to the army by war contractors.

The United States entered World War I after a powerfully orchestrated campaign to bolster patriotism and overcome the opposition to war that had been expressed throughout the country. It was not long after that war that the veterans, however they might at first have looked back on the war with satisfaction in "victory," began to feel betrayed, especially when the country sank into economic depression barely a dozen years after the war.

The most dramatic manifestation of veterans' disillusionment with "The Great War" came with the "Bonus Army" of 1932, in which more than 20,000 veterans, many of them jobless, their children hungry, marched on Washington to demand of Congress the bonus that had been promised them for their service in the war. Their encampment on the Potomac was destroyed by the U.S. Army using cavalry, infantry, tanks, and tear gas. Two veterans were shot to death and a thousand were injured by gas.

World War II was the "good war," a war generally supported by the people of the United States and still, to this day, regarded by the vast majority of Americans as a just war, a war necessary to defeat Fascism in Europe and Japanese aggression in Asia. It is hard to find a World War II veteran who is not proud of his participation in that war, persuaded that it was a just war.

Indeed, I enlisted enthusiastically in the Air Force, was trained as a bombardier, and dropped bombs on various targets in Europe. Only after the war did I begin to question the moral purity of that war. I still believed that something had to be done to resist Fascism. But my feelings about the war became more complicated. I came to see the bombings of Hiroshima and Nagasaki as only the culmination of a series of atrocities (the word is apt, I believe) committed by the "good guys," our side. The bombing of German and Japanese cities brought about the deaths of probably 200,000 children and a million adults, many of them women and old people.

I began to question the motives of the victorious powers and wondered: Did they enter the war to stop the Japanese from massacring the Chinese? To save the Jews from Hitler's extermination camps? Or were there other motives? The Fascists were as evil a phenomenon as one can imagine, but what of our side: the British Empire, the American empire, the Soviet Union under Stalin? Indeed, 50 million people died in the war. Did it bring a new world? Hitler and Mussolini and the Japanese military leaders were defeated, but there was still Fascism all over the world in various forms. Wars continued, with millions of dead, and an arms race between the Soviet Union and the United States now threatened the very existence of the planet.

In one of the interviews in this book with World War II veterans, Sid Podell, also a bombardier who flew in B-29s in the Pacific (I had flown in B-17s in Europe), reflects on his experience and on the wars that have plagued the world since then. He tells David Giffey: "Warfare, no matter what the nature of the state or its declared purposes, solves no problems." On his lawn, he has a sign: "War Is Not the Answer."

The other World War II veteran in this book, Charles Sweet, who was in the infantry in the Pacific ("Okinawa was mud. Okinawan, Japanese, American soldiers were rotting in the mud"), decided: "I can't think of a valid reason for war." Responding to the usual charge of being "unpatriotic," he says: "I don't like my government. But I love my country."

Whatever the moral complexity of World War II, the wars since then in Korea, Vietnam, Afghanistan, Iraq are devoid of any rational or moral justification, and the testimony of veterans of those wars, recorded in this volume, underlines that conclusion.

They are joined, in this collection, by a veteran of the Israeli army, Esty Dinur, who speaks out of a different context in another part of the world, but comes to a similar conclusion about the futility of violence in dealing with the problems of human beings.

Esty Dinur's appearance in this book testifies to the universality of a truth transcending national boundaries: That whatever problems remain to be solved in the world, we will have to muster all our ingenuity as thinking beings to solve them without massive violence. War, as that sign on Sid Podell's lawn insists, is not the answer.

– Howard Zinn –

CLARENCE KAILIN

Spanish Civil War

I was born August 20, 1914, here in Madison. My life as a pacifist and peace activist will no doubt be seen as strange and contradictory. I got my pacifist leanings from my socialist father, and when I was 20 I joined the Communist Party. Through them I learned all about the Spanish Civil War. I learned that this was not a local affair, but one that had international implications.

Spain's General Franco, in July 1936, rose up in rebellion against the legally elected Popular Front government with the hopes of overthrowing it quickly, restoring the former power of the Church, the landlords, and the military, returning the

Spanish people to their former condition of near-peonage. Because of the heroic resistance of the Spanish people, Franco failed in all of Spain's major cities, but he did take over other areas. As a result, Franco, by prearrangement, requested the military forces of Nazi Germany and Fascist Italy.

Hitler, with his aim of taking over all of Europe in his hope of world conquest, needed Spain. As a result, what started as a local civil war became internationalized. Calls for help by the Spanish Republic to the democracies of Great Britain, France, and the United States fell on deaf ears. To make matters worse, Great Britain and France set up a "Non-Intervention" committee with the express intention of isolating the Spanish Republic, but hypocritically allowing unlimited aid to the Fascist-held areas of Spain.

We understood that the defeat of Fascism in Spain was a necessity if World War II was to be avoided. At that point, the Communist International called for volunteers to fight for the Republic. Over 40,000 people from about 44 countries responded and became the famous International Brigade. During the course of the war, about 2,800 came from the United States. Like so many others, as a Jew who couldn't tolerate Hitler's anti-Semitism, I felt that here was a chance to strike back at Hitler. With another comrade from Madison and four more from Milwaukee, we were the first volunteers of about 35 from Wisconsin. We arrived in Spain on February 2, 1937. Our passports were stamped "Not valid for travel in Spain."

Two weeks later, with no training, I, the pacifist, found myself at the Jarama Front fighting against Fascism. Off and on for almost two years I saw death and destruction, which has been indelibly imprinted on my mind. Here were people who had been trained to kill and were supposed to think nothing of it. And governments spent untold wealth on armies and death-dealing weapons. Civilian areas were laid waste and the people suffered. We frequently fed the kids with our own rations. We didn't find war glorious, as it is so often depicted. In Spain I lost my dearest friend, John Cookson.

At least we did have a cause in defending the Republic from the Fascist invasion. It was, and still is, called "The Good Fight."

That didn't change my mind about war being a criminal abomination. I said that the United States offered no help to the Spanish Republic, hiding behind the 1935 Neutrality Act. During that war, Texaco Oil supplied Italy with enough petroleum products to remain in the war.

It makes a great deal of difference if you know what you're doing there, if you know why you went to war. Of course, after having been there one wants to avoid war at all costs because it's so destructive to everybody. For example, in World War I people were worked up into a frenzy to go defend our country and all this kind of stuff, war hysteria. Many of them were shell shocked from the experiences, which were terrible.

In Spain, while we had no training, we had a good, firm understanding of what that war was about, which a lot of people didn't. I was a member of the Communist Party at that time. I joined in 1935 and subscribed to their newspaper, *The Daily Worker*, which carried a lot of information about Spain and the Spanish Civil War. So we didn't go out of ignorance. We went out with a good deal of knowledge of the fight against Fascism because we understood the expanding nature of Nazi Germany, and that Hitler's aim, of course, was to conquer Europe and the world, if he could. It was a real, terrible danger. Spain was the first country. This was following the elections of February 1936 when the Popular Front came in. Of course, it changed the politics of the whole country. The progressive faction got itself together. There were seven, eight, or nine different political groups that came together and took power away from the church and from the big landowners.

Immediately, the wealthy people, actually Fascists, tried to figure out how to overthrow this government to get it back. So this counterrevolution, you might call it, began on July 18, 1936, led by General Franco and other generals. Their aim was to quickly overthrow the government and give it back to the old rulers, but the people in the big cities like Madrid and Barcelona and others just came out in the streets and resisted, and the coup failed. However, in anticipation of this, Nazi Germany and Fascist Italy were prepared to move into Spain, so from the civil war this suddenly changed. It became very internationalized. It became an invasion from those two countries. And of course Portugal was already Fascist, so it became a base of operations for the Fascists. This is how that conflict started. It had international implications because this was the first time in Hitler's rule that any country had stood up to Germany and Italy.

We understood what was going on, the difficulties that the Spanish Republic was having. Great Britain and France, and the United States as well, betrayed the Spanish Republic, refused them help, and in effect opened the doors to Germany and Italy getting in there. We understood then, and we said it many times and it was written in papers, that if the Spanish Republic should be defeated, it would mean the beginning of World War II. We were trying to stop that wider war.

Of course, it might have been different if Great Britain and France had listened, but their interests were otherwise, very typical of these imperialist countries. Anti-Communism was their key ideology, a fear of Socialism. We got no help from that area. As a matter of fact, France closed off the borders to Spain around March of 1937 so that it was almost impossible to get anything across from France to Spain. Anything in the way of war equipment and so on that had to be shipped had to be done through the port of Barcelona. As a matter of fact, several Soviet ships and, I believe, one British ship were sunk by Italian submarines. We were fairly well blockaded. We wound up with nothing to fight with. The war lasted, though, for three years, which testifies to the endurance and the spirit of the people.

This is what's so important. The political nature of the war and the spirit of the people in that struggle is something that should be preserved. We're doing what little we can. We have some books and a few of us who are able go out on speaking tours occasionally. Of course, we have our own publication, *The Volunteer*, which comes out about four times a year. This is very helpful to a lot of people. It's got a lot of wonderful information. We have the Abraham Lincoln Brigade Archives, which are located in New York University, which have a huge collection of information about the war. Of course, none of this compares with what the United States does when it wants to propagandize its wars.

These efforts at education, that's how we keep on going. There aren't too many of us left, though. There are probably about 70 of us American veterans left of 2,800. About 800 were killed in the war and the rest of us are dying of old age. I'm 93.

The Spanish Civil War was very unique and unusual, probably more so than anything else in the twentieth century. That's another reason why we're struggling to keep this whole history and spirit alive. Of course there were all kinds of resistance struggles around the world at one time or another, but this is something unique in the way of resistance.

Our fight was a fight against Fascism. From our standpoint it was an anti-Fascist war. Of course, the other side always tries to scream "Communism," but that new government had been anything but Communist. It was in many ways middle of the road, but the Republic was very progressive in comparison with what they had, with the monarchy that preceded it.

I was there 22 months. I got into Spain on the 2nd of February 1937, and I left roughly around the 2nd of December of 1938. Getting out was not a simple matter. We were able to take a train down into France, and I can't remember the town or the place where we stayed in France. I do remember we were put behind barbed wire. It was a little concentration camp. France, of course, had moved over to support Germany, and it was getting to be pretty right wing. They didn't mistreat us physically, but we lacked medical care and didn't have things. I had been shot very early in September of 1938 or the very end of August. I had no way of knowing exactly. The Spanish government decided to withdraw all the volunteers with the idea of maybe trying to put an end to the conflict that way, hoping that the Fascists would also withdraw their troops. But of course it didn't happen. We were withdrawn and the war continued. Germany wasn't interested in legalities or the niceties of these situations.

As for the U.S. government, if you were an important person and well known in the struggle, the McCarthy committees later called up a lot of our people to testify. They were asking the people to testify against their own friends and to betray them. Of course, the sensible ones wouldn't say anything. A lot of people went to jail, lost jobs, had their careers ruined. It was a hard time for a lot of people.

How we got along here depended entirely, if we were working, on who the boss was. If he was friendly, everything was fine. If he was very conservative, we had a hard time with him. I was lucky. I had a couple of good bosses and managed to survive. We [Spanish Civil War veterans] asked for veterans' benefits but we were just ignored. We were called "premature anti-Fascists." I don't recall exactly where the term came from. But that was just part of ignoring us. That was typical of what this country was doing all the time anyway, and had been doing, so that was not too much of a surprise.

A lot of us guys (I didn't because of injuries) entered World War II willingly still fighting Fascism. We had quite a number, but the government with their paranoia often did not allow Lincoln Brigade vets who were in the Army to get involved in any of the fighting. They put them off on some island somewhere out of the way.

There was supposedly a younger age limit for going to Spain. Some of them lied about their age. Some were 18 or 19. I think the average was around 25. I was 22. You had a very small number who deserted. We used to talk about it. Our idea was, "Well, if the war was too much for them to stand, go home." And that was it. There were a couple of them who were shot. Not very damn many. There were very few executions, at least within our own ranks, very few. So when we heard about it, we didn't like the idea. I don't know how you'd want to interpret that. An Army has to have a certain amount of discipline to hold itself together. But there was more of self-discipline than anything else. We understood why we were there. We had our own educational methods. We had political commissars who kept up on international affairs. We used to discuss what was going on. There were articles that came out about what was happening within the government. We weren't left in the dark too much, I'll tell you.

We were the first American fighting group that was inte-
grated. We had many black volunteers too. At one point, the
captain of a battalion was killed leading a battle. Here, you
had a black man in authority over white troops, which never
happened before in any American fighting situation. Of
course, so many of us were Communists and the fight against
racism was a key factor in our education. That made a difference in how we dealt with each other, and I never saw any
kind of racial conflict of any sort all the time I was there. Not
a hint of it. It was quite unusual. I can remember when I first
went into Spain, I had an unusual feeling of freedom that I
didn't have here. There was something different. That was a
pretty special situation. Being an anti-Fascist war, there was a
very high percentage of Jewish volunteers from the United
States. They had a special understanding. Here, we felt we
could get a chance to fight Fascism directly. My father was a
Socialist, and so I grew up with those ideas even from the
early age of six or seven. I was aware in a vague way, as much
as a kid could know or feel, about society and rich and poor.
Of course he hated the rich people with a vengeance. It didn't
make any difference if they were Jewish or non-Jewish, if they
were wealthy and made their money screwing people, he
hated 'em. He was very anti-Zionist.

Some people who were brought up with an opposite point
of view and had to change, had to do a lot of inner struggling
to figure out what the hell was going on in the world. What I
learned growing up gave me an understanding of how the economic system worked, how it created what we have. It just
didn't happen out of nowhere. This understanding made it
easier for me to accept what I was doing.

One guy from New York, a fellow by the name of Dave
Engelson, in the clique that I used to hang around with at the
front, told us a story of how he came from a very super-religious
family. One weekend his parents went away to visit some relatives, so he and his brother went out, and he and some friends
bought a piece of ham. They didn't know what it tasted like or
anything. So they went home and put it in the frying pan, ate

most of it, threw the rest in the garbage, and didn't think anything about it.

When the parents came home they smelled the ham and had a fit. They didn't know which dishes had been used. They threw out all the dishes, all the silverware, everything went in the garbage. They kicked the kid out of the house, and he was just a kid. So he had a soapbox and stood up in front of the tenement and began making a speech denouncing his parents. He wanted to come back home because he had no place to live. He had a sister, and the sister told the parents, kind of a fib, she said she was going to marry a Gentile unless they took him in.

I'd say about three quarters of the volunteers were like me in that they were Communists or very close to it, you know. So they had a pretty good idea of what the whole war was about.

We have an enormous amount of educating to do because most of the American public, I don't care if they voted for or against [George W.] Bush, doesn't know what's going on too much. We have a lot of work to do, especially us Veterans for Peace. We have the job of transforming peoples' militaristic kind of thinking, which has been with us for hundreds of years, literally. How do we do this? How do we reach people? I think those that are going into the schools and speaking to the children are doing a wonderful job. It is very important to get the young people to oppose militarism and to not accept the word of the military recruiters that are coming in. They seem to have a pretty free hand to do what they want. We're in a minority, and we just have an enormous job.

When I went to Spain my reasoning was purely political. I saw the dangers of Fascism, which were very real, and this drove me to it. From listening to Vietnam veterans and seeing various movies on the subject, I would say they had a very different experience than I did. In part, the nature of the war, and in part because they were deceived in why they went to war. This deception caused so much emotional harm to them. You can start even earlier with World War I. People went over there "gung ho," fighting a "war for democracy," and this led to emotional disturbances, what they call shell shock. I didn't notice this kind of a thing in Spain.

Here at home, it is easy to see this pattern of dirty politics: Since World War II, the United States was illegally involved in Vietnam, killing at least two million people and laying waste the land, to say nothing about the tens of thousands of Americans who died in that war. We spent at least $150 billion for no reason except trying to restore the old French colonial system.

We killed probably an equal number in the secret bombing of Cambodia. I can't forget the 1953 CIA overthrow of Mosadegh in Iran because he wanted to nationalize that country's oil, or the overthrow of the government of Guatemala to make things safe for United Fruit. How many hundreds of thousands died there since as a result? Must I mention our overthrow of Chile and the years of terror that followed?

There have been many other examples where the United States struck with impunity. I'm thinking of Grenada, Panama, and Yugoslavia; the attacks on Cuba; the billions we spent in Afghanistan. How about the mess we've created in Iraq, the struggle for oil and empire? Paying just for that could solve many of our pressing social needs here at home. This is why I've become more and more of a pacifist. We must find nonviolent, political ways to resolve international problems. This is one of the reasons I joined Veterans for Peace.

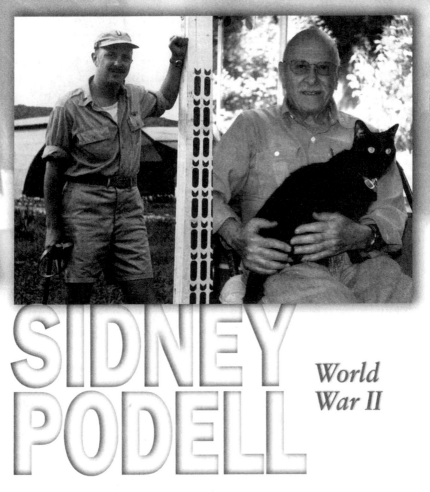

SIDNEY PODELL

World War II

I was born in Milwaukee, Wisconsin in 1920. I lived in Milwaukee. I went to school in Milwaukee. On finishing high school there, I attended the University of Wisconsin from 1938 to 1942. In 1942, I went into the United States Air Force with enthusiasm to participate in the fighting of World War II. I got on a train from Milwaukee and went to an induction center in northern Illinois, and then was shipped to Sherman, Texas. I knew all about German Fascism having lived in Milwaukee. I had observed the German American Volksbund, which was an indigenous native Nazi organization. I picketed at their parade as a high school student, and I was aware of Fascist developments in Europe, both in Italy and particularly in Germany.

When I got to the Madison campus, of course there was a lot of activity and awareness about what turned out to be the impending war. I had to register for the draft, and enlistment for people of World War II was just a step ahead of the draft board. I was attracted to the Air Force for some of the wrong reasons and some of the right reasons. Flying interested me, though I had never had any experience flying.

The Air Force training programs in which I participated were rewarding. My first assignment was to a photography school from which I received an appointment to Officers Candidate School. While waiting for shipping orders I met P-38 photo-reconnaissance pilots and decided that flying airplanes was for me. While in the Aviation Cadet training program, I was taken out of pilot training and transferred to a bombardier school. I graduated as a second lieutenant. After serving as an instructor and in view of the need for bombardiers in the B-29 campaign against the Japanese homeland in early 1945, I became part of a first-rate 11-person B-29 combat flight crew stationed on Saipan in the Mariana Islands. We flew 14 accredited combat missions, each about 3,000 miles of flight over water and hostile Japan.

On the very heavy bombers that I served on, the B-29, there were six officers and five enlisted men. The bombardier was in charge of the gunnery operation. I was responsible for arming the bombs on the way up to the target, and then aiming the bombs and releasing them as per the briefing instructions.

It was 1945 in the early spring until the end of the war, which ended so tragically in the two atom bombs that were dropped. That closed out my flying career. As a result of this military experience I personally suffered nothing like the post-traumatic stress that afflicts so many combat veterans.

I stayed overseas on the island of Saipan until the spring of 1946, and then was discharged. At the time of being discharged I was a first lieutenant and they urged that I reenlist. I would have received an immediate promotion to captain, and then with the same kind of recruiting arguments that they make today—pensions, salaries, promotions, "see the world," etcetera, etcetera. That didn't interest me, so I was discharged.

An added thing is that there was an opportunity to join the Reserve, the Air Force Reserve, which has some relevancy to what's happening currently where large numbers of reservists are involved in the second Iraq War. The recruiting appeal then was—and this was literally true and I did sign up—there were no duties involved, no weekly or monthly sessions to go to, no summer services, just join and the 20 years would start to run, added to the 4 years I had already been in service. At the end of 20 years, I would be eligible for the pension and so forth. I did sign up for that. It was as they represented, no duty involved. I took advantage of the G.I. Bill, went back to the Madison campus, and entered law school. Following graduation in 1949, I opened up my own law office, and began to claw my way into making a living for my wife and soon to-be-born two children.

At that point, the Korean War was heating up and I said, "Holy Mackerel, if I got called up it would be the end of my law career." So I sent them a letter: "Gentlemen, thank you, but I hereby resign." It wasn't done based on some lofty principle of being opposed to the war. It was on the selfish idea that it would have interfered with my law career.

Maybe that's just what Bill Clinton did when he decided that he'd rather go to England as a Rhodes scholar rather than serve his country in Vietnam. I must say I probably made that decision on the same level as the future president of the United States.

During World War II, I was in combat, I earned a few medals, I got a combat promotion, but after the war, following my discharge, like many veterans, I never wanted to talk about those experiences. I would change the subject when people would ask me for some of the details as to what I was up to in combat. However, I will say that after the fighting stopped, after we stopped flying missions, and after the two atom bombs were dropped, I did have one more flight in the B-29. I rode right in the glass nose. We flew over Nagasaki. And we flew over some of the other cities that we had fire bombed.

This is sort of an important background to my thinking today. Our targets were the center of built-up areas of cities. Of those 14 missions, only one was at what I would call a military target. All the rest of them, 13 missions, we salvoed. I triggered a toggle switch that released 20,000 pounds of incendiary bombs on Japanese cities.

Before the atom bombs were dropped, we had run out of targets. I knew as a bombardier having visited the bomb dumps on Saipan that we were planning on dropping 250-pound general-purpose bombs on rice paddies. There were no more military targets to hit in Japan.

I had read about some of the efforts the Japanese were making to surrender even while the war was on, and I had heard some of that even while I was overseas. When I came home I kept telling people my opinion that those atom bombs weren't necessary.

Based on my experience I can fortify that with something else that was very significant. When we got overseas in the spring of 1945, we were at an officer's briefing, and another bombardier asked the question of the intelligence-briefing officer: "If we're shot and we crash land in Japan, do we have to shoot out the bombs?" We all carried .45 pistols. The briefing officer said something that was very unusual. "No you don't have to do that. Matter of fact, if you get captured, tell them anything they want to know. Tell them where you were trained. Draw them a picture how the bombsight works. Tell them all about your family, your commanding officer. All that stuff about torture and you got to keep your mouth shut, name, rank, and serial number ... that doesn't apply here."

The reason, I concluded, for that unusual instruction was that we knew that the Japanese were completely defeated. That wasn't something I read. That was something I experienced.

As a returning student, I joined a veterans' organization that differentiated itself very significantly from the American Legion and the VFW and maybe other organizations. It was a new veterans organization that had different ideas on what the role of veterans should be in civilian society, and that was the American Veterans Committee. I joined the student chapter here in Madison and participated in their meetings and so forth until I left Madison.

The committee had an anti-war thrust, but the goal was to organize veterans to encourage United Nations activities and to help determine the role of the United States in the world during the post-war period. Within the organization there were many prominent members such as FDR Jr., Soapy Williams, Gaylord Nelson, and Jim Doyle. Membership divided into left wing and right wing. I believe the big issue that split the organization and ultimately led to its demise was the difference of opinion over the role of the Marshall Plan in the rebuilding of Europe and particularly the allocation of funds to countries that were pursuing anti-Soviet and anti-Socialist agendas.

After I left Madison, the organization just disappeared. It's gone. It was gone probably by the middle of the 1950s. There might have been 75 to 100 members on the campus during my time there (1946–1949). I was allied with those individuals that felt that we should not be buying influence in countries rather than letting them work out their own destinies. I guess I was on the side of the group that had misgivings at least about the Marshall Plan, if not actual opposition. After I got to be a practicing lawyer in Milwaukee, I lost all contact with that kind of effort.

I grew up during the "Great Depression." Every depression is a "Great Depression" if you're affected and afflicted. You have to understand that I lived in a family where we doubled up housing-wise with my father and mother; I moved in with my grandmother and my mother's unmarried sister. My father planted trees in the parks of Milwaukee as an alternative to getting what they called in those days "outdoor relief" where people went to a food center with a coaster wagon. Those were days of great privation.

With my so-called success in World War II, I rose in the ranks and acquired some leadership roles and some recognition, and then with the help of the G.I. Bill I became a lawyer. I was goal-minded only in terms of building my law practice, which I did. It was a very tough thing to get going because I opened up an office all by myself. From 1950 roughly to 1980,

I was the leader in a small law firm in Milwaukee that consisted of three shareholders, some lawyer employees, and a number of secretaries. I was so involved in developing that law firm and carrying out its activities that I was a member of no organization. I never ran for public office. I made some donations here and there to individuals and groups that I felt were commendable, like the civil rights groups.

On my retirement in the early '80s and my move to Madison, Wisconsin—which was the place of retirement that we elected to settle in—I was confronted with a very vital community, and audited many courses in the history department. I met all kinds of people that were interested in peace. Some of them had participated in the Vietnam protest movement.

I suddenly felt that some of my experiences in World War II had relevancy, and that I ought to speak out. I've been doing that now for the last number of years. I find that the Veterans for Peace group contains many individuals who feel the same way. They are veterans who have had significant military experiences in their lives who ask, "What was that all about?" looking back on it.

I find that I and most Veterans for Peace members are saying to themselves that we didn't accomplish very much as members of the armed forces, and that we have to make that clear to the youth of today. Those experiences are relevant. It wasn't a bolt out of the blue; it wasn't a flash of lightning. It was just reading history. I took a course in European imperialism as it existed in Africa and in India and in the Orient generally. It's very, very obvious how we were used to satisfy the advancement of what it turned out today to be corporate interests.

British imperialism, Belgian imperialism, German imperialism after World War I was not unlike what seems to me is happening in our world today, with my country providing the leadership. The whole history of oil in the Middle East, and the history of the Vietnam War as outlined by Alfred McCoy, whose course I audited, is impressive. It's plain as the nose on anybody's face what our interests were and who we cooperated with and how undemocratic, in every sense of that word, those military adventures were.

We don't have to go back to Smedley Butler, the Marine who looked back on his Central American experience as being worthless. We can look at our own experience. I even will tell you that with regard to the "terrible, horrible Japanese," there was a lot of logic in what they expressed about what happened to their interests in the Far East after World War I and the racism that they were confronted with.

The United States rushing off to war seems to me at this point in my life, in view of these experiences, and my personal experiences, and my education at advanced years, to say: "Sid Podell, you better get out on the street and let your presence be known and join these many good people that are protesting." So, that's what I've been up to.

There are many other issues that come up in one's life when you are in your 80s. All kinds of changes take place, many of which are not so desirable or happy. I've lived a very full life. I don't remember some of the post-World War II recessions because my economic activity was always growing.

Some very dramatic things have happened now in the last number of years. The first Gulf War was extremely dramatic. Intellectually to me that was absolutely not necessary. The Afghan invasion—we could talk long about that. We built up the Taliban. We created the problem. And then there's no solution to it at this point. It just goes on and on and on. Our troops are still there. They and their families say "why." And there is absolutely no future for any of the so-called principles that we feel our country ought to be advancing in the world.

The present Iraq War to me is absolutely pointless: the contracts without bidding, the corporate interests that are being nurtured and expanded. And, of course, there are the other behaviors of our government that are costing jobs in this country and the shifting of the tax burden to poor people away from wealthy, corporate taxation percentages. The percentage of the tax revenues raised in Wisconsin coming from corporations is reducing constantly. The latest thing we've had now is banks aren't paying any taxes by setting up offshore fake corporations. You can read it in the *Wall Street Journal* and the *New York Times* every day. There are major scandals.

With all of these elements of our society, and with the expansion of our military institutions, and the constant official pronouncements identifying opposition to these war efforts and these other events as being "unpatriotic," I feel I'm compelled to participate.

There hasn't been any cost to it. But I am also prepared to pay a price if that comes to pass because I want to stand in the streets. I want to stand wherever I can, with whatever energy I have, and whatever skills I may have. I want my voice to be recorded along with the people who I am now affiliated with in Veterans for Peace.

I just can't stay home when there's a meeting. I do go. I do speak up. The relevancy of my time and service as a vet, as an active member of the armed forces, I think entitles me to speak. On my lawn there's a sign: "War is not the answer." I'm entitled to put that sign in front of my house. I'm entitled to make that statement because I have been to war and I've been in combat.

Unfortunately, some of the biggest voices in expressions of blind patriotism are from people that haven't really wrestled with the threat of military annihilation. That doesn't mean that I'm disparaging them in any way. But I was there. I was in the front.

By the way, I will announce too that I was never the man behind anybody. I was the first. I was in the nose of that damn bomber and everybody else was behind me. When we hit the target, I controlled the airplane through that Norden Bomb Sight. Everybody froze until I said: "The bombs are away." So I'm entitled to speak up. I'm entitled to be heard. I think I would be less truthful to myself if I remained silent at this time of my life.

Although I'm not a physician, I joined the Physicians for Social Responsibility early on. I got some of their literature and I heard some of their speeches where a physician was saying, "If there's another atom bomb don't call me. I'll be either dead or trying to escape. The hospital isn't going to be there." That's just absolute logic.

If you had seen Nagasaki from treetop level like I did, there's no salvaging your interests or your life if you're in that position. When the Japanese surrendered, they were ordered to bring the geographic coordinates of prisoner of war camps all over the Japanese islands. They were ordered to print "PW" on the rooftops and, instead of bombs, we loaded up the bomb bays with food and clothing and medicines, and then we went over at very low altitude and dropped those supplies. After having dropped those supplies, then we went out "sight seeing." That's when I saw Nagasaki.

Veterans for Peace is offering an opportunity. There are other activities that Veterans for Peace has provided and will provide opportunities for activism to people like me. There's a recruiting program by the military in the high schools where tables are set up and recruiters come trying to entice high school graduates to join the military. We feel that there ought to be other points of view. They are omitting telling these youth what lies ahead for them. They're making grandiose claims and so forth. That will be another outlet for somebody like me to be doing things.

There are peace demonstrations of the kind that took place in Madison where, on short notice, just before the reinvasion of Iraq, 2,000 people assembled at the Orpheum Theatre, and another thousand couldn't get in. There were marvelous speakers and a program, people taking oaths against war. I participated in that. That was a real opportunity. There are some demonstrations and parades on the streets. I've participated in that. It's fulfilling.

At this point I'm a little bit influenced by Howard Zinn, the famous historian. Howard Zinn was, like myself, a bombardier in World War II, although he flew in Europe. He was very ideologically motivated to be in that world war as I was. Howard Zinn now takes the position that war is never justified. I'm coming around to that position. I do believe that an organization like the United Nations ought to have some coercive technology and method of controlling and influencing populations that are out of line.

For our nation to fire up and demonize, absolutely demonize, other societies, invade them, crush them, decimate them, that's not the way to advance the welfare of the American people. That's not the way to advance the ideology and the philosophy of the American Revolution and our democratic underpinnings which, by the way, we have to struggle to maintain.

Based on my experience in dropping incendiary ordnance, to use the military term, on Japanese cities, there is no doubt in my mind that had we lost the war against Japan, I would have been eligible for conviction as a war criminal. Imagine my surprise when I read that Robert S. McNamara, an architect of the Vietnam War, confessed to culpability for that war and told of General Curtis LeMay saying to him that had we lost the war against the Japanese, he would have been criminally liable for the bombing of Japanese civilian target cities as he [LeMay] directed. For me this is painful agreement even to this day.

Winning a war expiates one of guilt. The losers are always the criminals. When they talk about rules of engagement, the civilians, women, and children are military targets. They've been military targets in every conflict. The weaponry and the electronics are remarkable to be sure, but there has to be collateral damage. I think civilians have been the target of military campaigns prior to World War II, but not on that scale, in my judgment, with the Germans against Russians and against occupied countries in Europe, the Japanese with Nanking, the Spanish Civil War with Guernica. Civilians were the targets of that aerial bombardment at Guernica. They were fleeing on the highways and planes came over and strafed them.

If you are a fighter pilot and you're carrying bombs under your wing, and your major target, which might be a railroad yard or a factory is obscured, you can't hit your primary target, and you can't find your secondary target as per the orders or the briefing instructions—you don't come back with those bombs. You don't come back with a load of 50-caliber machine gun ammunition in your fighter plane.

You go after what is called a "target of opportunity." You dive down to the earth and expend whatever ordnance you have aboard your fighter plane or your light bomber, and then you come home. You don't ever want to land with a belly full of bombs. How discerning are you when you're diving at mach-something or other, on a ground target that you've picked out of your peripheral vision somewhere. Oops! Sorry, that was a hospital we hit, a school. It happens all the time. How can you regulate this? And how can these young men live with that after it ends?

Warfare, no matter what the nature of the state or its declared purposes, solves no problems. What remains after war are victors and vanquished, with the vanquished relentlessly seeking to be victorious. It never ends, despite advances in human experience. The enemy is always evil, uncivilized, and brutal. Pursuing the enemy always results in the abrogation of sacred human and civil rights.

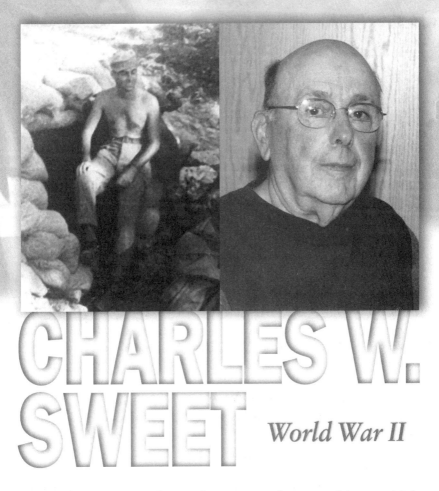

CHARLES W. SWEET

World War II

I was born and raised on a farm in southern Michigan, which is part of the story, because when I got out of the Army, I sold all my guns. When I was on the farm, almost every lad went squirrel hunting with a .22. I had a .22, a 16 gauge, and my dad gave me an old rifle, a musket from the Civil War. I didn't care what the value was. And I had a couple of pistols, you know, for target range. I just sold everything.

I didn't want guns around the house. If I was going to have a family, that was the main thing. I disliked guns because I was a machine gunner in the Army, and it just didn't set with me. And here I had hunted, you know, five or six years. It was September of 1941. I started as a freshman at Michigan State

College, it was called then, at East Lansing, Michigan, which was about 75 miles from home, and of course December 7, 1941, was our entry into World War II.

Early on, in 1942, the draft was instituted. Anybody from 18 to 37 was eligible for military service. I was 18. I finished out my freshman year. There was such a thing as an agricultural deferment, and I was afraid of that. But my dad was the kind that never talked or mentioned it.

So the fall of 1942, when I went back to school, I enlisted right away. I enlisted because I thought the Army couldn't be as bad as working on the farm with my dad, seven days a week, sunup to sundown. If it rained, you had to hoe corn. And I'd always say, "What good can one boy be doing in a corn field, you know, with a hoe you know, and cutting thistles?"

So I enlisted in the Army. The school term ended December 11, 1942, and I was in the Army December 12. I went directly to Fort Custer. Then I was sent to Fort Warren, Wyoming, for basic training. I came from there to the Army Specialized Training School here in Madison to learn conversational German. That was fine, but then I went to Military Intelligence Training School in Maryland for prisoner-of-war interrogation, and then cross-country train to Camp Stoneman, California, near San Francisco, and shipped out to New Guinea. The Battle of New Guinea was over then, but we were in the staging area there and then went to the Battle of Leyte, and that was winding down.

On April 1, 1945 I landed in Okinawa—not on the first wave, but on the third wave. I was there until September 19, 1945, and I was the only one in our group that went to Korea then. The Army of Occupation, Korea, not the Korean War. I was liaison with the Korean Bureau of Investigation in military. I lived in the capital and had a great deal. My first job was with the civilians in the offices in the capital that were in the Korean Bureau of Investigation, I was to make sure they didn't take any light bulbs home, because they didn't have any, and any toilet paper. That was my job.

Later, in February, I shipped back to Fort Lawton in Seattle. I was there two weeks, and it always bugged me, 'cause we were always on K.P. 16 hours a day, and the German prisoners-of-war there, you know, they would laugh at us because they only had to work 8 hours a day under of the Geneva Convention, and we worked 16. We were in the barracks next door.

They'd laugh and make fun of us, and I always remembered, because in some circumstances they knew English better than I did, they knew the "English" English, you know. I mean, they spoke very precisely. Then on April 3, I got out—it was Fort McCoy then. I took a train to Madison and then I went home to my farm in Michigan in 1946, the year after the war ended. I was only in Korea from September of 1945 until sometime in February 1946.

During the war, the main unit I was with was on Leyte and Okinawa. Leyte was the island that General Macarthur landed on. I was in 24th Corps Headquarters. When we went to Okinawa, they didn't know what to do with us. After the second or third day, we were artillery spotters. We went up in the Stinson L5s. We had these young Canadian pilots. They were Warrant Officers without fear. The Japanese put their artillery on the backside of the hill and then moved out and shot over it. And then they pulled back in.

Well, we spotted for three or four days until the main crew came that was trained to do that. Then we were guarding the airstrips. For the Okinawans, it was the only place they had to go. Okinawa was about 15 miles wide, about 60 miles long, and most of it was in the south. The Okinawans, all they wanted was a place to sleep, or food, or drink. And they thought if they went near the airstrips. ... but the Army engineers were building the airstrips. There were about 400,000 Okinawans when the war started. We and the Japanese killed about 100,000. Then they went to camps on the northern side of the island.

We were German prisoner-of-war interrogators. I was very good at German then. You couldn't speak English in class, eight hours a day. You make one mistake, fine. Two mistakes, and you were in Camp Carson, Colorado, in the infantry. So if I didn't know, I didn't talk. But I got into that class by taking a language aptitude test in the Army.

The hard part—it reminds me so much of Iraq—there were no front lines. Politicians in the United States announced that President Roosevelt had died. Harry Truman was President. June 6, General MacArthur, who wasn't even there, announced the battle was over. Big mistake. Worst mistake that was ever made. The battle wasn't over.

Our headquarters were in Nakagasuku Castle. It overlooked the Pacific to the east, and it was tall enough to overlook the East China Sea. It was that tall. But it wasn't a castle like I knew in geography. It had roads. In later days, we built a softball diamond on top. It was that big.

It was made of limestone and dirt. You know, it wasn't like a European castle. And we had all sorts of problems trying to defend ourselves. A lot of the soldiers went to examine caves to get Japanese rifles. Well, not me! We lost several men in our group because of grenades going off. I wouldn't be surprised today if there are Japanese in those caves that don't know that the war is over.

Iraq reminds me so much of that in the sense that we were an army of occupation. Before the war, the Okinawans didn't even have a police force. They were pacifists. They didn't bother anybody in this world. Yet we and the Japanese destroyed a fourth of them.

I was a tech sergeant, and I was in the first group that drew guard duty. And on the sides of the castle were these mammoth walls. There were inlets in there. We put a machine gun up there. Well, just to show you an example, I was on radio control in the radio tent for 24th Corps Headquarters.

And one morning, I think it was about August 3rd—I remember this day, good or bad. We were way up, and down in the valley on one side there was a meadow. The other side was the Pacific Ocean. I heard what I thought was shooting. I got on the radio. No response. So I opened the flap of the tent and I went out two or three times, and I just got nervous. I was trying to raise the 7 Division. This was about 5 a.m. I have a cot, and my carbine, and I looked in my tent, and here was a Japanese lieutenant with a hand grenade right here. And we looked at each other for a second, and I looked at my carbine. I couldn't reach my carbine. It was maybe a couple feet away.

And for some unknown reason, he turned around. He took two steps and pulled the pin. The flesh and bones came right through the tent side. And I thought, what if he didn't step back? What if he tossed it at me? You have normally three seconds on the pin pulls, you have three seconds if it's manufactured right. They aren't all manufactured right.

He had been shot, he was bleeding, he was confused, he didn't know where he was. I don't know how he got past the sentries; I don't know if he climbed a wall. We had 220 men in that castle area. And then the radio came on. It was 96th Division. "There is a Japanese infiltrator in the area." All I could say is, thanks a lot! These things happened all the time. The Japanese weren't going anyplace. They'd come out of the caves.

August 15th, in this country it was officially declared that the Japanese surrendered. But that didn't mean anything to these Japanese in Okinawa. They had no communication. They wouldn't even know. From June 6 until then, we always used to go swimming in the Pacific Ocean in the end part of July. To go down this dirt road, just down the hill, Japanese jumped out from the side of the road and threw a hand grenade at our six-by-six trucks. There were about 12 of us. A guy we used to call the Rooster, that son of gun reached down and tossed it back out. By that time, we all had our carbines with us, and everybody shot the guy, I mean, he was dead. The grenade didn't go off. And you wonder why I'm here.

I was in Okinawa from April 1, 1945, to September 19, 1945. The dates, you know, it's been 57 years. Leyte, it had to be about four or five months before Okinawa. About four or five months. And when we were done there, after we had guard duty and K.P. duty and security duty and everything, we had photo interpretation. The Navy would take pictures of the beaches in Japan and we photo-interpret them, you know, where all of the defenses were, and so forth.

But we didn't go there. We thought we were going there when we left Leyte, but we didn't know we were going to Okinawa. Our officers didn't know, they didn't know we were going to Okinawa until we went. There was no intelligence. The Japanese let all three waves come in. I was in the third wave. We weren't scheduled until later in that morning, it was April Fools Day. The first two waves weren't touched. The Japanese waited until all three waves were inside, and then they really let us have it.

The one unique thing about Okinawa was the highest rate of nonbattle casualties of any war we ever had. Over 47,000 soldiers just lost it. They weren't battle casualties. I mean, they just could not function. They didn't die there. They were shipped back eventually. But they lost—I forget the percentage.

What always gets me, I wasn't prepared. None of the soldiers were prepared—just like Iraq. Most of my buddies in the Corps called the Okinawans "gooks." I thought, why would you do that? There was a slang term, "Japs." I never used it. It was always, "Japanese." You know, that was my upbringing.

I was the only one in our group to go to Korea. For two weeks, I was liaison from the Army, from Seoul to Tokyo. I had that diplomatic pouch, and you sat in C-47s, you strapped along the sides. And the crazy pilots over the China Sea. Oh, they'd throw empty liquor bottles back on the floor, just to see how you'd react. It was typhoon season—it was always the typhoon season there—and it got so I volunteered for this just to get out, but after two weeks I got off. They just didn't have any fear. But those C-47s, I wasn't the only one on the plane, I was just the one who had a diplomatic pouch for Tokyo. Jeez, when I got there, I had a Jeep right there, and it took me to military headquarters and everything.

Churchill, Roosevelt, and Stalin, they determined in Korea that all the Japanese would go back to Japan. These were Japanese in Korea. And the head of the library was Japanese. He knew German. He was the greatest. He had a family, and before I left he had to go back by himself. And I thought, "That's war. There's nothing good about war." That's where I get all mixed up. And then I came back in 1946.

After the war I came back to Madison. My wife, I met her here when she was a student. She promised her dad she wouldn't get married until she graduated. Well, she graduated May 25, 1946, here at the field house on Saturday, and we got married in Plymouth, in Sheboygan County, her hometown, on Sunday, May 26, 1946.

I came back and I started school here, because I was called an Army student. I found a place to stay, 112 Orchard, and that's where I lived. I wasn't going back to Michigan State. I couldn't find a place to live. Housing was really something.

Mr. Thompson, who lived on Dayton Street, he had houses to rent out for people who had come to the University Hospital. They were here temporarily and had somebody in University Hospital. You know, they came from all over the state. I don't know how I got to know him, but when I came to meet Jean I saw "Rooms for Rent," so I went to his house and he sort of says, "Returning soldier." He was a man in his 60s or 70s then. Jean came to visit, and Jean had a ring. He says, "Oh, you're going to get married," and he says, "I'll give you a place to stay." I mean, just out of the blue! She graduated, but she worked in the zoology department as a teaching assistant at the University. I went in on the G.I. Bill, for which I am forever grateful, on $90 a month. Our rent was $35, no car, no insurance. Bus was a nickel downtown. Hey, I had more money than I've had ever since!

I studied accounting. And in 1947, I went to summer school. It was called summer semester then. For G.I.s, they wanted to get you through as soon as possible. Then I got a job right away working for the state as a traveling accountant. I traveled all over the state auditing cooperatives. I graduated June of 1948. I started working January 3, 1949. We went to Michigan to see what the job market was. I didn't want to get into the corporate world. I was a farm boy, you know.

So I worked there until July of 1988, 40 years. When I was 65, I thought, I'm going to retire from this. I retired in June 30, 1988.

But I went to MATC to learn computers because I wanted to do tax work for small business. I was in this class with 20-year-olds. Do you know how fast they went? It was called Beginning Computers. I stuck it out, I don't know how. I had a sympathetic teacher. She was wonderful. They called me the old guy. And I stuck it out. And then for 10 years, till I was 75,

I did small business returns. I didn't want to do individuals because I don't want to know their business.

I was 75, and I thought, I don't really want to work this hard. I had started in January doing taxes for a small business, a hair salon, a smaller restaurant, or something like that, and I would go into June. And then it was always the aftermath, all year long. I still have two or three farms, 'cause I could do farms, 'cause I understood it. I don't want to do them, and I can't charge what it's worth, but I can help people out.

I married Jean Holzschuh—the best thing I ever did in my whole life. She's got projects, and when she's involved, I say, "No more projects. I'll leave. No more projects!" And then she's on the History Committee for Midvale Heights. Next year it will be 50 years old. And there will be a history book. Guess who's working on that!

It's been mostly volunteering I do, since I was an accountant. I haven't volunteered for Veterans for Peace because I've got at least 10 volunteer projects and it takes time. I take tai chi six hours a week and we have a team that goes around doing demonstrations for seniors. That takes time and I'm the treasurer. I'm not complaining because I just want my health. Now that I'm 80, I want my health.

December 2002, Jean and I went to visit Debra in Brooklyn, New York. Deb is our daughter. She was working as a volunteer for the Not in Our Name national office in New York, and also the Refuse and Resist office. In the 1960s, the same time Debra was here, Clark Kissinger was a grad student here. While he was here, he helped start SDS, Students for a Democratic Society. He went back to New York. He organized that big veterans march on Washington. I don't know just what year it was. She worked in his office. We went to his office on Sunday. We were there Friday, Saturday, and Sunday, and she wanted to show us the office and everything. She showed us where everybody sat and where everybody worked. And we looked out the window, and there is where the World Trade Center used to be. I don't know between Jean and her daughter, what they said, but Jean said, "Let's organize a 'Not in Our Name' drive in Madison." So we came back and we started right in at home.

We thought we've got to have help. We'll go to the Madison Area Peace Coalition meeting, and Jean says, "I've never seen such an active group; everybody is so busy. We've got to do this ourselves." That's where it started. We just got started the second week of December, and my nephew, my namesake, died in Memphis. So I wanted to go, and I did. But then all this money was coming in, and I was the accountant, and we were in the midst of everything. I'm glad I went, but I don't like sitting in a funeral parlor where my name is on the plaque that says: "The funeral service is tomorrow at 10:30 a.m. in the chapel." I didn't like that. But we started going to the peace coalition meetings, and that's where I met Don of the Veterans for Peace, and I thought, "Oh, this is perfect."

My interest in peace activism began with our daughter. Jean, my wife, she started right then with Debra. I was just in the background, but I was there. Debra was the kind of person who would never hurt anyone. But yet, you can't change her mind when she starts out on something. She lived in Louisville and then she moved to Cleveland. Deb likes big cities and she was born and raised here on Woodside Terrace. We've been here for over 50 years, the same house. I don't move around much.

In high school, she was determined. When she was between her junior and senior year, she was going to the inner city in Milwaukee and working as a youth worker for the Lutheran Church. I supported her all this time. To show you what kind of person she is, Deb is a very frugal person. She, age 19, was living in Louisville, and she was going to Washington to get some sort of award, but she didn't have a winter coat. So I sent her like $30, which then was like $100. And Debra always wore jeans, a plaid shirt, and lived very modestly. I sent her the money and she sent it back. She says, "I don't need a coat." She could have bought food, besides spaghetti, and she could have bought other clothes to wear. I also remember that. She is just determined.

Charles W. Sweet   37

There were four youths in the United States that got this Young American Medal award. Two got the Young American Medal for bravery and two got it for service. Governor Warren Knowles picked her from Wisconsin. And she was one of the four in the United States that received the medal from the president in the White House. It was December 3, 1970. It was a turbulent time with a growing student anti-war movement in Madison and the whole nation.

This was in the White House and President Nixon said, "These are the good kids that don't protest their government, that do things."

She was the fourth one of the four. Well, when President Nixon presented the medal, she softly told President Nixon she didn't believe in his sincerity in giving her the award until we were out of Vietnam. This was in the White House, and he said, "Well, we're doing the best we can." We stood right behind her with our son, Jeff, and the families of the other three, and the press. The press wanted a picture of him with the group and he says, "I've got another appointment" and hurried out of the Blue Room of the White House.

J. Edgar Hoover is standing right behind her. Poor guy, he could hardly stand up. He was out of it then. He says, "My dear, you were wonderful." He took her hand. They took a picture while she was getting the award, but not with the whole group. Right after that we went to a dinner with the other families. The Justice Department gave us a dinner. We had a limousine move us around. But the family from Chicago shunned us. Their son had saved someone from drowning, I think it was.

I think it was a very courageous stand. I was surprised. I didn't know what she said because Deb is so soft-spoken. She said afterwards, "If he hadn't of provoked me, I was prepared to keep quiet." Jean, at her side, was the only one who heard her. The press did not, so they called her over when they realized how she confronted the president. The story was sent worldwide. It changed her life and our life in a lot of ways. What I didn't know prior, to that, my boss said, "I hear you're going to Washington." I says, "Well, how do you know?" He says, "Well, the FBI came to see me to check you out, to see if I was Communist." He says, "I must have given a good report!"

Debra still sees people that know her. Let's see, she was 19 or 20, and she is 52 now, and it set her pattern, and we followed it. Deb was going to Valparaiso University at the time, in Valparaiso, Indiana, and she was a real church kid. And she got into Christ College, where honor students could get in. She got a partial scholarship. Well, back here, she had been a Sunday school teacher. A committee from the Sunday school said she could no longer teach Sunday school because of what she said to our president. We've been her biggest fans, and with Not in Our Name, we were very successful.

I didn't talk about my war experience for 50 years. War is so terrible. Here is an instance. They surrendered in Europe when we were in Okinawa. When the news come that they had surrendered, there were 6,000 ships around Okinawa. When they surrendered, they celebrated with small arms. We ate alphabetically. I was S, I was way at the end, I wasn't even getting in line yet. And I heard these mess kits, something hitting 'em. Well, Bob Bentley from New Jersey, he was a pianist. He was dead. And we were celebrating Europe. Friendly fire!

Okinawa was mud. We were most fortunate after we moved to the castle. We got rid of all that. We didn't sleep in cots in the mud. The next year, the Okinawans, Japanese, American soldiers were rotting in the mud. You don't get over it. They just rot there. There's no … how can you … you can't even get them out, the medics can't even get there. Okinawa … I still think so. In Iraq, they have the heat. We didn't have the heat. We had the monsoon rains and the mud.

It was all hand-to-hand combat. Now, ours were spasmodic. We were on this side of the castle with the machine gun, and we had flares out on this meadow, so if something hit it. … I took a two-hour stint same as the rest of the guys. Just because I was a tech sergeant, that didn't mean anything to me. I think it was 1:30 or 2 a.m. the flares went up. And you had a spotlight, but I never used a spotlight, because if you use a spotlight, you're right behind it. The flares went up, and I took that machine gun and I just went side to side. And of course I woke up the whole camp. They came, and it was dark yet, and nobody was going out there. In the morning, we surveyed it, and I had killed two water buffalo. They had hit the trip wire.

War is so terrible. Any alternative is better. Every alternative is better. I go back to it, the soldiers were not prepared for anything once the battle is over. They always called me "college boy" good-naturedly, you know, and you were supposed to know everything. Well, I didn't. I was only a year off the farm.

I guess, I can't think of a valid reason for war, when you think what it does for people. Why does everything have to be war. See now, the flag infuriates me, not that I don't love my country, because I love my country more than anybody. I don't like my government, but I love my country. And the flag says, "Fly me to be patriotic." Now, as far as I'm concerned, we're still at war. I relate it to Okinawa. We're still at war.

I thought, with the flag, why be patriotic now? Shouldn't you be patriotic the whole time? I love my country. I wouldn't watch pictures of Vietnam. I couldn't watch it. If the radio was turned to war ... Somebody wanted to take me to see *Saving Private Ryan*, the movie. I did not go. That's the last place in the world I'd go, you know? It's too perplexing to me from the viewpoint of: I know what war isn't, and what it is, and the accidents of it.

Veterans may not be teachers in the way we know it specifically. But you have to live the life of whatever you do towards peace. Now, I can back that up a little bit by maybe going to Debra. When she wasn't allowed to teach Sunday school and, in effect, kicked out of church, Jean and I left, too. I was the treasurer. I was on their council. I was on their building committee.

I thought, I've got to believe in God. Jesus Christ said, didn't he say, "Blessed are the peacemakers." What happened, you know? My pastor was a wonderful guy, but he couldn't take sides in the Vietnam War. He would not take sides. We were good friends, and he could not take sides because he was afraid he would split the congregation in two. And he would've, but the council took sides. So my religion is to respect all human beings, do the best you can on the environment, and be an honest person. That's all I can hope for. I can't say I miss going to church.

To show you how odd it is, last spring was the 50th anniversary of this church, and since we were there from the beginning, we went to a service that was very nice, and the Sheraton had a noon banquet. You'd be surprised how many people still said, "What service do you go to?" I says, "I don't." "Well, what church do you go to?" "My own." But Debra taught me all of this. It's not without a price. I am not a forceful person, someone who can tell others what to do. It's just never in my nature. I had a very, very domineering father. He was English. He did like his father did. He raised his kids like his father did. My father sat here, and the serving plates were here, and his plate here, and he passed down what you were to eat. His idea of bacon was if it had any lean on it, it wasn't any good for you. You can't imagine the pocketfuls of food us five kids took out to the barn. You ate what was on your plate. And his favorite thing was, "the kids in China are starving." So we would always say, "Why don't we send 'em this food?"

I wish I could be more definitive about what I could do as an individual. I hope I have 20 years left. I'll fight against war every chance I get, by word, thought, and deed. And it scares the heck out of me, my grandkids are nine years old. That's my motivation. I could talk for hours and hours and hours. But it would just amplify some of the things.

Debra went back to working with the Walther League, a church youth organization, and we came back to Madison. Our postman delivered letters addressed "Deborah, Wisconsin."

We got hundreds and hundreds and hundreds of letters. I would say, 95 percent of them were positive. Debra says the heartening thing is all of her positive letters were from soldiers, all over the world. They were from all parts, from soldiers. She didn't get one negative. Now, isn't that strange, with the Vietnam War? There wasn't one negative letter. They took the time to write.

Now, I got a phone call, from the Veterans of Foreign Wars some place in Minnesota. The guy said, "We're gonna work to see that Debra's award is rescinded." Well, I talked to the guy. "Well," I says, "I was there. Were you there?" He says, "No."

I says, "Debra is very soft-spoken. Truly, she doesn't want to hurt anyone, you know?" Before I got through, after about 15 or 20 minutes, he was saying, "Well, you know, I'm going to talk to them and see if I can get 'em to change their mind." Can you imagine? I couldn't.

I don't care who is in government; I will always be against war, no matter what.

ROBERT
KIMBROUGH

Korean War

I'm Robert Alexander Kimbrough III. That's my official long title, but when I was in boot camp I got so tired of the drill sergeant at mail-call spitting out "Robert Alexander Kimbrough the Third" that I dropped my name to simply Robert Kimbrough, which I use for publishing, banking, registering, even though the government still insists that I be Robert A. Kimbrough.

On June 26, 1929, I was born in Philadelphia, where I was raised, although my parents were from the deep South. My father had taken his first two years of medicine at the University of Mississippi, then transferred to the University of Pennsylvania Medical School where he became an M.D. at age 22.

Both of my grandfathers were educated—southern Baptist ministers. They knew Greek and Latin and Hebrew, and earned Doctoral degrees in theology, so you could say that I come from an intellectually aware family. I grew up in the Republican atmosphere of Philadelphia's "Main Line." I remember going to my private school with Landon and Knox buttons all over me in 1936, but by 1940 I was able to laugh at Wendell Wilkie who, after he lost to Roosevelt, went around the world, and returned to say in amazement: "You know we really are one world." Well, I was ahead of him by that time. I was very much aware of World Federalism, and, of course, got very excited as the idea of the United Nations emerged from World War II, an event that had a real impact on me. Being a teenager, I was sensitive to the elevated morale of the citizens during the war who welcomed service people into their homes and picked them up while hitchhiking. It was a very open society. People today don't really understand that, in many ways, we were a happier country at war than we had been ever before or since.

Anyway, I used to write USMC on the edge of my textbooks and things like that, and I was disappointed when the war was over before I could join up. My father had sought a commission at age 42. When I went to college after graduating from high school in 1947, there were an awful lot of veterans on campus. These facts hit me in my macho soft spot, the romanticization of what you've got to do to prove yourself for your country. You know, they served and I had not.

In the spring of my freshman year, a Marine Corps recruiter came through selling something called the Platoon Leaders Class (PLC Program) in which you would go to boot camp for two summers, but have nothing to do with campus military training or ROTC. Here was my chance to join the Marine Corps. I did, indeed, sign up in April of 1948, and that summer and the next went through basic training. During the summer of the Berlin Airlift, we were told we may not get back to college because we would be immediately commissioned. The whole Marine Corps, regular and reserve, was on full alert.

The outbreak of the Korean War on June 25, 1950, made it clear that the minute I got my college degree I would be commissioned a second lieutenant and called up to active duty. The Marine Corps, unlike the Army and the Navy, makes all its new officers go through what is called Basic School after commissioning in order to acquire more indoctrination in terms of the Marine Corps: tactics, strategy, a breakdown of the kinds of intelligence, logistics, operations, administration, the whole show. I went through Basic School in Quantico, Virginia, in the fall and spring of 1951 and 1952.

I had requested and received orders to go into the Marine Corps version of underwater demolition training at Camp Lejeune in North Carolina, attached to the Recon Company of the 2nd Marine Division where, like frogmen, you go in to scout and clear beaches before landings. But in the early spring of 1952, when my commanding officer was going up to Headquarters Marine Corps in Washington to get his order changed to go to Korea, I asked him to do the same for me. He was successful and I was ordered to Camp Pendleton in southern California for three months of precombat training. And here's where two things converge. First, I really believed that we were fighting for the United Nations. We were going to try to reestablish the temporary dividing line between the two Koreas. That was the mission, the United Nations' mission. Even so, I knew that the U.S. government had installed as president of "South" Korea, Syngman Rhee, an old gun runner and war profiteer, who was just a puppet for the U.S.

I believed that my blue and white U.N. campaign ribbon was very important. I thought that this kind of military action was what the United Nations had to commit itself to in order to obtain ultimate peace. I tried to talk to my troopers about this and they thought it was a bunch of bull. One guy said, "Lieutenant, all I want to do is take my flak jacket and my Tommy gun and go back to Chicago and rob banks." Second, along with this U.N. idealism, I would finally get my chance to test myself and "to do my duty," whatever that means. As soon as I arrived in Korea, I was assigned to an infantry company on line. Sometimes you get more than you ask for.

Because I had gone to a private school and a private college, I got my first taste of the real people of this world, both in combat training in California and in actual combat. There's actually a little side story there. Toward the end of my tour in Korea, I went on R&R to Japan and was assigned a bunch of enlisted men for whom I was supposed to be responsible. Once we hit Kyoto, each was on his own. As we were coming back, one of the enlisted men came up to me and said: "You know, lieutenant, you don't remember me, but you used to kick our ass up and down those hills in Pendleton. We hated you. You were really one son of a bitch. But, you know, I understand now why you were doing that. And I hear from the guys that have served under you that you're okay." That was a nice thing to hear.

I became a pacifist my first day on line. I was first put in charge of the light machine gun squad, and my sergeant was showing me the line: the trench lines, the dugouts, the fields of vision, the fields of fire. Suddenly the Chinese side started shooting at me. And I thought to myself, "Why is anybody shooting at me? They don't have anything against me. I don't have anything against them." And I suddenly realized, "Hey, dummy, you're not in your backyard with your fingers playing 'boom-boom, you're dead.'" It came home to me: "This is not good."

A few nights later, our front was hit by a massive attack by the Chinese, complete with bugles. By dawn we had held them off, but one rifle platoon leader was killed and I took his place.

The 1st Marine Division was guarding the Panmunjom corridor where the so-called peace treaty conversations were going on. The eastern side of Korea along the 38th Parallel is pretty mountainous. But the western side, north of Seoul, is more like southern California, hills and flat land, and lots and lots of rice paddies. When you went out on a patrol, you pretty much had to stay on the dikes because of the rice paddies. So it was weird doing patrols and attacks and a lot of ambushes, being restricted both by darkness and the nature of the terrain.

For example, and this kind of thing happened more than once, from battalion, we got an assignment that filtered down to one squad of my platoon that had us going deeply behind

LONG SHADOWS

some strong points of land shooting out toward our lines from the hills where the Chinese were. It was a full moon. There wasn't a cloud in the sky. We had to go out on rice paddies. So I did what most platoon leaders were doing: We went out slowly in a spaced single line. Hunkered down in front of our own lines. I said, "Okay, everybody be at ease. Be alert." After an hour or so, I said, "Okay, fire." Everybody fired his rifle and we trooped back in. I called in a report that we had carried out our mission of assault. "No casualties. Many enemy killed."

Strictly speaking, I had disobeyed an order. But the order was insane. First of all, the mission was overly ambitious. But more to the point, any attempt to carry out the order was doomed because there was no way we could have approached the Chinese lines without being seen early and totally, because of the terrain and the weather conditions. What we did was what the troops and the front line officers called "shooting up a storm." You've got to watch out for your troops.

I was 23 years old—just 23—and I was in charge of a strong point, which meant I had a reinforced rifle platoon to defend an obvious corridor of attack. In total, I had 94 men under me: heavy machine guns, light machine guns, forward observers, some 60mm mortars. Here I was, the platoon leader of the 2nd platoon of "C" company, 1st Battalion, 1st Marine Regiment, 1st Marine Division. And those guys would do anything that I would ask them to do, which was very humbling.

After three months of pretty intense combat I came off line for the first time. I had been hit three times, nothing serious. After I had gotten all my troops in their trucks for the night-time replacement exchange, I just broke down and quietly cried. I had built up so much tension from the responsibilities and from the exposures and from the actions night after night. Some nights were very quiet. But you don't know that until the night's all over.

I was in Korea for a year, from June 1952 to June 1953. So I had one winter and, although we had little snow, when you're living outside in the rain, it can get awfully cold and damn muddy; the rice paddies, the higher ground, the dikes got awfully messy from snow, rain, and ice.

At the end of my tour, I was asked to be aide to a general in Hawaii. This was to kind of woo me into the regular Marine Corps. But I knew pretty much that I didn't want to have a military career. I wanted to get out and go to graduate school and teach English at the university level. I had been an honors student at Williams College and wrote a senior honors thesis that took me to libraries in New York, Philadelphia, and Cambridge, Massachusetts. So I really got into research. Even though I played football and joined the Maine Corps and boxed in the Golden Gloves, I really dug scholarly research!

While I was on the G.I. Bill at Stanford and Harvard, I stayed in the Reserves mainly for the extra money. But, in fact, it was kind of a boys' club. You'd go out and have a beer after your drill. After a while I realized that I was earning enough points so that if I stayed in I could get a modest retirement benefit. At the same time, politically, if I had run for president of the United States, I'd have been assassinated. I was for absolute unilateral disarmament. The United States should take the initiative and disarm. I still believe this, today.

I left Hawaii in December 1953, went on inactive duty and began the M.A. program at Stanford. Although I'd been an honors graduate at Williams, I knew my grades were not quite good enough to get me into Harvard. I had no illusions about Harvard. I hated Harvard and the "Ha-verd boys" and "Ha-verd" in general. But in terms of Renaissance studies and English literature in general, it had, at that time, the strongest Ph.D. program. After Stanford, that's where I wanted to be.

So I stayed in the Reserves and eventually became an adjunct faculty member at the Marine Corps Command and Staff College in Quantico, Virginia. I would go in civilian clothes with other Ph.D. types in the Marine Corps Reserve. And, one year, with a navy chaplain, I ran an anti-Vietnam War seminar at night. We went underground. There were a lot of midcareer captains and majors who wanted to think out loud and talk without being in jeopardy.

I taught literature, writing, and effective reading and listening, really basic stuff. I assigned *Heart of Darkness*, *Red Badge of Courage*, and books on what we now call global economy and resources. And, of course, most of my Marines thought that all the oil in the world belonged to us, and that's why the China Sea was so very important. What's new?! My curriculum was never censored. I never had to curb my anti-war sentiments. And I was never passed over for promotion. In fact, I was urged to stay in the Reserves to make brigadier general, but I was content to retire as a full colonel.

In Conrad's *Heart of Darkness*, when Marlow's going to Africa, he's on a ship taking him down the coast, and the French were having one of their interminable wars, and their warships were firing into the jungle. (I'm paraphrasing very badly here.) "Boom," the shells would go in, and nothing would happen. Nothing could happen. Well, these guys who had been in Vietnam said, "Wow. That's our story." You know, all this futility and all that destruction, they saw it. They felt it. These were junior officers, captains and majors, officers getting ready for their next promotion to either major or lieutenant colonel. They were all Vietnam combat veterans. The Marine Corps made sure that everybody got to Vietnam.

I had a long conversation with a senior colonel long before I was a colonel. He had had a little too much to drink and started telling me how the Marine Corps built up its forces in Vietnam by manipulating the Pacific Command and Headquarters Marine Corps and the Joint Chiefs of Staff. (Of course, Headquarters Marine Corps was in on it.) A small group in Hawaii created fictional events that were supposedly happening in Vietnam and that, therefore, the U.S. had better send a whole division in. Of course, the Marines could not just go to Vietnam; they had to be "invited" by higher authorities. It just "happened" that the Marine Corps had the 1st Division ready in Camp Pendleton in California. So, once invited, the move to the Far East began: first came the battalions, then the regiments, and then the whole division, and all the air and land support groups. It was a shameful, shameful story. Again, the senior people plan for their own glory.

The same thing had happened in Korea. The Marine Corps made sure every regular officer served, and some time after our battalion had gone back on line, I had a captain take over our company. I was still the rifle platoon leader of "Cynthia Deuce," but he pulled me out of my platoon and made me the executive officer of Charlie Company. His background was administration. He called me into his dugout, safely on a back slope, and he said, "You know, lieutenant, it seems to me that the role of the executive officer is that he does the strategic planning and I as the CO should take care of the logistics and administrative matters." This was a regular officer who wasn't very bright. He didn't know anything about infantry. This is a good example of how desperate they were to make everybody get "battle" experience. The same thing happened in Vietnam. And this is happening right now in Iraq. The Marine Corps welcomes war as a great training ground. Kill and get killed.

I still believe in World Federalism and that the United Nations ought to be supported, strengthened, and obeyed. The United States should be subservient. We should pay our dues and obey U.N. resolutions. That's what I believed when I was a teenager. That's what I still believe today. Frank Zeidler, the former three-time mayor of Milwaukee, has worked his whole life as an advocate for the United Nations and worked for world peace. A strong United Nations is the only way we're going to achieve peace and justice.

In January 1976, I went on the retired list after almost 28 years from the time I enlisted in 1948, and I have a pension that comes to just about $1,000 a month. I use it for things that I support. I don't need the money to live on. I feel privileged that I can contribute to the Socialist Party (S.P.), to the Madison Area Peace Coalition, to Clarence Kailin's going to Spain as a veteran of the Abraham Lincoln Brigade, and to many things like these. I can quietly support groups and people I admire and respect. It's money I didn't earn in the sense of going to the defense of my country and all that crap. It's an opportunity to use the government's money for people and groups that need it.

Actually, I did not have to serve. I had to get a waiver to get my commission and be put on active duty because during graduation from college I was in a serious motorcycle accident, as the passenger, not the driver. My injuries were such that the Marine Corps did not want me because I couldn't pass a physical. I actually had to pull strings and sign a waiver so I could get in. The same thing happened when I enlisted. I had had polio as a kid and I can't touch my toes. They didn't want to sign me up. I said, "Look, I play football, and you don't want to sign me up?" I got my waiver. Another thing: I didn't report my third wound because if you were wounded three times they sent you home. And I didn't think that was fair to my troops to do that.

I was hit three times by shrapnel, bullet, and concussion grenade. I was on line a total of about nine months. But that first summer was the hairiest for me. After eight months in the Rifle Company, I became the exec and the CO of the 1st Marine Regiment Heavy Mortar Company. The 1st Marine Division came off line in late spring 1953 for the first time since 1950, and I became the Liaison Officer between the Army's 24th Division and the 1ˢᵗ Marine Regiment, which was the back-up for the Army division, now on line in our old territory.

Ironically, the cease-fire was signed in July of 1953 as I was motoring across Kansas on my honeymoon on my way out to San Francisco to go for duty in Hawaii with the 1st Provisional Air Ground Task Force. That was kind of weird being in Kansas and hearing about the ceasefire. What was more weird is that after I got home and before the cease fire I could hear and read about combat the Army was experiencing in my old territory. Unreal.

It's not just my Marine Corps prejudice, but the Marine Corps is more fit for combat than is the Army. Toward the end of my tour, as I said, I had taken over the 4.2 mortar company for the regiment. (The regiment had anti-tank tanks and heavy mortar.) When the 1st Division was being pulled off line for the first time in the whole war, the 24th Infantry Division was taking over our territory. I had five pieces of motor transport equipment: a weapons carrier, a large truck, and three Jeeps. The captain who was going to take over my weapons, our firing bases, all that, came in with 34 pieces of motor transport equipment. He was more concerned about where he was going to put his vehicles than any concern for what the fields of fire were and what was going on up front.

Robert Kimbrough

A good friend of mine was in an Army division just over to the east of me. He was a hell of a nice guy and I hated to see him as a platoon leader. He did get his ass shot off. He survived, but it's different. The Marine Corps is different than the Army. Yet in the end it all amounts to the same thing: death—death of "enemy," death of civilians, death of ourselves.

Here is something that links Korea and Vietnam. A young man in my neighborhood came back from Vietnam, an Army captain. He was with the 1st Cavalry. I was the only one on the block he could talk to because people just didn't understand what he had gone through. We could talk. He had to have an outlet. Sort of what we are tying to do now in Veterans for Peace for new vets returning from Iraq.

The Marines didn't rotate by unit. We rotated by individuals. So every month, out of a company, say maybe five or six people would go, and replacements would come in. But I was very close to a number of those people. I kept in touch with them afterward. For instance, I encouraged a buck sergeant from the South to seek a commission without a college degree. Bright guy. Good man. So I kept in touch with him.

When the reporters and everybody over at the *Capital Times* went on strike (when the printers were being fired because all the typesetting would be done by computer) I supported the strikers and was very active with The Press Connection on the picket line and on the board as the treasurer. In short, what I felt in that pressroom was the kind of thing you feel when you're in the unit in combat. There's something about that kind of experience that is important to me. I felt it in football. You feel it when you're in a stage play. It happens when people come together, give of themselves while caring for comrades, all putting something together, together.

I sometimes jokingly say (and it's not really a joke) that I came out of my mother's womb organizing. They used to tease me in high school because I was always telling people to be more responsible. They started calling me "Responsibility." So I had my mother cut out a big red R and sew it onto a T-shirt. I went to school and waited for somebody to say, "Hey, here comes Responsibility Robert." I took off my necktie, unbuttoned my shirt, and there was that R. I know that I infuriate some people because they think I'm pushy, especially in volunteer organizations. Some have the idea that because they're volunteers they don't have to do anything. I don't see that. If you make a commitment, you make a commitment. There is something in my nature that leads me to do things.

In 1944, a sophomore in high school, I went door-to-door for Norman Thomas, because he was saying the things that I had instinctively come to believe on my own, in spite of my parents, who were the kind who say they're not political (which we know is a very political statement). It was true they were not Republicans or Democrats or ideologues. My father was a physician who practiced medicine, never owned a stock in his life, gave bonus money to his interns and his nurses, and spent every cent he got. Everybody thought he was a rich Philadelphia doctor. He didn't buy a house until 1940. We'd always rent. Money just didn't mean anything to him. It was the same thing with politics.

He very seldom talked medicine at home. But one night at dinner he came in and said, "I had an interesting visitor today. The president's wife came into my office, Eleanor Roosevelt." Because he moved in circles of people who would curse "that man in the White House" and all that sort of thing, and laugh at Eleanor's buck teeth and all that, he said, "She is the most charming, intelligent person I have ever met." He said, "I never noticed her teeth."

Mrs. Roosevelt was in Philadelphia because one of her daughters-in-law was pregnant and having a difficult time. The Roosevelts were a little worried and wanted the best obstetrician in the country. They were advised to call on my father. When she asked, "Can you come down to Washington," he said, "No, if you want me, you come up here." He didn't want any publicity out of this at all. But it did sneak into the papers that he had delivered two of the Roosevelts' grandchildren.

I guess I got a lot of quiet idealism from him. He was in ROTC during World War I, but the war was over before he could get "over there." So he pulled every string he could to get in the Army when World War II broke out. Of course, I thought he was an old man. He was probably about 42. He was directly commissioned as a lieutenant colonel and one of his first jobs was to take a train up to Canada to meet one of the first evacuation troop ships of wounded Americans and Brits, and bring them to hospitals in the United States.

Going up to Canada, his train got shunted off to a siding and nothing happened. He was in charge of the train, so he asked, "Well, what is it?" "Some big-shot person is coming through on the other track there." My father smoked. Smoked himself to death. He was outside the train smoking and this other train comes by slowly and stops. Eleanor Roosevelt gets off the train and asks, "Doctor Kimbrough, what are you doing here?"

I welcome my age. A couple years ago down in Washington with my daughter and her two kids and her friend and family, we went to the Roosevelt Memorial. I could tell them all these stories. And they had no idea who the Roosevelts were or about the Depression, the New Deal, and World War II.

I had read about Norman Thomas and went to his office in Ardmore, Pennsylvania, then a working class town in the middle of the Republican "Main Line." I got some pamphlets and was told where to go. And, of course, Norman Thomas would constantly rib Roosevelt for stealing the platform of the Socialist Party. At one time, about 1952, he said, "I guess I may have to stop running for president." But that Socialist-Democratic social commitment adopted by the Democrats in the 1930s and 1940s and supported by Eisenhower in the 1950s is almost dead in the water today.

Veterans for Peace was formed by some Vietnam veterans in 1986. Wisconsin had a chapter associated with the Twin Cities. In 1990, during the build-up for the so-called Gulf War, Vets for Peace stimulated the organization of a chapter here. Jim Allen, of course, was instrumental and he recruited me, and our chapter was formed in early 1991. There was a Vietnam veteran, stocky guy, pretty disturbed by the war, who was head of the chapter. We were never very big. Now, of course, Vets for Peace came alive trying to stop the "Attack on

Iraq," and we have a membership of about 60 and are now Chapter 25, the Clarence Kailin Chapter.

Sometimes I say I'm a pragmatic idealist, an atheistic theist, a pessimistic optimist, a realistic dreamer, and I guess there are other paradoxes I would have to admit to.

I remember when Ethel and Julius Rosenberg were found guilty of spying in the spring of 1951, and we knew they were guilty because the *New York Herald Tribune* and the *New York Times* told us that. I mean, there was no question about it. But then, this is really ironic, when I was in Japan on June 19, 1953, on my way back to the United States, I read in *Stars & Stripes* that the Rosenbergs had been executed, and I was shocked. I just couldn't believe that Eisenhower didn't come to his senses and revoke a sentence that far and permanently exceeded the nature of the "crime." Although I had lived in a peripheral political area, I knew that the execution was wrong, just totally wrong. Now the further irony is (I didn't know this until 1976, when I got to know Robbie and Michael Meeropol, the sons of the Rosenbergs) that Judge Kaufman, in sentencing the Rosenbergs, had accused them of starting the Korean War, and here I was in Japan on my way home when I read about their execution. I was shocked and angry about their deaths.

Their guilt was the received opinion. I was a victim of the kind of information we got. I subscribed to the *New York Herald Tribune* when I was in college, but I was more interested in what Red Smith had to say on the sports page and stuff like that. I knew the Korean War had broken out, and I knew the Rosenbergs were arrested and were guilty even before their trial because the media said this was so—sound familiar?

Time magazine was something I read. That's what you did, until you began to realize that glorified writing masks more than it reveals.

I never registered as either a Republican or Democrat when I was old enough to vote. But when I came to Madison in 1959, I actually joined the Democratic Party because I had entered a clean state and the "new" Democratic Party was led by Gaylord Nelson, Midge Miller, all those good people. And I'd come from Pennsylvania, where both parties were totally corrupt. In 1959, in this state there was a Republican Party and a Democratic Party. They stood for different things, but they each respected the other and conducted politics in an open and friendly manner.

Frank Zeidler, the Socialist mayor of Milwaukee from 1948 to 1962, in 1973 almost single-handedly declared the Socialist Party back into existence. Milwaukee was the national headquarters as well as the state's. That's when I joined the party and wanted the Wisconsin Labor-Farm Party to join the S.P. I still have some correspondence in answer to my suggestion: "No, we can't use the word Socialist. It's no longer valid. We can't use that."

It was Bill Hart, the Socialist, who got the Labor-Farm on the ballot. When we started our protests against the first Bush war, we founded the Wisconsin Network for Peace and Justice. At that stage, I started joining every left party and movement in the country. In 1991, Ron Daniels was running for president on the New Tomorrow ticket and I suggested to Labor-Farm that we ask him to run on our ballot slot for president in 1992. The answer was "yes," and I went down to Chicago where there was a meeting of Left scholars because he was going to make an address. I met Ron, Bernie Sanders, Cornell West, and a whole bunch of lefty people I'd never met. Ron said, "Yeah, sure, I'll run." He came into the state I think three times. In addition to Labor-Farm and New Tomorrow, there was the Progressive Network out of New Jersey, and then, when the Communist Party broke up, there was the Committees of Correspondence.

In June of 1991, I turned the annual membership meeting of the Wisconsin Network for Peace and Justice into a national convention. We had Manning Marable here as key-noter. That was a great coming together of all the lefties in the United States, and we were going to march away from the meeting with a new party. People would willingly give up their name, bond together, and do it. At the last session we had an open mike. The line was a mile long and all the speakers preached their own sermon. At that point I said, "Okay, I'm just going to stick with the Socialist Party." I know that the odds of our becoming a national force are infinitesimal, but the S.P. gives me what I believe in. The Eugene Debs story is a moving story. His life experiences made him a Socialist.

I was a *bête noire* on campus, a unionist, American Federation of Teachers Local 223, working for collective bargaining for the faculty and academic staff. I spoke out in the Faculty Senate, at regents' meetings, at legislative hearings, and in our United Faculty and Academic Staff monthly newsletter distributed to every mailbox on campus and in the capitol.

One of my most satisfying moments (I was president of the union several times) was during the second T.A. strike in 1980 when I was president. United Faculty didn't cross the picket line. We took our classes off campus. The UW tried to dock our pay, but the courts backed us. After the strike was over and the graduate students had effectively lost, I saw how two-faced my colleagues in the English Department were, how gloating they were. I got up at a meeting in H.C. White Hall and quietly said how ashamed I was of their behavior as adults, that just one level below us on the sixth floor, our T.A.s were now going back to work, and you're up here mocking them and gloating, and I'm ashamed of you. Charles Scott spoke up: "Kimbrough, when are you gonna grow up?"

I don't know what possessed me, but for once the light went on. I burst into a smile and said, "Scotty, if growing up means being like you, I guess I never want to grow up." I don't know where it came from. (Usually it's when you're driving home after a meeting that you come up with an appropriate zinger.)

Sometimes, I don't know. I get tired. But I think of Clarence Kailin; I think of Frank Zeidler. They really are my sustaining models. They're different from one another, but they never quit. And, you know, anything they want, they can count on me.

When I first when to Cuba in 1994, before the Brothers to the Rescue were shot down by the Cuban Air Force, it was a lot easier to get there. You would have to be a qualified journalist, so I became qualified as a journalist by getting a letter from Dave Zweifel at *The Capital Times* and one from the *Union Labor News* and one from S.P.-U.S.A. When I came back I wrote an article about how democracy was alive and well in Cuba. Dave Zweifel wouldn't print it. But *The Madison Times* took all three of my stories on Cuba, just as they had my five-piece article on the 25th anniversary of the Rosenbergs' executions. The mainstream press was not interested in Cuba or the Rosenbergs, but neither was the "left" media.

On the 25th anniversary of the Rosenbergs' execution, there was a lot of activity around the country. Because a videotape called "Invitation to an Inquest" is the best investigative reporting about how the Rosenbergs were railroaded, I arranged to have the video shown on WHA, to be followed by a panel discussion. WHA said we couldn't put the video on the air unless I had somebody from "the other side" on the panel, under the principle of so-called balanced presentation. I had to humble myself and ask my archenemy/friend Gordon Baldwin of the UW Law School. I could have said, "Screw you, I'm not going to compromise." But to get the tape on the air, I had to.

Charts show how all media and entertainment outlets are controlled by about five basic companies: newspapers, magazines, records, books, television, and radio—all for profit. I know it sounds corny, but there's a lot of wisdom behind a lot of clichés. "People before profit." It's that simple.

We don't have a sufficient sense of community. People are starving in this country. People are homeless in this country. It's not just a delinquent media. The media are the most visible enemy, but we as taxpayers are also delinquent.

I think, quite realistically, the way we veterans came together to renew the Vets for Peace chapter, really establishing the Clarence Kailin Chapter 25, generating vibrant energy from a diversity of people, is the key to successful, effective movement building. We need the committed unity of purpose that we have been talking about. That is collective energy, without words, where and when you don't have to say anything, the shared focus is just there. And it's personally therapeutic at the same time that it is communally creative and mutually contributive. If we can maintain a sense of mission for peace and justice, we may have a chance to reach and affect the larger community. The left is too defensive, too willing just to criticize. We must be on the offensive, positive and active.

JAMES C. ALLEN, M.D.

Korean War

I live in Madison, Wisconsin. I was born July 25, 1928, in Janesville, Wisconsin. I grew up in the small town of Brodhead, Wisconsin, a town that was probably fairly conservative at that point in history. I graduated from high school in 1946 and, while working at the post office, was drafted, in July 1952, during the Korean War. At that time I thought we were holding the Communists back and what we were doing was good for the world.

I went to Fort Sheridan and took some tests. Then I went down to Camp Gordon, Georgia, for a hot, miserable summer and eight weeks of basic training. As I look back on it now, I was very, very lucky. I was always a bookworm in the library studying a lot subjects. I knew something about electricity and radio. I had built radio sets from scratch and I could read a radio schematic. After basic training, I was sent to the signal school at Fort Monmouth, New Jersey. All the other guys in my class were radio and TV repairmen. They had been radio repairmen and then moved into television repair. Television was still new. We still had black-and-white TV and the exciting thing on the horizon was color TV.

The best schools I ever went to by far were Army schools. We had about 12 people in a class. We had two civilian instructors. They were engineers from Radio Corporation of America. We went over everything, starting out with basic electricity, AC/DC, then elements of radio, and on to advanced radio. Then we studied microwave, a new thing. Radar was the next class subject. When we went on to the radar sets to learn repairing, we would have two students and one instructor. Things were very complicated, but I'll tell you that, as one of my friends later said, I never went to an assignment in Korea where there was a breakdown that I couldn't fix.

The Army made excellent equipment. It was all laid out for easy diagnosis and repair. It wasn't all jumbled wires like commercial TV sets. Sets had test points so you could quickly analyze with voltmeters and oscilloscopes and repair them.

We finished schooling with friend or foe airplane identification. We would find a plane on radar and would send a signal at a certain frequency to that airplane. The airplane had a radio receiver. They would receive that signal and if they were tuned in on the right frequency, they would automatically reply back on their transmitter at that frequency and thus we would identify them as friendly. If that plane did not respond back you knew that it was not one of our planes. We changed frequency codes daily. The United States also learned how to apply this technology to tracking incoming artillery and mortar shells. There were about 12 in our class and 2 of us got pulled out for a secret weapon, MPQ 10, that had been just recently developed. There were 25 of these sets made by Raytheon Corporation. They were very effective when first sent to Korea. These sets could track incoming mortar shells.

Apparently with a mortar you fire and see where it lands, and then you sort of know how to adjust it for the next shot. If you had an incoming round you could turn on your radar set, then if they shot a second shell you knew where they were. Then you could relay this information to the artillery, which then would drop a shell on the mortar position.

The Koreans—and the Chinese, of course—soon learned we were hitting them more often than previously. They didn't know why, but they knew that we now had something new. These sets were put behind Marine divisions to keep them safe and secret because, sometimes, Korean divisions would disappear at night. They'd just totally disappear. Then President Syngman Rhee would go back to a village and surround it and load all the young men up in trucks and take them back to the front.

When I was sent to Korea there were 25 teams already there. I was on the 26th team. I got to Korea about two months after the war ended, to my relief. I was in a signal outfit and I spent the next nine months fixing radios. It was an easy and good life.

We were treated very well in the signal corps. I even thought about re-upping. But, you know, one thing bothered me. You just never know when some crazy world leader is going to get some wild idea, I just didn't think I was going to take a chance on this. I was smart enough to say I'm going to go back to school with the G.I. Bill.

I had been at Milton College two years after high school. I came back to Wisconsin and went to Platteville State College and then to Marquette Medical School. Then I came to the University of Wisconsin in Madison to study ophthalmology. I've been an ophthalmologist at the University of Wisconsin since 1960.

Most people don't think about peace too much unless it affects them or their family. They think they cannot do anything about the military and government.

We just got to try and make the world a little bit better. You know, we just got to try. We must do the best we can to promote peace. If you don't do it, no one else will.

I didn't question the Korean War. I didn't question foreign policy or anything. Nobody was questioning it, really, not in my small town. A few people were talking about it in a different way, for example, Joe McCarthy.

After the Korean War I started hearing rumors about Joe McCarthy. He wasn't quite the hero that the newspapers had portrayed him. I remember hearing at Marquette that he used to invite himself to speak, and the priests used to say, "Well, this drunk just wants to come to Marquette University and use us as a stage." You started hearing rumors like that from people.

Joe McCarthy was a good politician. I remember working in the post office when he was elected in 1948. Back in those days people didn't get much mail. Just before the election we got all of these postcards. "Who is this?" He had sent a postcard to everybody in town. We had never seen this ever happen before from a political figure. We spent a couple hours sorting all these postcards. People picked up those postcards and voted a day or two later. I've often wondered if that won him the election.

I think all we can do is be a witness—that we are people trying to prevent wars. I think it's interesting that growing up in the 1930s, the VFW was a real anti-war organization. Oh, yes. I mean we had just come through the terrible slaughter of World War I. Everybody remembered World War I. No way were we going to war in Europe again. World War I was like Vietnam, a war for no good reason.

And that guy Roosevelt, what the hell was he trying to do, putting those destroyers out there convoying goods because you knew damn well they were going to get torpedoed someday. Then we would be involved in war, and most of the veterans' organizations were strongly anti-war. It's strange when World War II kids came home they all had a different attitude. "We did something good." It changed. These World War II guys felt that they had done something special.

We were fighting Hitler and we were in a good war and good came out of it, the "good war." Before World War II,

Republicans were anti-war. They said, "Stay out of the war," and, "It's the damn Democrats that always get us into war," and, "We're going to stay out of World War II for damn sure. Democrats got us into World War I and we got all these casualties and big debt."

I never heard any anti-war sentiment during the Korean War. Korea was just a clean-up operation, I guess, for World War II. It's interesting because after World War II, the troops in Japan and Germany had a hell of a good time. Oh God, that was the life. I knew all these guys. They had a wonderful time, like my sergeant. He'd been in the Far East for 11 years. He had no intention of going home. Privates were making 75 bucks a month, and for 25 bucks you could live in Japan and get a house and a hooch girl and she'd buy the groceries and you lived off base and you went down to the military in the morning and walked around and saluted somebody. In the afternoon you played golf or did something like that. It was a good life. We were the kings. If you wanted a taxi fare you jumped in a taxi and when you got out you said go to hell. Everybody, even the privates, was living the good life.

Our signal corps captain who was orienting us before we went to Korea said when the Korean War started, they took rations for two weeks, but mostly they took flags because they figured as soon as the North Koreans heard the Americans had landed, the war would be over and they wanted to be prepared for a big parade. What a surprise.

You know, these wars never turn out like some people think, like they're sold.

In Korea, the important thing was to get your tour in, keep your head low, and stay alive. You just went over and hung out for nine months, stayed alive, got your points, and went home. If you were in a combat zone nine months, you got combat pay. They said they used to pull the tape measure out and measure every morning where the shells landed, so they could put in for combat pay. The guys in my signal company said what they liked to do was go up to the front line and stay in a bunker overnight and then got credit for two days in a combat zone.

Growing up, the only media I knew was the *Chicago Tribune*. I mean now we have different points of view. In World War II, as soon as that war started, there was no dissent. I mean, everybody said, "We're going to have to win this." There was never anything said against the government or any admission of mistakes. MacArthur was an idol and when Truman fired him, half the country was ready to fire Truman.

Then in July of 1952, Eisenhower said, "I'm going to Korea if I get elected." He put out a public rumor that, "Dammit, you guys have got to settle over there. We've got the atomic bomb and we might just use it." I wonder what role that played because that was about the time they started peace talks at Panmunjom. The troops really quit fighting as soon as those peace talks started. Then Harry Truman says, "Hey, this war's not over yet, send those guys out on patrol at night and keep them fighting. We've got to show them that we're tough, that we aren't sitting around, we're going to be in a tough bargaining position."

The Korean War was just like now. We don't know how we're going to end the Iraq war, or why we can't end it. It always has been the same for the last 50 years. We just got tired of fighting in Korea with no end in sight. Vietnam was the same way. We were spending money and lives and didn't know what the end might be. We didn't want to go fight China. Both sides were tired. I think the Korean War just petered out on both sides. Vietnam was the same.

I think we'll just struggle through this damn thing for a number of years, then get tired of buying bombs and seeing the casualties come home. Then we will say we won it and go home.

Our leaders are responsible, always have been and always are. They want to be macho. Way back in World War I, it was Wilson saving the world. My dad went to France to save the world for democracy. It was the same.

My grandfather said the war was good for farmers. "We're making good money on the farm." The farmers did well. They did damn good in World Wars I and II.

I told my children never to join the military. They were in their teens around 1990, and I thought the first Iraq War would be four to eight years, like Vietnam. Bush thought the second Iraq War was going to be short like the first Iraq War.

Becoming an anti-war person was a very gradual process, starting with the Vietnam War. I gradually began to see the world in a different way. As time progressed, I saw the failure of the Vietnam War. I saw us invade Grenada. Then we invaded Panama, and I just thought, "all these wars do not make sense."

Then the Iraq War came in 1991, and that made even less sense. I had kids growing up about that time, and paid more attention to what might be coming on the horizon. My son and I went to Washington on a peace march in January 1991. We saw a group of Veterans for Peace members there and jumped right in. I joined Veterans for Peace and have been a dues-paying member ever since 1991.

I always have felt guilty that I wasn't more of an anti-war person in the 1960s, although I was a sympathizer. I was involved with my work and I enjoyed my work. I just didn't pay attention to it. I was like most of the people in this country now, saying it doesn't really affect me. I have worked on some campaigns for presidential peace candidates. I've been trying to make up for my past mistakes in a way.

I think you have got to keep these organizations alive between crises. I've seen Veterans for Peace member numbers go up and then go down. Same thing happened with organizations like the War Resister's League, the Fellowship of Reconciliation, and Women's International League for Peace and Freedom. After wars end, membership starts to decline and members start blaming the leadership. Why is the leadership not doing this or that, why are we falling apart?

Veterans for Peace was born in the 1980s. The Veterans for Peace guy who started it was a man whose brother died in Vietnam. At first he thought that had been the heroic thing to do, then gradually changed his mind over several years.

A bolt of lightning did not convert me to the anti-war movement. I stop and think, listen and read about things before I change positions. The fact that I was a physician did not particularly influence my view. We got some casualties back, and I took care of some of the Vietnam veterans. Some of them were badly shot up and I helped a few of them. No doubt it had some influence on me, but we didn't have a big influx of bloody casualties ever get back to Madison. They were more rehabilitation types of cases by the time they got here. At that time, the VA hospitals were not a direct back-up system for the Army hospitals.

After the Vietnam War, they changed the administrative structures between Department of Defense and the Veterans Affairs Hospitals so that they can ship people more directly to the VA Hospitals. I just had a communiqué from a VA hospital nurse out on the east coast who said, "We're working from seven in the morning until seven at night with all kinds of terrible causalities."

Walter Reed is an Army hospital. Many go to Germany first nowadays from the battlefield. Walter Reed is the best-known Army hospital. We had other hospitals in World War II in Battle Creek, Michigan, Colorado, and San Francisco. We even had casualties in the Stevens Hotel in Chicago in World War II. Causalities usually go to an Army hospital first and then come to VA hospitals. Army hospitals can get overloaded. I knew an army nurse that ran the eye ward at Walter Reed during the Vietnam War. I think she said she had to clear out 20 patients every few weeks to make room for more casualties on the eye service.

One of my ophthalmologist friends who just got out of the Army a couple years of ago says that because of the body armor, ophthalmologists in Iraq are working like hell because they are taking care of injuries to the faces of survivors.

I remember Max Gaebler at the Unitarian Meeting House saying about 25 years ago that we've made a little progress in the last few thousand years because in the old days when the conquering army came in, they usually killed everybody in the city. Now we just say we want to kill the soldiers. We're making a little progress, I guess. That's my hopeful note. Now even the military says, "Well, we're trying to hold civilian casualties down. We're just blowing up bridges and things." A little hope.

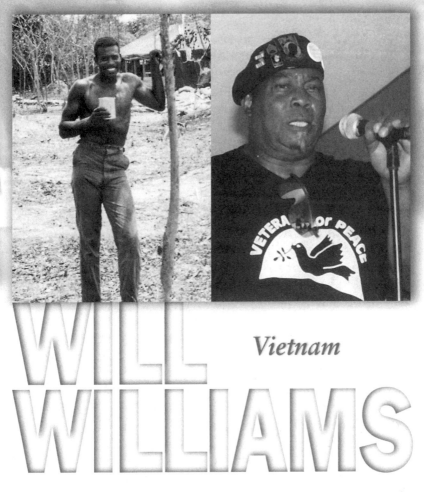

WILL WILLIAMS

Vietnam

I wonder if I would have been worse off than I am now, or if I would even be alive now because coming out of Mississippi when I did as a teenager, I was young with a lot of hate. If I had come to Chicago or New York or somewhere where I would have been around people in the Panther Party or any other group, it would have been easy for me to join. I think that people could have played with my head at that time. I would have joined and I would have been just as dedicated to that as I thought I was about the military. So I often wonder, suppose that when I graduated from high school, if I had just moved to Chicago or somewhere, what the outcome would be. I know if

I had been in touch with people like that I probably wouldn't have joined the Army under any circumstances. I wouldn't have. All I needed was a little tilting, someone to push me a little either way.

I try to equate that with the Vietnam experience. I think now that I'm better off that I did go in the service and go to Vietnam. I grew up a lot. I learned a lot about life during that time. I learned to appreciate it more and I learned respect for people in general from those experiences where, had I not gone, I wouldn't be doing what I am trying to do today, speak out against it. All it would have taken is for someone to talk to me during that time period. At 18 years old, I had gone through depression about Jim Crow. I knew I hated it. It wouldn't have taken much for me to join the Panthers ... or some other group ... Malcolm.

I couldn't have marched with Dr. King at that time. I know that to be a fact. I didn't believe in being abused by anybody. During that time I didn't understand, you know, how people could just march and have people put dogs and fire hoses on them. I knew at 18 years old there was no way in hell I would have tolerated that. He probably wouldn't even have let me in the organization.

It took a lot of years to really find out where he was coming from, the message he was sending. Back then I didn't know anything about Gandhi, and I'd see people being abused by Jim Crow. I couldn't have taken an oath saying I'd be nonviolent. So, therefore, I couldn't have gone with him. But if Stokely Carmichael had come up and handed me a weapon, it would have been easy for me to go out in that direction. Rather than fight in a war across the sea, I would have been fighting one right here in America.

I was young and my mind wanted to move me but one way, and that's that. I'm not going to take this crap from anybody. I didn't understand it; I really thought Dr. King was a nut in those days to allow himself to be abused for no reason other than being who he was. I couldn't understand it. Since then I know where and why he did what he did and the way he did it. I understand it now. But that's 40 some years after the fact, you know, that I began to be aware of why he believed in nonviolence. Why he and the followers accepted that abuse. That's what's so hard now when you think back to those days when he was out marching and how he drew people. He was like a magnet, he drew good people from all walks of life, people with a heart for justice and equality. I can see how he became a threat to this society and to this government. What I can't understand is why now people can't see that same thing happening that he spoke of.

It's like a prophecy, what he said. Much of it is being fulfilled today. And yet, you don't see the people coming together as they did back in the 1960s. Think about it, his speech in 1963, August of 1963, at the Poor Peoples March. After that, many of his own people began to turn on him, when he started talking about Vietnam in 1967. And the torch was dropped, and even now most people, I think, many people think of his speech at the Lincoln Memorial as the greatest speech he ever made, his "I have a dream." But the one that was more touching for me was the one he did at Riverside, where he went from a racial thing to a human thing, the value of people's lives all over the world, not just poor people that are black people. I don't know; I see that many people lost that spirit that he had. They dredge it up once a year and celebrate his birthday, and it's a big thing. They give out Martin Luther King awards to somebody because they did something.

The spirit of his work is not there, of what he was doing. That's the sadness of it. It touched me a lot when we wanted to pass out literature that said "Not In My Name" and we weren't allowed to because the King coalition, the people that set this up, said it would take the thunder from this celebration. In reality, I believe that had he been alive he would have been there passing out the literature himself. The people see that it's politically right to celebrate Dr. King Day when, in reality they don't give a damn about what his message was nor do they try to carry that message any further. It's just another day, a day that they get off work.

Vietnam made me. I grew up fast in Vietnam. It made me look at life, at all people, as being sacred. There's the pain that I never shake from it. I know I'll never get rid of it. But

I also learned that nothing can make me change the way I feel about myself, what I stand for and what I'll do. I know that in Vietnam I wasn't myself. I'm not the person now that I was then.

It's partially due to the brainwashing you get in boot camp. The other part is not taking the position like, "I'm not going to go in the service and be a pawn for the government." It's hard to determine which was right and you can't say either was wrong. Hell, I think some good can come from both of them. I think the good for me from that experience was that it made me love people more, made me value life more, made me stronger in a sense. You look at the other side, the guy that went to jail, he was strong at that time because he refused to go and do what I did, which created problems for me because I did.

There's no winning anything in war. I believe that in a war no one wins. I think I have learned how to take some of the worst things that happened to me and try to find good in them. Even in the worst, I believe there's a glimmer of hope and good. I think that's what keeps me going. When I think that once people lose the feeling that there is hope, a chance, then you're doomed. The minute that you feel that you can't do anything to change something, they're doomed.

That's what had happened throughout the years in this country, that because of the political system, the way it's set up, the way it's run, many people don't take part because they feel that "what I do is not going to change anything, therefore I won't do it." When you have that feeling you lay down, you haven't stood up. And the only thing that you can say about people with that ideology is that if they don't do anything, it's a fact that nothing will change. That's what worries me about this country, that in many people that attitude has formed. They wallow in despair when things don't happen the way they think they should. They feel left out because they feel their leaders, their elected officials, don't listen to them. So they just sit back and say, "I'm not going to vote, I'm not going to be a part of this because I can't change anything." They're the loneliest people of that mentality. If they can't come together on one accord for some reason, there'll always be the status quo, nothing will change.

Too many look for instant gratification. We want to see results right now. The possibility of what we are doing in the peace movement, if it lessens the chance of my great-grandkids going to war, then we've done something. It's got to be our legacy that we changed this system just enough to where people now believe that war is not the answer, to look at the real issues that cause war.

What I'm saying, it's the issues beyond the lies that the media put out: "People hate us because we are free. They hate us for what we've got," rather than looking at the real causes of why people in other lands don't like America because of the American policies that have oppressed them for years.

You can see it throughout the World Trade Organization meeting in Mexico where people stood up. All of this goes back to what Martin Luther King said. He talked about how those oppressed throughout the world, all men, at some point, they will rise up against the ones that were oppressing, and it's happening. People are too content not seeing the real reasons of why people feel as they do about this country.

I feel we're bullies. I feel that neither party will lead this country in the direction that it should go because they both are hung up on capitalism. They support the same ideas; one is just a little more progressive than the other. Republicans will throw you a bone with no meat on it and the Democrats will leave a little meat on the bone. But they are no different. Their ideas are the same.

What are the reasons of war? We spend all this money building weapons to go and fight rather than looking for solutions to eliminate war. And I don't think it's a hard equation to figure out. I don't think it's hard to pick that up. Treat people and do to people all over the world the same as you, the individual, want to be treated. If you wouldn't want your daughter or son to work for Motorola or somebody for 30 cents an hour, why would you want someone in a foreign land to do it so your profits could be higher?

My grandmother Safroni was Seminole. She had much to do with the way I think now. I believe she spent more time with me than she did my siblings. Sometimes I thought she was being mean to me because she always wanted me to do this or do that. She didn't think I would grow up to be a man, reach adulthood. She saw a lot of hate in me. She saw what was happening during those times when I was growing up.

She said the hate would destroy me, cause me to be killed because she knew that I wouldn't tolerate what was happening back during that time in Mississippi. When Emmett Till was killed she saw the same thing happening to me but for different reasons. She instilled in me that there was a way to harness that hate, to turn it into something positive. That was something that took me over 45 years to understand. When I talked about the military, she didn't think I should go. She didn't tell me not to, but she had an old canteen, one of the old aluminum canteens they used to fill in the evening with hot water, wrap it in a blanket, and stick it at the bottom of the bed by their feet to keep their feet warm in the winter. And in the morning the water would still be warm and she would wash up with it, wash her face. That's the only thing she told me that was good about the Army, she held this canteen up. I didn't understand at the time what she meant. I had no idea. Then when I graduated, I went with her blessings.

But it was many, many years before thoughts of the things that she had told me as a child growing up had been buried in the back of my mind until the year 2001. When I finally got in contact with a cousin of mine, she lived in Mississippi, who I hadn't seen in over 40 years. I was just a kid the last time I had seen cousin Lily. We went down, spent a few days with her as soon as I found out where she was. But then, she came up here probably a month later. We were sitting on the front porch talking about Mississippi in those days, my childhood. She started talking about my grandmother. It was like an awakening. Things started coming back. Many things that Lily had heard her say started bringing back the memories of when I was a kid and how she took me more or less under her wing. And I began to wonder, "Why did she do it?" I finally began to realize that she had me doing all those things not because she hated me. At that age, she understood me more than I understood myself. She saw something that she knew would destroy me if I allowed it. She tried to get me on the right track.

When I talked to Lily I began to understand it more. And then, looking at Lily she reminded me of my grandmother because her features, her bone structure, her facial features were the same. She would be talking about things with me, looking through her, looking to my grandmother.

Then the Trade Center stuff happened and after talking with Lily, listening, and seeing what was happening after the Trade Center, the Pentagon, the planes, I finally told myself what they were doing. This administration was taking that day, September 11, which was my birthday, and making it a bad day. I don't know if it was confusion or anger. I saw them beating war drums. Even to go to Afghanistan I felt was wrong. And using this day as a reason, and hearing people say that September 11 is a day that you will always remember.

Hell, I had remembered September 11 since I was born. It was my birthday. And what I saw on TV about the towers falling struck me as being a tragedy, as catastrophic.

I don't think it touched me the same as it did a lot of people because I had seen death and destruction and I knew that what happened here was something new for America, that we had been shielded in this bubble of security shielded by the oceans. We couldn't handle what people throughout the world handle every day. I had learned from Vietnam that all life is sacred.

I'm speaking of the populace now, after September 11 people seemed to be bloodthirsty. I saw them not valuing the lives of people. The same way I had done when I was in Vietnam and I was fighting. I didn't value that person. It never crossed my mind that their lives were just as precious as mine.

There were several times during 2001, after September 11, that I thought I had never really stood up for what I knew was right while laying the blame on the problems dealing with Vietnam. Part of it might have been that same rut that people wallow in, that I couldn't change anything. Then Tammy Baldwin came to a town hall meeting out here in DeForest. I went to the meeting with the sole purpose of speaking to her about SOA [School of the Americas] because I knew what was happening at the SOA. I did ask her about the SOA, but I was more concerned that we were getting ready to go into Afghanistan and the reasons behind it. From that day forward

I started watching stuff build. I could see where the administration was laying the foundation just from looking at the snippets that you would see in the news. That hurt even more because they had taken this day that was supposedly a tragedy and used it while I think people were at their lowest. That's how I got involved with MAPC [Madison Area Peace Coalition] was from that town hall meeting with Tammy. It was the first time I had joined any peace movement or anything and I was skeptical. I think my wife, Dot, had a big part in me actually joining MAPC. Because when I came back from the town hall meeting I told her that I had met these two people from Madison Area Peace Coalition that wanted us to come down and listen. I don't think I would have gone if she hadn't said "Maybe we should go and see what they're about." I went thinking that they were like a stop the war group, like many groups sometimes they'll take up an issue but once it has gone different from what their idea is, they drop it. So, I went myself to listen to MAPC and I think I did ask the question, "Were they in it for the long haul?" Then I explained what that meant to me, fighting for equality, for peace and justice throughout the world, not just to stop the war in Iraq, but also to try to stop the reasons that war happens, by changing politics. So after I saw that's the direction they were going, I joined. If I had seen that they had focused on stopping the war in Iraq, I wouldn't have joined.

In the 1980s I was in a situation where I didn't want to be part of anything. If I hadn't been married, I would have been content just living out in the woods alone. I didn't want to be around people. I was dealing with a lot of Vietnam in the 1980s. I was having a lot more flashbacks and nightmares. I wasn't dealing with it well. So I wasn't part of anything. Even during Desert Storm, I was watching CSPAN one night. At the time Canada was against the U.S. going into Iraq, and I called Canada to support the New Democratic Party that was against this. I spoke with these people in Canada and sent a letter to them because they were the only ones that were against it. The Democrats here were right behind Bush One.

When I saw the New Democratic Party in Canada that was fighting it, telling about the lies that Bush had told, it made me call them. I needed somebody I could talk to that felt the way I did, even though there might have been groups here in Madison that were vocal about it. I wasn't a part of them. I know that they had groups that actually came out and organized against Desert Storm. But I was still in that tunnel created by Vietnam in the '80s. I think back when I called Canada, it was the beginning of where my mind was coming back to reality. I didn't connect with anybody in Madison. I didn't bother to watch the news or see what was going on. And then when it started, I was watching the bombing at the end of Desert Storm when the U.S. murdered the people that were retreating and I went back in the shell. I couldn't deal with nothing no more. It was like I spent a week living in Vietnam all over. It reopened that part of my brain that I had sealed off for so many years. It made it harder for me to deal with what was going on with myself. It was even harder. I was sleeping less. I didn't want to be a part of anything. I just wanted to be out of the loop. September 11 changed that.

I just reached a point to where I couldn't keep it in any more. I reached a point where I didn't care if I was in a vets group that believed in waving the flag and was against people who spoke out. I didn't care from that point on because I found myself after September 11. I found out who I was, what I stood for, and that there's nothing on this earth can make me change back. You can take everything else but you can't take my heart, what I believe, and that's the ground I stand on. That's why I joined MAPC. I felt it was something I had to do. There's nothing this government can do anymore that will change me from who I am, like they did in the '60s. They twisted my mind. But they can't do it any more. I found myself, I have my identity. Nothing anyone can do that will change it. I think if I was of the age I am now when the draft was going I would say "No." I'd steal my grandkids out of the military. I'd do whatever it takes to keep them from going. If it means take them somewhere in the back woods and we'll survive out there together, I'll do it rather than see them go.

I feel that our young people are being misused. I use that term that many people didn't like once, and I say that I look at them now as being underpaid mercenaries. Even though it's not their choice to be, but what the government is doing is using them for the same purpose mercenaries are used where they get paid to go and fulfill the policies of anyone that's got the money to put them there. I feel that our young people now are in that position. They're not defending the Constitution. They're defending the corporate interests throughout the world of those who own the corporations or control the leaders in the government.

That's what our young people are doing. They're low-paid mercenaries. If they wanted to be mercenaries, they could have chosen to join the mercenaries and made big money. I wouldn't call them mercenaries like it was dishonoring them. It's not dishonoring, it's the truth, and they're doing what they have to do. But the government is the one that is making them mercenaries. Those young people that took the oath, took it for the same reason I took it. But they're not being used for those reasons.

I haven't pledged allegiance, none of that stuff since I came back from Vietnam. I know after I came back that was one of the things that made me different from the vets groups that I'm in. I told them before I joined that I didn't pledge allegiance, that I didn't respect the flag. But I know that deep within it were the ideals that I didn't express until after 9/11, 2001.

So, I think the seeds of me, myself, my identity, what I believe, were planted by my grandmother. And it took Lily, cousin Lily, too. It was like she put a little water on them, along with the Trade Center and watching this administration twist things to get the support the same as they did in Tonkin Gulf. My interest became more in coming out physically speaking against what was going on. It was not a hate for America. I love America as a country, but love of America to me means exactly what it says: I love this country. I love everything about it except the policies that are destroying it.

When we went to Vietnam we were chumped by this government. The veterans that don't stand up now don't have the guts for some reason to admit, "I was a sucker." They're living in a world of denial and trying to justify their reasons for being there and causing harm and death to those people in Vietnam. They are still searching for some justification rather than facing the reality of "I was a chump." That's the main barrier between those veterans and us that speak for peace.

I feel sorry for many veterans because I know many are going through the same pain that I went through. But I can't understand how they still have that hate for people. The experience I brought back from Vietnam is one that I am sad about, and at the same time I realize that experience made me come back to the reality of who I was before I went.

Coming up in the family, my mother taught us to love. Even though I knew what she meant and she used to say the same thing that Dr. King later said, you know, turn the other cheek. My mother believed in the Bible. I had a grandmother that saw within me that I wasn't one to turn the other cheek. Even with that hate I still had love. I loved people, but out of love I will kill people. It sounds funny but even now I don't worry about myself as an individual. Even though I know that violence is not an answer if Dot, if my daughter, or one of the grandkids was in danger, it wouldn't be hard to bring hate back, to use that violence. Not in the sense that I did in Vietnam but more or less in the sense to protect them.

It doesn't even have to be family. I remember when we lived in Chicago there was an old Irish guy that tended bar a block from where I worked. One night I was standing out in front of the building and there was a guy tried to stab this old guy. I ran over and took the knife from the guy just from instinct. All I knew was this old guy was a bartender and I knew that this guy had no reason to be trying to take his life. So, in that instant I could have easily killed a guy that was trying to kill the bartender or do whatever. I think something within makes one react, not just from military training or brainwashing, but what we have to do to survive.

I never said I was a pacifist. Even though I know deep within that violence is not the answer, it still bothers me a lot that I'm capable of committing it, but for purposes other than I did in Vietnam, out of love. Sounds crazy, don't it?

I hate to see anybody get messed over by anybody. I used to fight all the time, and most of the time it wasn't because someone had done something to me. But, if I saw someone doing something to others, I would intervene. That's one of the reasons I stopped drinking alcohol. Not that I was alcoholic, but I think alcohol had a lot to do with my intolerance. I made up my mind on my own to quit drinking.

When I went to PTSD counseling, it was because I lost so many people that I loved that I'm afraid to get close to people again. But I don't know if that's altogether true because I do the same thing for people I don't know.

Life itself is sacred. I mean life for you, for me, for the Israelis, for the Palestinians, the Iraqis, the whites. I hope the situation never comes where I see part of my family or anyone in danger. That's one of the reasons I didn't do civil disobedience. It was out of my own fear of not knowing how I would react if a police officer came up to grab me. It's not because I would mind doing the time. Part of it is because of growing up in the South, seeing my people being abused by the officers that are supposed to protect us. I haven't forgotten that.

So I walk away from stuff and I always try, since I came back to my senses, to try to stop a problem before it starts. I don't put myself in a situation where my actions could be adverse to what I believe. I think it's noble for people to do that, to do civil disobedience. But, with the struggle I've gone through from childhood up, I also see a side to where it might be detrimental to the movement, to myself, or even to the officer that's trying to arrest me. Too many memories. I don't know what my mind would do if I had the occasion where I did challenge some of the officers and it came down to a physical confrontation.

In the first speech that I made on the square, I said I could see why we were called unpatriotic and these different names. I explained how I had put in a 1049 request to go back to Vietnam because of the protesters, not because they were wrong, but I didn't understand at the time why they were doing what they were doing. I felt they were wrong. Once I learned, I knew they were right, and I looked at them as being the heroes and I still do.

I think those people that went to Canada or went to jail rather than joining the army are heroes because they took a stand at that time. So to me that's more heroic than what I got medals for. It doesn't bother me that people say I'm unpatriotic. It used to. But, it doesn't anymore. I know who I am, I like who I am, and there's no way you can make me think I'm anything other than who I am. If I had known that in '62, I never would have joined the military. I never would have taken that oath.

I don't look at Vietnam as a bad experience in its entirety because some good came out. After Daniel Ellsberg released the Pentagon Papers every citizen of this country should be keeping a close eye on this government and what they're doing.

It's really hard to talk about Vietnam. A lot of it is really hard when I think of some of the battles. It's hard. Not just talking about it but after just thinking about it. It doesn't go away right then. One of the things that is hard was, a friend of mine, Ellsworth, who died, who I was trying to save.

We had been out on a search and destroy mission. We used to monitor each other. All of us did a lot of patrols. We would monitor each other. When one would go on patrol the others would go up to the FDC shack and listen to the reports coming.

This one night Sergeant Womack went out. We were listening in the FDC shack and they called for indirect fire because they were being followed. They were denied indirect fire because there was a friendly village in the area. They weren't that far from our camp. You could actually see the tracers. Then it stopped. Next morning we went out and found everybody dead and mutilated except Sergeant Womack. We found out later he had been captured, and we started tracking him along the river. We knew they were taking him to the north from intelligence from the villages. So while we were tracking him we got hit. Ellsworth had gotten hit, and every time somebody tried to go to him they were wounded or killed because "Charlie" had a fire lane right to where Ellsworth was. I told my grenadier, the M-79 guy, I told him to cover fire for me because I was going to get Ellsworth. So I started out in a low crawl. I came to 15 feet from Ellsworth and he pulled his weapon on me. He said he knew that he was going to die and he would kill me before he would give "Charlie" a chance. So, I stopped. I started crawling back.

Since then I wondered if I hadn't hesitated, could I have saved him. Did I put too much value on my life when he told me he would take it when trying to save his? Could I have got him to medical help, and would he have survived or would he have pulled the trigger on me? I'm struggling with that question. I think about it, it hurts all over again. It's the question I need to answer and I don't know if I can.

I knew that he was dead. He did die, and the question lingers ... should I have done more? Would he have actually done what he said? Would he have killed me? That's hard, because I think he would have. I tell myself I think he would have done it, but then I think I'm just saying that to try to justify it. And I try to use other means to make it easier. The way he was hit and shot up he wouldn't have been normal. But then, who am I to make that decision?

When I think about that incident, it takes me to the present. I think about how many of those young people over there fighting now would experience something similar, and come back to this country, and later on in life find out that this war was a lie, that they went because of lies and deception. I wonder how will they deal with it? So many of the young men who were wounded say they would rather be there with their comrades.

Are they saying this because they're still brainwashed or is it coming from their heart? It intensifies that anger I have against what's going on now when I think of those experiences I had and see that the young today are going through the same things.

We're repeating the cycle that could have ended if people had only taken heed to what Martin Luther King said, or to what Kennedy said in 1962 when he said those who make peace impossible, make violence and war inevitable. I don't think they learned a damn thing from it. To filter the information that people get, that's what was learned from it. That we cannot allow people to have access to information that is negative toward our ideas and our causes, therefore, we'll control the information they get. I see this happening again and again until people come out and demand that this system change, because America cannot stand following the path they followed throughout the years.

It must have been 1969 at Cam Ranh Bay, the blacks got irritated because they were being pulled out of their MOS and were doing the dirty work on the base like humping ammo, regardless of MOS. They got ticked off about it, and I remember what actually started it was a movie. I think it was *A Hundred Rifles*, the movie with Jim Brown and Raquel Welch. It had this scene where Jim Brown hugged her or something while she was under the water tower, and some racial slurs started. That's all it took to tip it because the idea was already there that there would be a riot. I was in an MP unit, and I refused to go up to take part in anything to try to quell it.

I don't know how they finally settled it. I know the guys had machine guns up on the hill. The ammo dump was down in a valley, and the regular base was down, and up on the hill they had a lot of the supplies, the meat and all the other supplies were up there. The black guys took the high ground. They hauled ammo up there and set up machine guns and dared the MPs to come up. It was planned. It was well planned and well organized.

It was bad being a black man in the military. In Cu Chi, if people were wounded, if you were black, nine times out of ten you would get patched up if you were able and go back to the field, back on your regular duty. If you were Caucasian, you would go to brigade or something else, but blacks, they never got sent back to the rear.

There wasn't a whole lot of racial stuff between the individuals themselves, the soldiers. It was just at the higher levels that you would see it.

The medals I think were given according to color also. When I got my second Bronze Star people said I should have gotten a Silver Star or a higher medal. They had other people there that I know didn't do anything and they got medals, high medals.

As a matter of fact, my company commander got a Congressional Medal of Honor and he skipped out when we really got hit. It was a matter of who wrote the citations, what they put in it.

When I first got there, I didn't see them as Vietnamese. I'd been brainwashed. I saw them as the enemy. I had no regard for their life. I used to call them "gooks," the word that I hate to hear now. It bothers me when people use it. But back then, I was doing it.

It took a lot of years for me to realize that I was doing to them the same thing that had been done to me in Mississippi verbally. That word "gook" is the same as being called a "nigger" in Mississippi, and I was guilty of it. So it just reinforced the fact that I was brainwashed, that I was used as other veterans are used. I hadn't realized that the system had beaten my brain to that point where I didn't see people as people until many years later. Even as bad as things were in Mississippi, we were taught to love people, that God made all of us, that we all are connected, we are part of the earth. I was taught this and I believed it.

In boot camp all that stuff was pushed to the back of my brain and this other crap came in it. Part of the reason I survived is because when I first went in service, I was fighting every day because I could hit a white person and not get hung. I didn't need a reason for it. It was just venting anger that had been penned up in me for all those years in Mississippi, but in Vietnam I couldn't depend on blacks only.

I was squad leader. My men—one was just as important as the other. Blacks didn't get any breaks from me because they were blacks. I was not hard on whites because they were white. I treated them the same, even though at times I hadn't been treated the same. I felt you need to have that cohesiveness, that closeness in order to survive. I had both black and white people asking to come to my squad because they knew I would stand up for them. I had blacks that tried to take advantage of it, coming in because I was black they thought they'd get a break, and I let it be known that "No, you got to pull your weight."

If history had been taught as it happened, not only would it eradicate the need for black history month, but it also would have enlightened the young people on the lower end of the economic scale, not just blacks but all people, about this government, what it's doing, and they wouldn't be so apt to go and join thinking it's patriotic to do it if they know the real reason why we've been engaged in all these wars.

I see young people when I go in the schools and talk to them. Any chance I get I talk to a young person. I often wonder if this kid knew that this country was on this imperial quest, would they still want to join the military? If they knew the true reason that we are involved all over, could history have changed their perspective of what's happening now? I think it would have.

I think the dots could be connected simply by reading history, what happened, what this country's done in so many different places. If you read that, then I think the brain tells you to look farther, and you would learn, you would connect it.

We didn't go into Vietnam mainly because of a Communist threat. We didn't go into Iraq because ... we didn't go into Nicaragua because ... we didn't use the CIA to overturn these governments for this or that.

I think young people are intelligent enough if they had all the information, that they would make the right decisions. I think if that history was taught, it would affect young people in different ways. I don't think the government would be in the shape it's in now if the real history was taught because I think as a rule, the populace of this country wants to do the right thing. I really believe that, but I think many don't know what's going on.

MIKE BOEHM

Vietnam

I served in Vietnam from 1968 to 1969. I was stationed first in Dau Tieng for about three months and then in Cu Chi. That job meant a lot to me. It was the first time in my life I had been treated with respect. I rose from Spec 4 to staff sergeant within a year. I worked in G-3 Plans in 25th Infantry Division Headquarters. What our office did was to act as liaison between different combat units. We were fielding calls from units all day. Say Company A had information of enemy activity in Company B's territory and they wanted to send a patrol in. They would have to go through us. We would get permission from Company B and then Company A could go in. But before that we would have to notify the ARVN, the South Vietnamese Army, our air force, and our artillery to make sure that everybody knew where everybody was. Luckily, we made no mistakes that year I was there, so there was no one killed or wounded by friendly fire.

I didn't go over there to fight Communism or to bring democracy to the people, I didn't know anything about democracy or Communism. I went to Vietnam to please my father. I'm the oldest of seven kids and all of us had been badly abused by our father. As a result, I had no capacity for empathy for the Vietnamese people, or any ability to think through my decision to go to Vietnam. I drifted through a year and a half in Vietnam and I came home to Mauston, the small town where I had been raised.

The person I have become was formed out of child abuse. I don't feel sorry for myself but I do recognize the path I have taken in life, or the path that was chosen for me, is a direct result of my finding a path to healing. Vietnam and child abuse are so linked together as motives for the direction my life has taken that I could never separate them.

It wasn't until a few years later that I started catching on to what I had been party to in Vietnam and it all came together for me the summer of 1977. I had been going to Madison Area Technical College where I was taking a two-year college entry program. I was receiving money from the G.I. Bill to be able to go to school. The summer between those two school years was when everything fell in place. I went to my mother's house, went to the attic, got my uniform, medals, and everything, and threw them into the garbage. When I went back to school the fall of 1977, I went to the veteran's representative and told him I wasn't going to accept the G.I. Bill anymore because it was blood money. He was furious because that wasn't playing the game. You go to war, you take your "bennies." But other than that small gesture, there wasn't anything else I could do because it was a done deal, the war was over. It didn't take long for me to learn that Vietnam was not an aberration. I started looking into our history, looking into all of our military and economic interventions around the world, and the more I learned the more I started backing away, retreating from being involved with this society until I reached the point where I lived in a shack with no plumbing or electricity for about seven years.

People misunderstand people like me who live in shacks. I've been asked a number of times "Oh, you mean like Ted Kaczynski?" Or they think that those of us who lived in shacks were lost, that we had been so overwhelmed by the circumstances of our life that we couldn't interact with society. That wasn't true in my case because I wasn't isolated. I had my circle of friends. I just refused to take part in most aspects of this society because I saw no value in this society. Or at least the values that I saw were not values that I wanted to take part in, all of this death and destruction to basically allow us to shop 'til we drop.

Most of what I'm saying now took quite a bit of time to articulate. On the surface it looks like I have made decisions impulsively but that is not the case. Intuition, informed by an overwhelming need for spiritual balance, inner and outer, has been the driving force behind what I choose to do.

Living in the shack was a healing experience. It was during that time that I found a broken violin in the trash, got it fixed up, and that's where I learned to play the violin at age 40. It was during that time that I did rehabilitation work with wild animals through the Dane County Humane Society. People brought in more than just cats and dogs. They'd find squirrels or whatever, and a group of people like me did the rehab work. I took in squirrels, foxes, deer, hawks, owls, vultures.

That was very, very satisfying for me. There were a lot of wonderful moments with them. One day I had three baby squirrels inside the shack. They had already been weaned. When they're really young you have to feed them with syringes with Similac or something like that. But they'd been weaned. I fed them nuts and vegetables and stuff. And they were just tooling around the shack and I'm sitting next to the stove playing my fiddle. They all started climbing on me because I was "dad." At one point all three of them hopped on my left arm. So they were busy eating away with their tiny little tails curled up like they do, sitting on my arm as I was playing the violin. I have a vivid, vivid memory of that.

Loneliness was a problem occasionally, but loneliness can be a problem no matter where you live. Up until that point in my life I had gone from job to job hating all of them but never understanding why I hated them, getting into trouble in many of them because of my overreaction to abuse and authority. I got fired from six different jobs. So I think living in the shack was a very important transition period.

It was while living in the shack that I learned carpentry. I used to pick up this kind of high-end glossy magazine for home-builders called *Fine Homebuilding*. And in 1991, I believe it was, at the back of this particular issue there was a short two-paragraph article by Ruel Bernard, a carpenter from outside Albany, New York, who was calling on other carpenters to come with him down to Puerto Rico to help rebuild after Hurricane Hugo. And I thought, "Yeah, I want to do that." So I called him up and he immediately started telling me about the political situation in Puerto Rico, and I said, "Ruel, I'm going down there for humanitarian reasons, not for political reasons." I was really hard on him. I wouldn't want someone like me on one of our projects. So we get down there and I discovered that Puerto Rico wasn't just one island. Puerto Rico is made up of one large island and two small islands, and one of the two smaller islands was where we worked, the island of Vieques. What I learned there, that the island was divided into thirds and the outer two-thirds were used as a practice range by our navy, just fanned the flames of hatred. Everything we learned as children, to know good from evil, had been turned on its head, white was black and evil was good.

To be put in a position to commit evil or to support the commission of evil, how do you live with that? How do you ever trust your institutions, religious institutions, education institutions, people, your parents?

I got down to Vieques and I talked to the people there who were trying to live under these conditions, with artillery shells and bombs raining on their tiny island. Vieques is about four miles by 22 miles. And, of course, regularly, shells would go astray and somebody would be wounded or killed. The real problem, aside from the flat-out disruption of daily life, was the chemicals released over a period of 60 years. Cancer rates are high. Hearing all that was like pouring gasoline on the fire for me because I had already had all this hatred in me anyway. The big difference this time was putting bricks together in that context. I remember flying back to Madison and just feeling euphoric. It just felt so good. I had never done anything like that. I didn't know that a positive response to all this evil was possible. Even though that response was small, just putting a few bricks together. So the first thing I thought of was: "I wonder if I can do this in Vietnam." I hadn't realized Vietnam was that close to the surface of my consciousness.

I got back to Madison and started asking around and ran into Judy Ladinski, who told me about an organization in California that was doing similar work. The organization is called the Veterans Vietnam Restoration Project (VVRP). What they had been doing since 1988 was building health clinics in Vietnam. The government in Vietnam would determine where a clinic would be built. Then VVRP would start fund-raising, writing grants, sending out funding letters, and so on. When they had the funds for the clinic they would then put out a call for American veterans to come over to Vietnam and work alongside the Vietnamese to build a health clinic. It was a very good concept because it was a practical, useful project and healing at the same time. So, I called them up and got on team four, which left California, I believe, in early February 1992.

We were there two months. There were 12 of us vets and one other guy from California who was a grad student. He was doing his Ph.D. dissertation on the effects on American veterans upon returning to Vietnam. He had us filling out forms. He was observing us while we were there and so on. The 12 of us had never met before. We came from all around the U.S. and gathered at a place called Magic Mountain north of San Francisco. That name should have been the clue right there.

I think all of our reactions ranged from being a little nervous to being terrified about going back to Vietnam. For myself I was nervous. But after three days in Magic Mountain, going through every new age, touchy-feely, bonding process, we were ready to go to Vietnam, anywhere. We wanted to get out of Magic Mountain.

The location of the clinic we helped build was in Xuan Hiep village, Dong Nai province in southern Vietnam, about 60 miles northeast of Ho Chi Minh city. The 12 of us were supposed to work with the Vietnamese, side by side. But they were getting there at dawn and working to dusk. So they were working at least 12 hours a day, seven days a week, and we'd show up at mid-morning and quit in mid-afternoon. It was hot. I had forgotten how hot it was there. And here we are, middle-aged, out-of-shape American men, you know, trying to keep up with the Vietnamese, and it was no contest. Watching the Vietnamese build this clinic using just these wired together hand tools was an amazing process. That 10-room clinic was built, begun and finished, in three and half weeks.

The effect on me from being back in Vietnam was completely unexpected. I felt driven to come over and do this thing, to build this clinic. I thought I had no trauma from Vietnam, at least as far as I understood trauma at the time. I felt the men and women who were traumatized by the war were the ones in combat. I think some of the nurses had worse experiences than combat troops. I thought the guys I was traveling with, many of whom were in combat, were the ones that were traumatized from the war, not me. I worked in an office during the war. My weapon was a telephone. But I had a lot of problems being back. After I was back in the U.S. and I was able to sort out all my emotions, I realized that the problems I was having came down to a very simple question: "Why?"

I got to know the guys I was traveling with and I heard their horror stories of the war and their horror stories after the war, drug abuse, alcohol abuse, suicide attempts, and for some of them, hoping that coming back would somehow lay those demons to rest. Then I would hear the stories of the Vietnamese. The man who was in charge of working with us was very tense working around us, very unhappy, chain-smoking all the time. It turns out that his whole family had been annihilated, obliterated by an American bombing raid, and because his family was essentially vaporized, he couldn't bury his family. All he could do was take soil with their flesh mixed into it and bury that instead. Working with us was his job. He was under orders. It was really hard for him to be around us because it brought up all those memories. It was that kind of story that I kept hearing over and over again.

It's one thing to read a story like that here in the U.S., safe in our own country, our own homes. It's quite different hearing that story standing on the soil of Vietnam, even for a non-combatant like myself. So it all came down to "why?" Why all this death? Why all this pain? Why all this suffering?

I was not easy to be around because I was lashing out at people for no good reason because of all that rage and grief. I was also bursting into tears. Usually I'd find a place by myself when the tears came. Finally one evening, I think toward the end of the construction process on the clinic, I was lying on my bed at the resort place that they put us in. And what rose up out of that stew of emotions was to go to My Lai. By that time in my life, My Lai had come to represent the whole war.

When the clinic was finished, five of us traveled on to Hanoi by van and on our way north I insisted we stop at the My Lai Memorial. Not all the guys wanted to. The My Lai Memorial was constructed on the site of where part of the massacre happened. Shortly after the end of the American war in 1975, construction began on the memorial. It's a very emotionally wrenching place to be. What I did was go to the main monument, which is a cluster of figures designed on the old Stalinist concept of rage and resistance via the up-thrust fist. It's tough to be there. I had brought my violin with me to Vietnam because I couldn't speak the language but music transcends that, usually. I played taps as my offering to the spirits of the dead. It is a military tune, but taps has always meant to me farewell and rest in peace. It was for everybody, not just the Vietnamese. Everybody. It was tough, you know. We were all crying and my hands were shaking so much I had the vibrato I've never had since. All I can say now is that I think it helped. It was something I had to do. And it was impulse or intuition that led me there. Logic didn't bring me to that place.

As soon as we got back, five or six of us on that team were asked to be on the new board of directors for VVRP. I leaped at it because I wanted more of whatever that was I had just experienced.

In December 1992 or January 1993, I received a call from Carol Wagner. She said she worked with Global Exchange and she was in Madison selling off her share of a company called Earth Care Paper. She said that she had led a study tour to Vietnam the fall of 1992. This study tour was of women only, so their hosts in Vietnam were the Vietnam Women's Union. This was six months after we had been there. She said that she was going to be showing slides at the Friends Meeting House, and would I be interested in coming to see them? She was obviously a very good organizer because she knew people who were interested in Vietnam, Betty Boardman and Joe Elder. Through them she learned of other people like me who were interested in Vietnam. A number of us showed up at the meetinghouse. She showed the slides and during the presentation told us that one of the places they had visited was My Lai. When she finished the slide presentation she told us that while they were in My Lai they had received a proposal by the Quang Ngai Province Women's Union to fund a micro-credit program for the poor women of My Lai based on the Grameen Bank concept. She told us that while Global Exchange philosophically supported this kind of endeavor, it's not something they actually fund, so would we like to start an ad hoc group, and she suggested a name, Madison Indochina Support Group, and take on this proposal. Sure, we thought, that was great. So that's where my involvement in Vietnam came in again. My Lai was coming back into my life again. We agreed to take this on, Betty Boardman, Joe Elder, and some others and I, and during 1993 we began raising funds for this project. I didn't know squat about organizing or fund-raising or anything, so we had garage sales and events like that to raise the money. My mother had a bake sale. She baked cookies and cakes and bread and sold that. She raised over $400. We only needed to raise $3,000 but we didn't quite meet our goal so I paid for the shortfall.

That was our first My Lai loan fund. I was back in Vietnam December 1993–January 1994. On January 10, 1994, I formally handed over the funds for the My Lai loan fund to the Quang Ngai Province Women's Union. It was a modest beginning, and because the initial funding was so small it was actually creating problems within the village. I got a letter from the

Women's Union, the provincial Women's Union, a couple of months after I had gotten back in 1994 telling me that this initial investment of $3,000 was not enough. What was happening was that a handful of women were receiving loans and having their lives improved but hundreds more were on the outside looking in with no access to the fund. It was creating a lot of tension within the village. So would we, Madison Quakers by this time, be able to expand this fund by $10,000?

Thinking back now I was so caught up in the moment, I hadn't realized how historic this was. My Lai has been evoked over the years for this atrocity or that atrocity. Look how many times it came up just during the Abu Ghraib scandal. And yet, nobody has dealt with it. Think about all these years My Lai has been bandied about yet whenever My Lai comes up in a conversation what's the context: rage and grief or denial or finger pointing. "Somebody's got to be blamed for this." It's like having been caught in a closed loop. We're caught in all these different dysfunctional emotions dealing with My Lai rather than ever facing the reality of what that meant to us as a people.

We Americans live with these myths about ourselves that are so completely divorced from reality and one of these myths is the magnitude of our goodness. Our goodness is so vast, so deep that it's genetic. We don't have to even think about our actions, whether they're right or wrong because we are Americans. Therefore what we do is automatically right. That makes us inhuman. What else could it be? Every human being on this planet is capable of evil. Until we address that, we're never going to deal with what happened in My Lai or Abu Ghraib or anything in between. What makes this project so historic is the very fact that we have put that aside. All that hatred, all that grief, denial, recrimination, we've put aside. As a result, we have been able to take on the responsibility for what happened at My Lai, a responsibility our government has refused to accept in a peaceful, inclusive way.

I look at the photos of those early meetings of me with the Women's Union and I realize that I hadn't a clue of the impact of what we were accomplishing together. Over the years we have developed a very strong relationship and, in fact, four years ago I was made an honorary member of the Quang Ngai Province Women's Union. I have my own little laminated card. They had fun with it. When it came time to put my name in there they asked "Mrs. Boehm?"

These are rural areas the women live in and the uses for their loans reflect that. They use their loans for raising cows, raising pigs, chickens, ducks, shrimp farming, producing cassava flour, retail business, sewing. The concept, since it is based on the Grameen Bank, is for loans to go to poor women only to start up small businesses. The loans are repaid and then given out again to other poor women.

The hardships these women have experienced in the past and still live under are almost unimaginable. Mrs. Nguyen Thi Lan from Pho Khanh village is one example. Phan Van Do, the coordinator of the Vietnam projects, and I go back to each village shortly after it's funded. We do this because we believe that relationship building is easily as important as the economic aid itself. We feel it's very important that we come back to meet with the women who receive these loans. We can get to know them and they get to know us. Instead of being some distant entity that is tossing money their way, we want them to know we are real human beings interacting with each other. The soil in that village is basically beach sand so it's difficult to grow crops with any value, fruit trees, for example. Mrs. Lan's idea, which was very innovative, was to start a nursery growing eucalyptus trees because eucalyptus will grow anywhere. As Phan Van Do and I walked around her nursery with her we noticed she walked with a limp. At one point Do asked her what had happened. She said that in 1972 when she was 14 years old she stepped on a mine and lost her leg. A few years later she met a young man who, also in 1972, had stepped on a mine and lost his leg. They felt that because of that shared trauma they understood each other better than others could, got married, and had two girls. He died many years ago leaving her to raise the children by herself.

We have friends here in Madison who are single parents, single mothers raising children, and we know how hard it is for them. Imagine a single mother in Vietnam living under these horrendous conditions, trying to raise her children by herself, but as she told us her story, there was absolutely no anger from her—no anger, no sadness, just enthusiasm that at long last she could borrow money and improve the lives of her children.

When you think of the cult of victimhood we have in this country, where if you stub your toe, you call the ambulance and then the lawyer, or maybe the lawyer first, it really points out how strong these women are. I have so much admiration for the strength of these women to endure and move ahead. I put myself in their place and I know I'm not that strong.

The story I'd like to finish up with is Mrs. Pham Thi Huong from Truong Khanh village. We established the loan fund in this village about seven years ago now. As with the other funds we had set up, Do and I went back to visit shortly after the fund had been implemented. After we arrived she took us to her cow pen to show the cow she had bought with the loan she had received. She told us that she had done what every woman does when she buys a cow, which was to have it artificially inseminated. Once the calf had been born and weaned, she could sell the calf, pay back the loan, have the cow bred again and she's on a roll. Like most women in her village, her house was made of mud: mud floor, mud walls, thatch roof. Words don't describe how poor she was. She would answer our questions in a monotone but there was no life in her.

The day before we came up to Truong Khanh, Do had told me that this village also had a massacre. And sure enough as we drove up that next day they had their own memorial commemorating their massacre just like the My Lai Memorial. All these years our government and our military have been trying to portray My Lai as an aberration and of course it wasn't. I've since heard of many other massacres. At one point Do asked Mrs. Huong if she had been there the day of the massacre. I watched as she responded in Vietnamese and then burst into tears; she couldn't speak anymore. She said yes, of course, she had survived the massacre but that her aunt and two of her children were killed. The massacre at My Lai was begun and over within four hours. The massacre at Truong Khanh took place over a period of two days. The G.I.s kept coming back and killing anyone they saw, but mostly they were trying to hide the evidence so they burnt the bodies and partially buried them.

It was days before the villagers felt safe enough to come out, unearth the bodies and inter them properly. Bodies rot quickly in tropical heat and the last thing Mrs. Huong said before she broke down was, "I cannot forget the smell of the decomposing bodies of my children." What can you say in the face of something like that? We spent a fair amount of time with her that day and while she was walking and talking, to me she seemed dead inside. I was wrong because two years later Do and I were back visiting Truong Khanh village again and Mrs. Huong and Mrs. Du, chairwoman of the village Women's Union, were on a motorcycle outside the village eagerly waiting to lead Do and I around the village to show us the improvement in the lives of the women over the previous two years. I kept looking at Mrs. Huong. I couldn't believe she was the same person. She was laughing and talking and her eyes were bright and shiny and alive. Do started talking to the neighbors, trying to find out how this change came about. They said that once money started coming into her house through the sale of calves, that at long last that crushing burden of poverty lifted enough where she could begin to heal. If somebody had told me this, I wouldn't have believed it.

I would have thought it's just another new age, something-for-nothing spiritual event. We went to visit her again last year and she now has a new home, a beautiful new home, cement and brick, cement floor, nicely painted, nicely furnished. She now has a herd of five cows and three water buffalos.

We have now funded loans in 16 villages and have provided more than 3,000 loans to poor women. Every year, depending on our funding, we expand into more and more villages.

Last year was the 10-year anniversary of the relationship between the Quang Ngai Province Women's Union and the Madison Quakers and myself. So the Quang Ngai Province Women's Union had a ceremony to commemorate these 10 years of working together. There were a number speeches by ranking Women's Union officials, but the speech that meant the most to me was by Mrs. Tinh Minh Oai, who at the time was vice-woman of the Quang Ngai People's Committee, one of the highest ranking political positions in the province. She said two things that meant a lot to me. She said that the Madison Quakers is the only organization doing humanitarian work in Quang Ngai Province that touches the people's heart. And she said Madison Quakers is the only organization allowed to work with the ethnic minorities in Quang Ngai Province.

There are two extremely sensitive issues for anybody working in Vietnam, these are religion and ethnic minorities. There are 54 ethnicities or ethnic groups in Vietnam, the vast majority being the Kinh, the Vietnamese people. The 53 other ethnic tribes live up in the mountains throughout Vietnam and they have been treated by the Vietnamese over the centuries like Native American people have been treated in the U.S. Outside forces have exploited that hatred by the ethnic people toward the Vietnamese. Our CIA used them to fight against the Vietnamese during the American War. Outside forces have been coming in since the end of our war to try to foment uprisings by the ethnic people against the Vietnamese government.

The Vietnamese government is careful about who is even allowed in the central provinces to visit these tribes, much less who can work there. It is a testament to the trust they have in the Madison Quakers that for the last four years I have been asked to help fund ethnic villages in Quang Ngai Province. The last seven villages in which we have established loan funds have been for ethnic tribes. The difficulties in establishing programs in the ethnic villages are much greater than in Vietnamese villages. There is very low education within these ethnic tribes. In Truong Ke village in the last 200 years, only one boy has graduated from high school. The conditions under which people in the mountains live present more difficulties.

An example of these conditions can be seen in the story of Mrs. Pham Thi Ru from Truong Ke village. We met her four years ago. She lived in a grass hut with a mud floor. She looked to be around 80 years old but we could only guess because she didn't know how old she was. When we went to see her four years ago, she said that in January of that year her last surviving son had been killed by lightning. Two months later her last surviving grandson was killed by a poisonous snake. This is life in the mountains.

In 1989, Morley Safer went to Vietnam to produce a segment for *60 Minutes* called "The Enemy." He had access to all the old high-ranking officials, but the man who stood out in that segment was a teacher of English from Hanoi named Nguyen Ngoc Hung. His English was very good, of course, but he was also very compassionate, very charismatic. As a result, he was brought to the United States on a speaking tour promoting peace, friendship, and reconciliation. That was the first time our "enemy" had come to this country to speak of peace, friendship, and reconciliation. I can't imagine the strength and courage it took for him to do that.

One stop was Madison, and from there local veterans took him up to the Wisconsin Vietnam Veteran's Memorial called the Highground. On top of the hill at the Highground are a number of statues, but down the slope from the statues is a memorial that seems to have the most impact and potential for healing for the Americans, the Dove Mound. One reason for the potential for healing from this memorial is that it was designed intentionally to infuse some form of spirituality because it was inspired by Native American effigy mounds. Hung was brought down there and told that the Dove Mound is a powerful source of healing.

I talked to the director of the Highground and he told me that he and his staff have come to the Highground in the middle of winter and they have seen where somebody had come in the middle of the night and walked through the snow to lie down on that mound. He was also told this is a place to go to remember your friends who were killed in Vietnam and who are still missing in Vietnam. When Hung heard that last part he took incense he had brought from Hanoi, placed it on the mound, lit it and then said a prayer for his younger brother who is one of Vietnam's 300,000 missing in action.

Up until that point I heard that many of the vets who were there were furious that the enemy had been brought to their sacred site. But when they saw him do that, burn incense for his younger brother, many of them saw him, for the first time as their brother. They understood very well, the importance, the emotional impact of somebody who's missing in action. A poem was written a few days later that ended with "I looked into the eyes of my enemy and saw myself. To kill him would be suicide, to love him would be salvation."

Three years later, in 1993, when we were busy raising money for the My Lai loan fund I heard that Hung was being brought to the United States again. I arranged out of my own pocket for him to fly from California to Madison. Because I was angry that all we could ever talk about was our pain and our suffering. As if we were the only ones affected by the war. I thought at least the people of Madison are going to hear the Vietnamese side. It was while arranging for his visit to Madison that I heard for the first time the incident at the Highground three years before and I thought, "This is it. If we are ever going to have an honest relationship with the people of Vietnam, the foundation upon which it rests must come from some deep fundamental level within ourselves." And that is what I felt this incident represented. Unbeknownst to me Hung had been feeling the same way. That was the inspiration for the first peace park in Vietnam, the Vietnamese–American Peace Park.

Over the years, people from around the world have been inspired by this concept of the peace parks. It was 1993 when Hung and I discussed the possibility of a peace park. Two years later, on May 11, 1995, we had the groundbreaking ceremony. With us that day was General Pham Hong Son. General Son is the brother-in-law of General Vo Nguyen Giap, who was the commander-in-chief of the Vietnamese military that had defeated first the French and then the Americans. Having Giap's brother-in-law with us turned that small ceremony into something much grander. At one point, I stuck my hand out to shake hands with him and he pushed my hand aside and gave me a hug instead. After giving me a hug, which, incidentally, is very un-Vietnamese, he said, "Most countries around the world continue to teach the younger generations about the horrors of war by building war monuments. We are changing this tradition by building a monument to peace."

A few years later, U.S. Ambassador to Vietnam Pete Peterson came to the Vietnamese–American Peace Park to plant his tree and he said, "Mike, this peace park is an example of the exchange of love and mutual respect between the people of our two countries." Now these are pretty remarkable words coming from a man who had been shot down over North Vietnam and held as a prisoner of war for six and a half years, tortured much of that time. Six months after the ground-breaking ceremony we held the dedication ceremony on November 11, 1995 for this peace park. Thirteen veterans flew from the U.S. to attend this ceremony. One vet wrote to us after he returned to his home and said, "As I stood on that hill after planting my tree and embracing my former enemy, I felt I had finally begun to heal."

Six months before this dedication ceremony, while working on the My Lai loan fund, I was introduced to a man from Quang Ngai Province named Phan Van Do. Do, who is also a teacher of English in Vietnam, became the project coordinator for all of the Madison Friends projects. He's become my teacher, my role model, and my brother. We were introduced by the Quang Ngai Province Women's Union in May 1995 when they asked him to translate for me during my visit to My Lai. We spent the day visiting and interviewing women who had received loans in order to evaluate the success of the loan fund. At the end of the day, a number of us went to nearby My Khe beach to review the loan fund and talk about future loan funds. At one point I mentioned I had to be back in Hanoi to attend the groundbreaking ceremony for the Vietnamese–American Peace Park that was going to be constructed north of Hanoi. There was a bit of silence at first. Finally Do asked me, "What is a peace park?" I said both of our countries have plenty of monuments to war. This is a monument to peace so there will be no statues, no artillery pieces, just trees, flowers, shrubs, and fish ponds, just a green living monument to peace. They were stunned.

For more than 3,000 years the Vietnamese have been driving out invaders. They've driven out the Chinese nine times. They defeated the Mongols twice. They've driven out the French, the Americans, the Thais, the Cambodians. They have war memorials all up and down their country. They have never conceived of the possibility of a memorial to peace. So after I described this future peace park, there was kind of a barrage of questions from Mrs. Ho Thi Hanh, Chairwoman of the Quang Ngai Province Women's Union and Phan Van Do. Finally Do turned to me and asked, "Can the Madison Quakers help us build a peace park for My Lai?" So, the second peace park was inspired by that first one built north of Hanoi.

Over the years, I have witnessed some powerful reactions to this concept of a peace park, especially the My Lai Peace Park. We dedicated the My Lai Peace Park on March 16, 2001. Twenty-five Americans flew to attend the ceremonies and to plant trees. As with the first park, we paired off with our Vietnamese counterparts to plant trees together. To plant a tree, you really have to have hope for the future. To plant a tree with your former enemy, what kind of hope does that inspire? After planting the trees at the My Lai Peace Park, we went to My Khe beach for lunch and shortly after we got there a man from Ireland showed up, Brendan Jones. He said he was really disappointed because he had heard about the ceremonies for the My Lai Peace Park but didn't know where to find us. Do and I arranged for his own private visit to the My Lai Peace Park. He came back a while later, fairly subdued, at least for an Irishman. A couple of months later I got a letter from him. He said, "Mike, you asked me what I thought of the My Lai Peace Park. When I saw those beautiful trees growing out of that barren soil and the villagers taking their lunch under those trees, I thought there is hope for peace in Ireland." It's remarkable how this idea of former enemies coming together to build a peace park on the site of a horrible killing ground is touching people beyond just our two countries.

We have been building a series of primary schools over the years. We had constructed our first three-room primary school by the end of 1998. Shortly after that I was showing slides to a Girl Scout Troop here in Madison. When I show slides to kids, it's kid stuff: "Here are the children of Vietnam, here is what they look like, here are things they like to do. See, they like to play soccer just like you do. And here is a small school that we just had built for them. But the school doesn't have a toilet." Well, this was mind-boggling because these girls were already struggling with the fact that most people in Vietnam can't just go into their house and turn on a faucet for water. They kept coming back with, "You mean they can't just go into their house and turn on a faucet for water? How do they get their water?" Then they hear me talk of a school without a toilet and that was just inconceivable. They took it upon themselves, with the guidance of their den mother, to write a $500 grant. They used that $500 grant and their Girl Scout cookie money, gave me the money, and asked that we build a toilet for the school. There was enough money left over so we could also fund a new well, build a holding tank, and install new plumbing. I like getting kids involved.

It wasn't long after that when we began raising funds for a much larger eight-room primary school. That building was dedicated on March 17, 2001. Included at each ceremony are speeches by the various officials, and the People's Committee speeches never change. Politicians are the same all over the world. They make their speeches so safe it's like listening to white noise. You grit your teeth and smile and wait for them to be over. After their speeches, though, a little girl came up and said that Uncle Ho Chi Minh taught the people of Vietnam the importance of education, so on behalf of the school children of My Lai she wanted to thank the Madison Quakers for their help in building this school and hoped for more help in the future.

Last year we funded and dedicated a second eight-room primary school and had a group of almost 40 former anti-Vietnam War protesters from Japan take part in the ceremonies. They planted their own tree in front of the school and held hands in a big circle around the tree when they were finished. We're now raising funds for one final eight-room building and that will complete the need for classroom space for My Lai for some years to come. Once that's finished, we'll start moving into other villages building schools.

Sisters Meeting Sisters came about as a result of a visit by Madison Mayor Susan Bauman to El Salvador in the fall of

1998. Arcatao is one of Madison's sister cities, so Mayor Bauman went down visit Arcatao. While she was there, she met with women's groups who talked with her about the different issues they were working with, such as the maquiladores, the sweatshops. One of the projects they talked to her about was the micro-credit program, the loan fund programs that they were struggling to make a success. Mayor Bauman was asked why not bring the women from My Lai to meet with the women of El Salvador because our loan funds in Vietnam have a very high success rate. In 13 of the 16 villages that we have funded in Vietnam, the repayment rate of the loans is 100 percent. That's better than you could say about banks here in the U.S. Mayor Bauman thought that was great idea and when they returned to Madison I was contacted because of my relationship with the Women's Union in Vietnam. In January 2000 I was sent down on behalf of this newly formed project, Sisters Meeting Sisters. When I met with women's groups in El Salvador and we discussed this idea of the women from Vietnam meeting with the women of El Salvador, I didn't say this is what we're going to do. I said this is our idea, what do you think? The reaction was immediate and emotionally charged. The women had tears in their eyes as we discussed this possibility. Just meeting the women of Vietnam, they told me, would revitalize their organizations because the women in El Salvador are former guerillas. The women I met and the guerilla movements of Central America, in Nicaragua, El Salvador, Guatemala all look up to the people of Vietnam for having won their revolution.

The women from both countries immediately took this idea much further. They felt they needed to discuss a wider range of issues: domestic violence, sexual violence, women in government, and women in the work place were some of the issues that would be discussed when they met, but the issue both women's groups came back to repeatedly was healing from the trauma of war. By the end of that first year they had exchanged a very powerful series of letters. Each of the letters was an articulate plea for the women of the world to unite to end the fratricide of war.

Mike Boehm *103*

One of the meetings with the women of El Salvador took place on the Rio Sumpul. For folks knowledgeable about the war in El Salvador, the most well-known, infamous massacre was the El Mozote massacre on the Rio Sumpul, but there were massacres all up and down that river. In the mid-1980s the El Salvadoran government, frustrated with not knowing who was the guerilla in the village and who wasn't, would come in and massacre any village that was suspected of harboring guerillas.

One day in El Salvador in 2000, I was seated in a circle with four women, Esperanza, Tita, Esmeralda, and Adela, on the riverbed of the Rio Sumpul. It was the dry season. Esperanza was telling me of a massacre that the four of them had survived. Esperanza was leaning forward just a little, not looking at me but telling me how years before the four of them had fled the El Salvadoran government troops when they were spotted coming to the village to kill everybody. As they fled the government troops, they were stopped by the river, which was much higher at the time. As they swam across, the government troops opened fire on them with their M-16s. Hundreds were killed. Esperanza's son, Alberto, was 9 years old at the time. He made it across the Rio Sumpul, climbed a small hill and watched as the government troops would become weary of firing their guns and hand them off to other soldiers to continue the killing. When Esperanza finished telling me this story, she said she had given testimony of this massacre all over the world, including the Vatican. But, she said, this was the first time she had given this testimony at the site of the massacre itself. She reached down to the riverbed and picked up a small stone and handed it to me saying, "Please give this to the women of My Lai as a symbol of today's testimony." Before these women had even met they already had a powerful emotional exchange.

After I returned to Madison, I thought of that day and I thought of all the times I've been in this position over the years, sitting in women's kitchens or pig pens or cow pens or rice paddies or the Rio Sumpul. Women suffered as much as the men did, but their suffering goes unacknowledged. In the midst of all the killing, they still made the meals for their family.

Just having heard their stories I'm having emotional problems, yet these women actually lived these stories. How could they live through these horrors? Instead of succumbing to the trauma, they move ahead raising their children, trying to keep their communities together. I hold their strength in awe, that they were not only able to survive, but also to focus all their energies to moving ahead.

The Grameen Bank was created years ago to give loans to poor men and women to start small businesses. They would pay the loans back and then the money would be loaned out again. A few years after they initiated this program, they realized loans to women were much more successful than loans to men. Women, in general, are focused on family, community, and problem solving rather than resorting to violence. Of course, there are exceptions, such as Madeleine Albright and Condoleezza Rice, the female men. Still, women have strength that men don't acknowledge or comprehend. I was open to accepting this strength, but I didn't begin to understand the depth of this strength until I began working directly with women in Vietnam and El Salvador. I saw their lives and heard what they had endured and yet they still looked to the future, not for themselves but for their children. It's one thing to read about this, but I only experienced the reality of this strength when I began working with women.

In my second visit to El Salvador, I was asked to go to Guatemala. It's a five-hour bus ride from one capitol to the other. Women from Guatemala wanted to hear more about the Sisters Meeting Sisters project. One of the women I met in Guatemala was Manuela Alvarado. Once we had talked through the issues of Sisters Meeting Sisters she said to me, referring to Guatemalan society, "If this society is ever going to be saved, it will be the women who save it." For me, this applies to every society around the world.

All these projects will keep expanding as funds come in every year. All of these projects were inspired by requests by the people of Vietnam through the Women's Union, People's Committees, and education authorities. We feel the Vietnamese know much better than we do what their needs are, and we have Phan Van Do overseeing all the projects making sure the money is being used the way it is supposed to be used.

The one project I started myself was an art exchange between the children of My Lai and Madison. The children of My Lai began this exchange back in 1996 by making drawings for me to give to the children of Madison at Marquette Elementary School. The children of Marquette made drawings for the children of My Lai, and now this project, the Art Penpals Project, has expanded to include many elementary schools in Madison and some from other parts of the country. It's more than just a cute project. The idea is to get the kids to know each other. The children certainly enjoy it. When you think about how little we know our next door neighbor, you begin to realize how little we know of people on the other side of the world and, therefore, how easy it is to go to war with them. If we get our children to know each other a little bit, maybe making war with others will be a little bit harder in the future.

If we are willing to sit down with humility, which is tough for Americans, to listen and to learn from each other, anything is possible. There is an "us versus them" mentality in this country that has persisted for many years. In the context of the war in Vietnam, this has played out as "us against the soldiers," "us against the protesters," "us against the Communists," and so on. This dichotomy exists in my own family, and so I see my family as representing our country. My younger brother is also a Vietnam veteran and, in fact, our tours overlapped. We even had an in-country R&R together in 1969. Years ago, he told me that the humanitarian work I was doing in Vietnam was treason and the last thing he said to me was, "If you love those fucking people so much then move there, get out of this country." I don't blame him for his hatred for the Vietnamese because what he experienced in combat destroyed something inside him, but this split is not necessary. I believe we could sit together and come to understand each other's realities. That is what I see, co-existing realities rather than one side versus another. If we could acknowledge these coexisting realities rather than continually pitting ourselves against each other, we could actually come to understand each other, and with that would come acceptance.

The trauma experienced by many of our soldiers in Vietnam has been well documented. The trauma for many of the people protesting the war in Vietnam has never been acknowledged, much less documented. The extreme manifestations of this trauma, such as the self-immolation by Norman Morrison, were noted but never examined, and so the pain and sacrifice of the war protesters continues to be dismissed. This theme, trauma from the war, has come up over and over during the years I have been working on these projects in Vietnam. This trauma is responsible for the resistance by American people to reinvolve themselves with Vietnam even after all these years.

Vietnam and the work I've been doing there have forced me to grow up. I've learned to let go of the need for immediate solutions to dilemmas I faced and to begin to learn to think of the long term, to think in terms of decades instead of days. Learning to think this way, while painful at times, has come to be a blessing. I look at the peace movement, for example, in the context of all human history rather than focusing on the day-to-day struggle. What I see now gives me strength and hope for the future. The 100 years or so of organized peace movements is an almost unmeasurable length of time it's so small. Of course, it seems like we have learned nothing from the war in Vietnam, that we have just repeated the same mistakes in Iraq, but that's because the profound change that's needed is not going to happen overnight. Thirty years in the context of all human history is, relatively speaking, overnight. We need to keep in mind what has happened in the last 100 years is completely new in human history, the United Nations Declaration of Human Rights, for example.

To keep our strength, to continue our struggle for justice in the world, so that future generations have something to build on, we need to recognize and cherish hope wherever we can find it. None of these problems are going to be resolved tomorrow, or next year, or in 10 years. As long as we continue this new process then, the sky is the limit. We have shown what can be done, what is possible, through our work in My Lai and our relationship building in My Lai. Hope has arisen from the ashes of My Lai. And if hope can arise from My Lai, it can rise up anywhere.

Mike Boehm   107

Over the years, I have been asked why is it that I have been able to move beyond the trauma of war and so many other Vietnam veterans have not. My answer is that I haven't had to move beyond the trauma of combat because I wasn't in combat. If I had been in combat, it's very likely I would be just as damaged as the other veterans, like my brother, and I wouldn't be doing this work in Vietnam today. The only difference between my brother and myself, or the guys who committed the massacre at My Lai and myself, is that I'm lucky. I wasn't there that day. I remember how messed up I was as a 19-year-old. If I had been at My Lai that day, it's very possible I would have participated in the massacre. This isn't something people want to hear because if they hear me say this about myself, then it means that they too could commit horrible crimes, and that's a place most people don't want to go.

Americans have certain myths they live with about themselves, and one of them is that they are incapable of evil, that as Americans our goodness is so deep it's almost genetic. So we don't have to examine our actions because we're Americans, and therefore anything we do is automatically right. We forget that we are human like every other human on this planet, and as humans we have the capacity for evil like every other human on this planet.

DENNIS McQUADE

Vietnam

When I was drafted my name was Dennis Butts. I changed it in 1976. I had gone to Ireland and became more familiar with that side of the family and decided to change it. I was born in Madison and lived on the East side my whole childhood. My dad, Charles Butts, worked at the Madison Kipp factory for 36 years. My mother, Doris, was a domestic in people's homes. They were Democrats. My dad actually was kind of radical, but he never was very active. He was never afraid to think for himself. That kind of became a model for me. He really did do a lot of thinking on his own.

During high school I hung around with six guys. All six of us ended up either in Vietnam or the South China Sea. Some people say nobody they knew was in Vietnam. That seems remarkable to me when so many people were going.

I campaigned for Kennedy. I felt real badly when he died. I never considered myself to be a gung ho patriotic person, but more a Kennedy-type Democrat when I was younger. My family was too. And so when your country asks you to do something, you do it, like Kennedy said. That's what I felt.

One of the things that I really remember is that my father, especially since I was an only child, didn't want me getting killed in the war. When he started finding out about Vietnam, we had a friend, a doctor, and he actually talked to my dad because he was quite worried. The doctor said, "Well Dennis has these medical problems. You know I could probably get him out of the military." My dad told me that, and I understood where he was coming from, but I got angry and said that I would never do anything like that. That would be lying. There are people dying in Vietnam and if I have to go, I go.

I was 19 when I was drafted. I just turned 19, and when I got to Vietnam, I was 20.

He was very worried about me when I was drafted. I was drafted in December 27 of '65. I ended up in Fort Lewis, Washington with the 3rd Brigade of the 4th Infantry Division. We were training as a unit to go to Vietnam. I ended up training for nine months with the Fourth.

I was put first in the Davy Crockett squad, which was a tactical nuclear weapon, a field weapon mounted on a jeep that had a range of about four miles. I was placed in that unit for a few weeks and then they put me in the 4.2 mortars. As I think back, and as I developed my thinking, because I was in that unit and trained somewhat on the gun, I became aware of how close any war is to becoming nuclear. The Army has all these tactical nuclear weapons and that's probably the way it would start, with those weapons. Since then, I've been very fearful a lot of the time that the United States, especially now in Iraq, could use their tactical nuclear weapons and it could start a nuclear war.

But I ended up in the infantry in the four-deuce mortar platoon. We trained for nine months at Fort Lewis, Washington, near Seattle. We went over on a ship and ended up in Vietnam on September 21, 1966. We were sent to the Michelin rubber plantation owned by the Michelin Tire Company. It was about 65 miles long and about 10 miles wide and near Dau Teing, Vietnam. We had our base camp there and one of the first things that made us mad was that we found out that we weren't ever going to get mortared or attacked in the "rubber," we'd call it, because the French who owned the plantation were paying the Viet Cong not to mortar us, because they didn't want to lose their rubber trees. They were worth a couple hundred dollars each, and we soon realized just how much we were worth, that the rubber trees were worth more than we were.

I'll never forget my feelings seeing the French that were the foremen and the administrators of the rubber plantation driving by in Corvettes sometimes as we were walking, and I thought, why are we here protecting this giant corporation from Communism? And the complete irony, from what I've heard, is that the Michelin Plantation is still there. Even under Communism, the Michelin Plantation has survived.

When I was in the 4th Division, I first pulled a lot of perimeter duty on the berm, the border around the base camp. That was where I first saw some civilians being shot. I saw a 15-year-old get shot when he was urinating. The man who shot him did so with a grenade launcher. He knew that he was out urinating because he had a lantern, and they were told that if they were using their toilet at night, that they should use a lantern.

It was sickening to see how my conception of John Wayne, the Army, fighting for America, was not what I had thought it was. Civilians were killed. We treated anybody who was dead as a Viet Cong. The one way you were certain someone was a Viet Cong was if they were dead. If we killed them, we were not always sure what they were before, but once they were dead, we counted them as a Viet Cong. So I think everyone is familiar with the body count, the way that the United States kept track of how many people died, how many so-called Viet

Cong and North Vietnamese and often civilians were killed. They counted bodies all the time to show we were moving forward in Vietnam.

If there was any firing and there was a certain area that we had fired into, then someone would go out and count the bodies and turn the numbers in to command. All the command centers would then turn them in to Division. Division would turn them in to Saigon, and they had all these body counts. Anybody that was dead, I'm not kidding, it's absurd, but if that 15-year-old had been killed (he actually didn't die, he was wounded pretty badly), he would have been counted as a Viet Cong. That's how absurd it was.

Also, while I was on the same berm I witnessed a man fire a 50-caliber into the village. There were some people wounded. There was a lot of screaming in the village. I could hear that. All of this deeply sickened me.

So I stayed in the mortar platoon and eventually we exchanged troops with other divisions. We exchanged a lot of troops with the 9th Division, so I ended up going to the 9th Division. When I was with the 9th Division, I was put in a Reconnaissance Platoon. That was totally different. In my previous mortar platoon, I was usually in the base camp.

In the Recon Platoon I was scared a lot more. I went out on walking night patrols. I was living the life of a rifleman, a grunt, in Vietnam. It became even more horrible. I did not like the military. I was very upset by what I had seen already, and I started to see other things.

One of the things that happened, which had a profound impact on me, was when I was with this Recon Platoon. I was with another guy who had an M-60 machine gun. That day I happened to carry the ammunition for him. George Childress was his name. He was carrying the machine gun. And that day they gave us a new lieutenant. We hadn't had a lieutenant for a while. They gave us one and he had been trained recently. He had never been in the fighting, and they sent him right out in the field.

Then they sent us out to this junction. It just symbolized the whole Vietnam War for me. There was nothing there but jungle. And yet there was a crossroads there that was called

Baldwin's Junction. Baldwin was our Colonel. The rumor was that 50 men had been killed fighting over this junction, but nothing was there. There were no buildings. There were no crops. There was no VC base camp. And they sent us out there.

I was with Childress and this lieutenant was with us, and about 10 other guys. We went up the trail. We got near Baldwin's Junction, and sure enough, there was a sniper. He started firing at us. We were at the back, Childress and I. The lieutenant was in about the middle. The lieutenant called for the machine gun and so Childress and I ran. I had the ammunition. He had the M-60, and the lieutenant, when Childress ran by, said, "Go over there and spray that area." Well, I ran by and he says, "Where the fuck are you going?" He didn't seem to realize that I had the ammunition. And Childress ran and he stepped on a big mine, a huge mine. He was just blown up and was killed. There were also six or seven other people wounded, one pretty badly. I'll never forget that. They then called in air strikes for this sniper.

Then they had us dig, we got about 50 meters away and they had us dig a 10-inch deep foxhole the length of our body in the ground, and then they called in the air strikes. They just pulverized this whole area, which had been pulverized many other times. I remember being more afraid of that than I was the sniper because, I knew from being in a mortar platoon that people make mistakes and they call in the wrong coordinates. The ground just shook like it was a trampoline. And I was scared. I was really scared. Luckily I got out of that unit. I was transferred.

But probably for the next 10 years, I had one of those survivor complexes. I kept thinking, "Why did that lieutenant stop me that day? What kind of fate saved me when Childress died and I should have been there with him?"

But also from that incident I realized that that it had been completely useless. There was nothing of any value there. There was no winning or losing. A person died and six or seven were wounded. When I went to Vietnam I wanted to survive, but after all these things had happened, my whole mind-set was, " I want to survive." Nothing else mattered.

Dennis McQuade   ·   *113*

So I didn't volunteer for anything. I didn't do anything that would make it any more dangerous for me than it had to be. And a lot of people were acting that way at that time. I even went with some sergeants on patrols in the 9th Division that we were being sent into similar places like Baldwin's Junction, completely useless places out in the jungle where you were sure you would be attacked. And we would go out and call in co-ordinates of the location, but we were usually about 400–500 meters away. And we would say we were there, that we had checked it out and nothing was there, and we would radio back. This was at the E-7 platoon sergeant level with certainly officers aware, and just saying, why should we go in that area. There's no reason.

I also was placed with a mortar platoon down in the Mekong Delta and one night I saw a bunch of guys firing illumination rounds, which are rounds that have flares and parachutes. And they were laughing and drinking and they were setting the flares so they would land on the village and burn down the huts. I remember saying to a sergeant, "What the hell is going on? Why aren't you stopping this?" And he made an obscene gesture toward me. He just acted like: "What the hell are you doing talking to me like that" and ignored it. At the time, everything around me seemed absurd and horrible, and yet that incident probably was just another day of the horror that is war. And I just said to myself, "I want to get out of here."

I came back home after a year and seven days in that country, September 28, 1967. I came home to Madison. I was home about a month and the Dow riots were happening in Madison, the Dow Company that made napalm. And it was crazy. I had heard there was a lot of rioting in black neighborhoods in Milwaukee, and that upset me. But here it was in Madison. There were people out protesting. There was some police brutality as far as I remember. I actually went down and took some Super 8 movies, I had a Super 8 camera, and I took some film of the protesters. It was kind of my way of asking: "What's going on? I want to figure this out."

Because I was living in Madison, I couldn't escape the war. I would have had to move away. It was obviously something that was not going to go away for me. Then I got a job at Oscar Mayer's in the research department about a month after I got back. The day I went there, they had me share a locker with a guy named Dave Wheadon. And when I opened the locker door, there were his antiwar posters. And I just looked at them and I didn't say much. I was teamed with David to help with the research. We were the peons on the research team. We shoveled the meat, ran the machines, cleaned the machines. And Dave trained me. And we worked at night.

Eventually the topic of the war came up. He was curious. Here's a veteran coming back. We both later found out that management had us share the same locker, whether it was intentional, or just because we were doing the same stuff, and he had to train me. They thought it would be hilarious, that I would probably end up fighting Dave or attacking him, verbally at least, telling him what an asshole he was, or something. And I ended up becoming a very close friend of his. Dave explained a lot of things to me very slowly in a calm way at night sitting around at Oscar Mayer's, about what his interpretation of the war was.

He had been to the demonstration on October 25, 1967 where Timothy Leary tried to levitate the Pentagon ... very famous ... 25,000 people. ... And he told me about all these things. I became still more curious. I started taking classes at MATC in the college parallel program. I took some of the courses, even in an English class you could be writing about Vietnam. You couldn't escape it. So I had to write. I took some sociology. I ended up working at Oscar Mayer's and going to school part-time about two and a half years.

I started seeing posters that there was a "Veterans for Peace in Vietnam" organization in Madison about 1968. Probably in early 1969 I started going to demonstrations.

Another thing happened to me during this time, which really had a profound effect on me. One day in May of 1969 I went to the main library in Madison. As I walked into the library, I could see there was a lot of commotion down the street on Mifflin Street on a Saturday afternoon. So I've always been drawn to that kind of thing. I want to find out what's going on. So I went down there and it was the Mifflin Street block party, the first one. I ended up staying around and I witnessed the conflict when the police came and tried to get the partiers to shut down the music. They disconnected it and then there were riots, and I saw this, and I was in the middle of a riot.

I had another friend at Oscar Mayer's who had a motorcycle and I went out to see him and I said, "You know there is a riot in downtown Madison at a party. You want to check it out and see what's going on?" I was 21 years old. I mean, now I would try to run the other way if there was a riot. We went down there and we parked the motorcycle on West Washington. It was cold, so he gave me his leather jacket, which had captain's wings on it from the military. He wasn't a big biker guy, but he had this leather jacket you wear on a Harley. He had a big Harley.

So we went there and it was really bad. We walked around a bit. The police were driving down the front lawns of Mifflin Street and Bassett Street, as though they were streets, because the streets were barricaded. The people were on the lawns, and police would go 40 miles an hour. People were being beaten. There were protesters throwing big bricks at the police. We said to each other let's get out of here. This is really bad.

So we went back to the motorcycle and as we got to the motorcycle there were four cops with helmets and billy clubs. They looked at us and said: "Where are you guys going?" I said, "We want to get out of here." And one of the cops sees the captain's insignia, and he grabs me by the lapels of the leather jacket and he says: "Why are you wearing this military stuff? You couldn't get in the military if you tried."

I started yelling at him that I had been in Vietnam. He said, "You're a lying fuck" or something, and they all started beating me. So I was beaten. I later went to the hospital. I had a lot of welts. I was arrested for disorderly conduct. I went to jail that night, and then when I got out of jail I went to the courthouse part of the building, and my name wasn't listed with those arrested. I eventually found out they had dropped the charges.

My father, who had always been kind of rebellious himself, went down to the jail and demanded to know who the police were, who had beaten me. I had no knowledge of this, and he almost got arrested himself, because he was so angry that I had been beaten up.

I think that it was really good that I had him as a father, because he supported me in most all the directions I started taking.

Another thing that really influenced my political outlook happened when I spent the summer of 1970 in Mississippi doing educational work. One day a group of us, both black and white, ate together in the black-only area of a bar in Tunica. When we left the bar and drove down the highway, we found it was blocked by two police cars with six police officers standing behind them pointing rifles at us. They put us on the ground and searched our car and us. They arrested the driver for drunken driving (he had one beer) and put him in jail, and they threatened us. We eventually got him out, but the event politicized me a great deal.

Also, I remained in Vets for Peace. I marched in demonstrations. I was on the radio a few times on talk shows, such as Papa Hambone's show and various others. We had marches. They had a Memorial Day parade in Madison, the VFW, and we weren't invited. We tried to get in it. They wouldn't let us. They didn't want us. So we went up there. We wore our fatigues. We had plastic M-16s, and we would do guerrilla theater sometimes just stopping people saying, "Are you a Viet Cong?" And eventually during one of the parades one of us got attacked. I wasn't, but someone was physically attacked by one of the VFW. So it was pretty testy times. It was quite testy.

Vets for Peace in the 1960s were just local. We got incorporated. I think it was officially called Veterans for Peace in Vietnam. I remember we went through incorporation with the

Secretary of State's office. It was a statewide organization. There were vets from other areas of Wisconsin who came to our demonstrations. There were a lot of World War II veterans. They were very good role models for me because they had been through World War II, which was supposedly a war that was much more positive than Vietnam. But they were still against war.

There was one man—I'll never forget him, John Cappon—who was a World War I veteran, who was in Vets for Peace in the 1960s. He was a great guy. He had real stature. He was white-haired. He must have been in his 70s. He was always smiling and very peaceful and wore the Vets for Peace hat. He just had an aura. I thought, all those years ago this guy went to World War I and then he became a person that's fighting for peace.

There could be a lot worse ways of living your life, and so he became a great model for me. He always went to meetings. A lot of people still remember him if you talk about Vets for Peace in the 1960s.

When we went to Washington for Dewey Canyon, a Gold Star mother from Middleton went, Marcella Kink. She was anti-war. She was the woman that, at the October 1969 moratorium in the field house, gave a very moving speech about her son being killed in Vietnam. Then she was recruited by the peace movement and was a spokeswoman many times. She went to Washington with us. I have pictures of her outside Arlington trying to lay a wreath at the graves at the cemetery in Arlington. So there were other people that I greatly admired that I came in contact with when I was in Vets for Peace in the 1960s and early 1970s.

I started hearing there were national things going on and this interested me a great deal. I thought the veterans should do something nationally. There wasn't a lot of interest in Vets for Peace, at least initially, for national things. Chuck Goronson pretty much kept Vets for Peace together. He was much more interested in things like the anti-war referendum. He helped organize that, although he would not have been opposed to national actions.

I took the responsibility of contacting the Vietnam Veterans Against the War, in New York, and asking them if we could take part in their demo. And they said, "Well, why don't you just join and be a chapter." I said, "Okay." And they flew somebody out and they met with myself and some other people. A friend of mine, Rick Larson, who was in Vietnam and was one of the six people I was in high school with, he returned. He was my roommate. We lived down on Bassett Street, and had long hair, and were going to UW-Madison.

When the VVAW flew out to Madison, they brought a couple of guys, and Jan Crumb was one of them. They met with us, and then I just said, "Well, I'll continue to be a coordinator." We sort of were like Vets for Peace but we also had our own meetings. There were about 20 of us in VVAW. We always worked with Vets for Peace. There really was no conflict. That was in 1971.

The first thing VVAW did that was national was Operation Rapid American Withdrawal (RAW), which was a march from Morristown, New Jersey, to Valley Forge. It was retracing one of Washington's marches in the Revolutionary War. We did that. We marched 100 miles. John Kerry was there. He spoke. Jane Fonda was there. She spoke.

We did guerrilla theater along the road, and this whole thing with the plastic M-16s. On a Sunday morning in small New Jersey towns we'd walk through when people were going to church, with our jungle fatigues and our plastic M-16s and we're passing out literature. "This is what it looks like to the Vietnamese people seeing all these 100 men walking through their town and checking people out." We'd pull guerrilla theater. Some of us dressed as Viet Cong or civilians, and we had them interrogated on the main street.

The second thing that I took part in was the Winter Soldier investigation in Detroit from January 30 to February 1, 1971. I testified about the things I had mentioned earlier, the atrocities, I really thought the whole war was an atrocity by this time.

John Kerry interviewed me before I was interviewed officially. And then he was the moderator for my panel so I got to talk to him and meet him. Of course I didn't know he'd be a future candidate for president. But, I always thought the guy would go far. It's not surprising to me that he did, because I was pretty impressed with him.

The whole thing about the Winter Soldier was that it was really preparation for a larger demonstration in Washington. I also went on that, the Dewey Canyon demonstration, which was in April of 1971, where 1,000 Vietnam vets protested. We camped out on the capitol mall and Nixon tried to get us off the mall with a federal court action.

The whole argument was over whether we could camp or not. The federal court said we had the right to protest, the first amendment right to protest and stand on the mall. We couldn't sleep because it's not a campground, so we stayed on the mall.

We marched. I'll never forget it and I have picture of it. A helicopter flew over when we were marching to Arlington to lay wreaths. Years later I was reading the biography of John Kerry and learned it includes things about Dewey Canyon. The guy who wrote the book went through the Nixon tapes where Nixon recorded every word he ever said in the White House.

I was so happy to read that we were just basically enraging Nixon. Nixon was asking for reports every half hour on what we were doing. He was sending people out to watch what we were doing. And that was Nixon who flew over in the helicopter. I just smile to think that we caused Nixon this much trouble. Basically some grunts that fought in Vietnam were causing the President of the United States all this trouble. So I participated in the Dewey Canyon and continued a while to participate in the Vets for Peace when I got back home.

I also should mention another thing that happened. I woke up one morning and heard an explosion in Madison in August of 1970. It turned out that someone had blown up Sterling Hall, the UW Physics Building. It turned out to be someone I went to high school with, Karl Armstrong, he was in my class. I remember thinking at the time that although I would probably never have done anything like that, I completely understood Karl, the rage he felt. This scared me because it made me realize all the rage I had. I had angry thoughts about the government, Nixon, and the military. It could have taken me somewhere I just didn't want to go.

I did seek therapy. I had counseling at the time. I also decided to enter social work. I ended up graduating in social work, and then entered the master's program. That was 1974. I ended up getting a field placement at the VA, the veteran's hospital, on the psychiatric ward. In social work you get a field placement in graduate school. This I thought would be very interesting, but I should have known it would be very hard. There were guys acting strange and angry mostly, whom I was working with on the VA psych ward. One of them was a friend of mine, whom I went to high school with. He had a dog and he couldn't come on the psych ward unless someone took care of his dog, so I ended up taking care of his dog.

He wasn't real close to me in high school. He was an acquaintance. But he became a friend. It was very hard for me at the time because the staff called him a psychopath. He was becoming kind of psychotic. But the staff was calling him a psychopath. I didn't know at the time what was going on, but he later became fully disabled from post-traumatic stress disorder, actually 10 years later. He was very angry.

I really couldn't deal with the VA. I also became very angry. I tried to make it positive by setting up a change project where I said that instead of analyzing or labeling all the veterans, they should try to just work with their behaviors. Of course I had no idea that it was post-traumatic stress disorder they were trying to deal with, or I would have been a famous man, had I been able to figure that out.

I did get my masters in social work. I went to work for the university as an advisor for special students. I worked with a lot of veterans that were returning, but I really started to back off from politics and in April of 1975, the war ended about the time I got my first job. I was so thankful it ended. I was very happy. I celebrated that it ended. I just dropped out of politics for about I guess, three or four years. Then I started auditing classes from a professor named Harvey Goldberg who was pretty well known on campus.

He was one of the best lecturers that the university ever had. He was very charismatic. I told him one time if he was doing anything politically that I would I like to get involved with it. I was still angry. And he was talking about the anger of the oppressed and that attracted me. So I joined a political group he was in, the Mass Party Organizing Committee. Basically for two or three years we tried to organize a socialist party in the United States. That was quite an experience. It ended up not going very far, but I really realized in studying socialism that it was something I really agreed with. I ended up visiting Cuba for a few days in 1978. I saw that they weren't the pariahs and the terrible people that the U.S. was portraying them as. I think there should be an election in Cuba, but the people, at that time anyway, were pretty happy. They had health care. They had jobs.

I became very involved with politics again and ended up working for Medical Aid to Central America. My wife, Carol, and I worked with them for a couple of years. We raised money for Nicaragua and El Salvador. We went down to Nicaragua. I saw first hand in Nicaragua in the early 1980s how American dollars were oppressing people by supporting the Contras against the Nicaraguan government, which had been freely elected.

I was still very angry. And then time just passed. I kind of got into my own life. Thank God I didn't always have to be focused on saving the world and stopping war. I ended up getting involved again when Grenada was invaded, I don't remember what year that was, there was still a chapter of VVAW and I went to them and we had a meeting, and we decided we'd have a ceremony in the capitol on Veterans Day. We had George Vukelich speak. We had a ceremony where we would have a body bag brought in. I was one of the ones who carried it into the rotunda on Veterans Day. A lot of people brought roses. We'd have all these speeches. Jim Wachtendonk sang some songs. He was a veteran. We had that. But that was during the 1980s. We did that even after Grenada ended for a few more years.

Somehow after that I got interested in meditation. I studied with about three or four different gurus and teachers, some of whom I attended workshops with in New York and different places—in Madison, too. I started meditating. I have to say, and I've talked to other veterans who have said this, that's the one thing that helped me get rid of the rage—even though I still had the same analysis of what the United States was doing as far as pushing its might around the world to control and to keep the multinational corporations in power.

I became calmer. About 10 years I meditated. I meditated every day. I don't do it every day anymore. I meditate about once or twice a week, and I'm hoping to get back into it more. But the peace is there. Meditating brought me peace.

Then Iraq started happening, and I saw this was turning out to possibly be another Vietnam and even potentially worse because there are a lot more countries involved. I thought, even though I have my own work with being a social worker and my meditation, I really wanted to get back involved with the anti-war movement. So I was really happy when eventually I saw signs saying Vets for Peace was having meetings.

I was really happy to become involved with Vets for Peace again. I participated in some protests when Bush was threatening to go to war with Iraq. I became very concerned with the way that the U.S. is still fighting a war where there are no body counts, because they just are killing a lot of people there. When I really read in-depth stuff about Iraq, I found a lot of people that were being killed were civilians.

And it was a preemptive war, which I just think the United States should have never initiated. We hadn't done that before, and we should never have done it in the first place, no matter what we would gain by that. It has put us down a path that I think is just too treacherous. It's scary to me to think that we could start a war to bring democracy to a country. And Bush was also lying about, or else was misinformed about, the weapons of mass destruction, and so forth.

I've been very pleased with Veterans for Peace. I've not given it the energy I gave Vets for Peace when I was 24, but I have a couple teenagers, Miguel and Beto, who keep me busy. I'm hoping that when I retire that I'll be able to give Vets for Peace more energy. Even now I'm trying to give it more energy. It's a very good organization. I'm glad I'm in it.

Besides the meditation, counseling, and being a social worker, I think that continuing to fight for peace really helps bring peace to me and a lot of other people who are doing it. It's something I try to teach my boys. They're pretty anti-war.

I'm basically, in my core, against all wars. I wouldn't completely call myself a pacifist because I probably respect people's right to defend their own country. It may mean I'd take part in defending my own country if it were invaded. But, I still am opposed to war. It's a horrible thing. It's never positive. It's always very negative. That's the only thing it can be.

I hope that I can do this until I'm 85, maybe longer I hope, because I think there's just a tremendous need. Over the years I've also shown my slides of Vietnam, and have added some slides of the peace movement. It started out with a first grade teacher, Cate Lyman at Hawthorne Elementary. We showed it to first graders.

I remember going in there when Rambo was big, and talking about Rambo, and then what I did in the Army. At that level we didn't talk about the killing and the death, but we talked about how the war really wasn't so glamorous. You end up filling sand bags all day long. You end up working in the kitchen. You get dirty cleaning trucks. John Wayne, when I was young, was just an outrageous misconception of what a soldier is. It's farcical that soldiers ran around in World War II movies and they didn't even get dirty. When John Wayne was out fighting, lying on a Japanese beach, he would have a pressed uniform when he got up.

Wars are a lot worse than that. They are bloody and horrible and full of death. One of the worst things wars do is lower people's level of morality. They can't help but do that. There's a common denominator for morality that lowers a great deal because there's so much death and everybody has to excuse it. It is lowered for everyone. The whole culture becomes that way. That's one of the most horrible things for me.

I saw some terrible things. For a time I became accustomed to it, and that's really sad. All war, even if it's a war for a so-called good cause, does this. There's no way it doesn't. People lower their levels of morality.

I think what we try to do in Vets for Peace is try to remind people there's a higher level of morality that we've got to keep, that war is really horrible and here are guys that were in the military who can tell you about it.

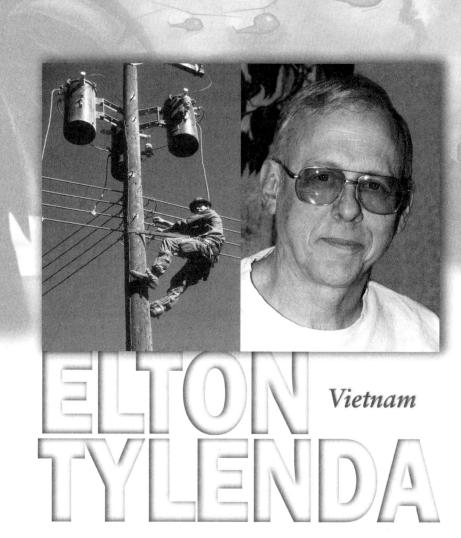

ELTON TYLENDA

Vietnam

I had a deferment, was not interested in war or the military. No one in my family at the time had been in the military. I was suddenly undeferred without explanation. When I persisted in knowing why I was undeferred, I was assigned a government attorney and still got no answers. The lack of answers and a slip of the tongue strongly indicated that something was amiss. I was in business at the time, and my accountant set me up with a heavyweight attorney, another client of his. He charged me a lot of money for a retainer, and assigned his right hand man to investigate. Days later this man directs me to meet him "on the steps of city hall for a conference." When we met there, he said

127

this would be our final meeting, that his boss wouldn't pursue the case any further. When I asked why he said: "Mr. L. has political aspirations and taking your case would be political suicide." He shared the results of his investigation with the condition that it would be said only once and would deny it if I made it public. The results: there were fraudulent deferments protecting the sons of the wealthy. Someone had called the draft board asking why I had not been drafted and threatened to expose them if I wasn't drafted. Bingo—I was drafted. Weeks later I discovered that a mentally unstable family member (through marriage) was the one who had called.

I was head of household and putting a younger brother through college. I owned and operated a rapidly expanding electrical business at the time. I was able to get a deferment on my own, meeting with a group of old gentlemen at the draft board by candlelight because it was the night of the huge East Coast power blackout. I thought I had gotten a lucky break, but when I showed up they were all there. On the merits of the case they opted to defer me. But in the spring of 1967, I was sacrificed to save the sons of the rich. I felt it would be life threatening to pursue the case any further.

I tried to get into the Seabees, and there was one opening for a high voltage lineman, electrician. The problem was it would take something like 29 days to do the paperwork, and I had only 30. The guy assured me it would work out. Well, it didn't. It was a couple days late so I ended up in the Army, Fort Dix, and when I got through and we were issued our MOS codes, no one knew what mine meant. I had to wait until I got to Virginia to find out what I was in for. I think we were the first Army group trained to be high voltage linemen, electricians. In fact, we were trained by the Navy. Ending up a lineman after all was so weird that I took it as a good omen.

I was a reluctant draftee. I was not into the military. I was just making it through. I thought my only MOS was high voltage lineman. I didn't realize I had a secondary MOS that the paperwork indicates I'd been trained for—combat engineer. A lot of us were products of McNamara's "expedited training." We got all our "training" in a single morning in a huge warehouse. I had come in later, one of the last ones to come in. I was on time but the place was packed and I could barely see.

An officer was running through the drill: "This is the M-60 machine gun, this is how you load it, this is the safety—everybody got that?" There were a number of us in the back: "Excuse me, Sir! We can't even see it from back here." He glared at us and repeated more loudly: "Everybody got that!?" And some of the officers started closing in on us, and we realized real quick that it wasn't going to do any good to say anything. Our morning "training" covered the basics including the grenade launcher and common explosive devices. From way in the back I could barely see what he was holding up! Weeks later, several weeks into the Vietnam tour, I was with three others on a volunteer mission—we were half drunk and stupid enough to volunteer. It was night and the only weapon between us was the M-60 machine gun in the back of the jeep. There were four of us and two were E-5 sergeants and none of us knew how to operate that weapon in the dark! That was a sobering experience. Much of my military experience was unbelievable, some of it absurd. I couldn't figure it out, couldn't wrap my mind around it. I still can't.

I started to think back. ... Those days as a boy out in the woods when these wounded veterans from World War II— totally disabled some of them—would be hunting near our home. I was a good listener, so they talked to me. And I remember this one guy talking about the atrocities that he witnessed—not by the Germans but by Americans. I listened and I remembered it, and he showed me his horrible scars. He was shot so badly in the back. Huge red scars. In the end what he told me didn't register.

I watched TV. It was all about American war heroes, so his experience was just too dissonant, but it stayed in the back of my mind. There was another incident when I was a teenager. A few days before what I still believe was a suicide (officially it was called an accident), my high school teacher and mentor told me something unforgettable. He was a bit drunk, and again I heard it but it didn't register. I don't know who else he had talked to about this, maybe I was the only one that he talked to about it. But he said he was in a unit in World War

II that went all the way from France to Berlin and they never took a prisoner. They tortured 'em and murdered 'em—every single one. Not a single prisoner was taken or handled as a prisoner. They were all executed. And he told me that he almost missed getting his state teaching position because the SPN code on his military record indicated that he was from an outfit that committed atrocities. It was a very difficult struggle for him, and he was gentle. You wouldn't know that he had been in the military unless he told you. So there were these stories from people I believed, but it didn't compute because what I got at home and through the media was the hero stuff. I used to make model B-17 bombers, and had them hanging on the ceiling, and fantasized about being a war hero. Everything encouraged that, what I heard on TV, from people in authority, what my other teachers said.

By age 21, I began to question all that and was not very happy about being drafted. I almost went to Canada. I came so close. To this day I don't know exactly what tipped the balance because I was agonizing at 1 or 2 in the morning, deep in the woods. I had a wooded area at my disposal, and it was agonizing. I was very incisive in decision making back then, being in business and all, so whichever decision came down, I would have gone with it without hesitation. It went down on the side of going, but just barely. When I confided that to my then girlfriend—it just blew me away. She said, "Oh, good, because I wouldn't want to be dating a coward." I was really taken aback by her response.

I think my mother was quite tickled that she had a warrior in the family. Most of my family and virtually the entire town were flag wavers, believed in authority, thought the president wouldn't lie, and that sort of thing. I don't think they were aware of the struggle that I had deciding whether or not to go. They just thought, well, of course, there's no problem.

I don't recall seeing a protester until I got to the induction center the first time for tests and there was a group of protesters. I had never seen actual live protesters before. Well, I didn't know what to think of that. But one thing that did make an impression on me when I was inducted was the two people who refused to take the step forward. The response from the sergeant—there were two sergeants as part of the detail—was extreme rage. The two civilians were dragged away behind closed doors, and I had a strong feeling they were beaten. This was chilling to me, and I never forgot it. I guess I didn't, at that point, think of not taking that step forward. And no one else knew that they would refuse. One was right beside me. He never said anything about what he was going to do. These little things started to add up, and I began asking myself some troubling questions.

We had some heavy pep talk sessions when we were told that we were soon heading out to Vietnam. And these wound-up officers, I presume just back from the war zone—at least that's what they led us to believe—were talking about how badly the people wanted us there, and how we'd be doing this great service. It was powerful stuff, and they were very excellent orators. And, well, you kind of get hooked on it.

We shipped out, literally by ship—the USS General John Pope, as I recall—out of Oakland because we had all this heavy gear, this construction gear, and I guess for whatever reason we had to go with it. It was an old rattletrap of a ship with no stabilizers, and it was quite a trip across the ocean. When we hit high seas there were a lot of very sick people.

There was a weird incident quite a ways from Subic Bay in the Philippines where a soldier died. He went into diabetic shock, and they had nothing. There wasn't supposed to be anybody on board with that condition and they had no supplies. So the medicines were dropped by a helicopter in the middle of the night. I happened to be up on deck. Nobody told us what was going on. We found out the next morning because my unit had K.P. duty and the dead body was in the freezer in clear plastic.

Due to regulations regarding the body, we had to stop at Subic Bay, which was an unscheduled stop. We went out of our way. Because of the delay we got news in the *Stars & Stripes* that peace talks had begun. Some people were disappointed because, oh, the war will be over before we get there. As I recall, this was in 1968, just a few weeks after Martin Luther King was assassinated. The death tolls and casualty tolls were incredibly high, a fact I was noticing with some dismay and wondering what was up ahead.

We got into Cam Ranh Bay. Our group was actually composed of several small units. One got off at Vung Tau. There might have been one other stop, and somebody went up farther north. But we got off at Cam Ranh Bay, the unit that I was with. It felt like an American city, and so it threw me off. There were one-armed bandits. There were cafeterias. It just didn't seem real with the music, all the comforts of home. That didn't last long.

We got loaded on a convoy and told not to worry for the first day because we were heading into a "friendly" city. I remember the officer saying Quy Nhon, on the coast. We did get to Quy Nhon and an incident there was burned into my memory. We were headed out of the city, I think we were already through the city heading out, and a group of unarmed women were throwing stones at us. And if they could have killed us they would not have felt bad. The anger ... I could hear a little bit of broken English about "G.I. Number Huckin' 10, go home!" Others spoke entirely in Vietnamese, but it was like powerful angry, angry stuff. And we were armed by this time. And the canvas was down on the deuce and a half, so we had to dodge some pretty good sized stones, and they were flung with all their might.

It so stunned me that I just said out loud, "If these are the friendlies, I sure hope we don't meet anybody who's really pissed at us." And everybody cracked up for a second, and then there was total silence. I don't think we said another word for half an hour. I mean, we were just told how happy they were to see us, and we had just gone through a friendly city, they told us.

When we reached An Khe in the central highlands, the orders concerning our small unit hadn't arrived. There was no paperwork. They had to find a place for us and wouldn't let us work the highlines unless there was an emergency. We went to another camp and played baseball, day after day after day. And they almost didn't have a place. It took quite a while for them to find out who we were legally, and put us to work.

Then another bizarre incident occurred. I had a background in electrical but I'd never done high voltage lineman work, never worked that kind of voltage hot. We were supposed to have civilian engineers hired by the Army to guide us. The one who was supposed to be working with us at An Khe never showed up. One day he did show, and this floored us. He showed up on a motorcycle, black leather jacket carrying an AK-47. And he said, "Hi, I'm John Henry." And I don't remember him saying I'm your engineer. I don't think he gave a shit about what he was paid to do. He had other business.

He said, "If you guys are looking for a good time and you want clean women, come down to Sin City and the girls on the left side are mine, and they're checked once a week. It's cool. You know." And he says, "Seeing you're my guys, I have a house out in the country. You're welcome to come out and visit."

This was so bizarre, and by this time we had a vehicle. I think we had already stolen a jeep. To get a vehicle that you weren't requisitioned at the start took one year's worth of paperwork. And the same was true for any major part pertaining to our highline equipment. It took a whole year to get a replacement. What happened to the other group farther south, their unit was disbanded because a single part broke. All of them were due back home in less than a year. It was mind boggling to me coming from a business background at the time.

At any rate, I learned about the black market. John Henry sounded like a bogus name to me, but everybody knew him. If you just said John Henry they knew who you were talking about. He had a house, a real house stocked with a bar, with power, air conditioning, a number of young women who followed him around. We did visit him and he said, "What would you like?" And I said, "It's a hot day, what have you got to drink?" He said, "You name it." So just for the hell of it I said, "How about a Scotch and amaretto?" [Claps hands.] Anything you named he had it. It was like New York City.

There were all these things that didn't jibe with the pep talks. Other officers were trading real estate. Anyplace that was really decent was owned by Americans, and they would trade them back and forth to other officers, would rent them, for these huge monthly payments, and then they could have their women come and so on, on their off time.

I spent the bulk of my tour in Pleiku farther north, and learned about some really ugly things. One of them was the sport killing of Montagnards, the mountain people, by this fellow who drove an earthmover, one of the big ones that can turn sharply from both the front and the back. When the Montagnards would walk along the edge of the road they thought once the vehicle was mostly by, they were safe. But just then he would work the back end and drive over them with those huge tires. I was the jeep driver for our lieutenant at the time and overheard the discussion. That's how I came to know about it. The soldier was told not to do it again. That's all! Apparently he had killed a lot of people over quite a long period of time before he was told to stop it or face legal reprimand.

They were gentle people, the Montagnards. When I did guard duty I had a captain give us our orders. It was getting dark fast and we had a long way to trek in the dark to get to a remote bunker. There would be one Montagnard to three Americans in some of the bunkers. This captain said if I get any reports that those Montagnards have been abused, you're going to wish all you had was a court martial to deal with, but first you're coming into my tent if I get your name and number. He was screaming. I think he meant it. Apparently there had been a lot of abuse at An Khe. One night our Montagnard did not show up, and apparently it was because he was abused the night before by some other guard detail. He came late, very late. I had no trouble with them. I had some of the friendliest meetings with Montagnards because they were so up front. But they were black, and the units mostly, the people I was with, were from the deep South—Texas, Georgia, and all in through there. Some were very racist; I mean a racism that I could not understand not having been raised in it. It blew my mind.

That sparks a very sharp memory. In Pleiku we had a good deal because, I have to assume, the officers in charge of my unit smoked pot and did other things. We always got warned about "surprise" inspections day or night. So we smoked a lot, and one night of heavy pot smoking, I saw this guy from Georgia, one of the more racist people I have encountered, faced with a situation. In the little cubicle there was only room for one more person to join the pot party. There was a black guy and a white guy, and he apologized profusely to the white guy. He said, "I'm sorry. We don't have room." And the black guy was invited in. That blew me away. And they really came to like each other. So pot smoking was a good deal. With the booze I saw many people get ugly, and load their weapons and try to kill each other. I had one guy put a .45 in my face. He was a decent young kid but he just got wacky with booze. But the pot-smoking people were cool.

We had TDY status, temporary duty, and we were never really accepted. We remained outsiders. We worked in all the camps but didn't know any particular unit any better than any other, so we could get away with things. I mean our MOSs were weird. Nobody knew what they were. We were a special unit for the Army and it wasn't clear what officer was in charge. That worked to our advantage from time to time. When lower ranking officers ordered me to do something dangerous I responded by saying, "Colonel so-and-so has ordered me not to do that." I got out of it. It was taking a big chance but it worked. Not long into the Pleiku venue, I was looking toward survival. I was pretty turned off. The more I saw and heard, it just got crazier and crazier, and I did not believe that the people wanted us there. That was a joke, a sick joke, but you didn't want to dwell on it. We were all counting the days we had left in country and hoping for the best.

During the day we had a lot of Vietnamese working inside the big camp called Engineer Hill near Pleiku. They were supposed to be "friendlies." I went one time and one time only to get a shave from one of these folks. This woman got real careless with the straight razor. Looking back, I have flashbacks about this, I think she was fighting the impulse to slit my throat. It still gives me a chill. I was too naïve at the time to realize how close I came. Later, one of the male barbers was shot while attacking the camp.

I was there after Tet in 1968, but the people were traumatized everywhere I went. When I was out on guard duty, I had people who were edgy, and if you did something unexpected or made a loud noise in the dark, I mean, these guys, you really had to calm 'em down. And as part of an apology they would say, "Well, a few weeks ago this camp was overrun and I'm a survivor, and so don't fuck with me. Just be cool." The tension was still there. I felt very lucky that I came over by ship. That gave me 23 more days beyond Tet.

I saw some very gung ho people. I tried to steer clear of them, and I was able to because of my status. With some, if you indicated that you weren't pro-war, there'd be some shit going on, some heated argument. But I believe that most of the people I was with were draftees and who were just putting in their time. The folks in my small unit were especially slack, with the focus on partying and, when sober, on survival. But some of the units that we interacted with were very gung ho. The company commander at Engineer Hill was looking for rank. He was either a captain or a major at the time, I don't recall now. He was volunteering units for some real bad shit. I remember one guy from our hooch who put a .45 bullet through his own hand to get out of a detail. He's the one who told me what was happening maybe two days before, and then, all of a sudden he has this "accident" cleaning his .45. It was a bloody mess.

At the start there was one exception in our small unit, the sergeant. He was more into military discipline and at times would pull rank. I recall some group punishments for our slackness. It got kind of ugly at one point where things got out of hand. But I think we mellowed him out a bit. At company muster one morning he caught me saluting with the finger. He just glared at me. In another case he didn't report me AWOL when he could have. So he turned out to be a decent fellow after all. I'm quite certain that he got involved with black market activities related to the NCO club and the Vietnamese women who worked there after dark. Late one night at his request I accompanied him while he returned the women to Pleiku City. I don't know what was on that truck along with the women but there was an incident at the main gate that night that had him really worried. I refused to get involved any further after that.

It was unbelievable at times. I don't know why I was picked, but for whatever reason I became the lieutenant's jeep driver. The jeep our guys had stolen in An Khe, we brought it up to Pleiku. It had phony paperwork because he had a connection with a higher-ranking officer. So I became his jeep driver for a time. We were high on Engineer Hill and there was this beautiful lake, Ben Ho, to the west, and there was this one narrow driveway that went down toward the lake. We didn't know anybody who had been down there. This beautiful day, we're out driving and he says, "Let's take a look." So I drove down, and about a half mile along we see black pajamaed Vietnamese running in every direction. So, my God, total shock because we're not far from the main camp. So I spun the jeep around and came tearing back up, and the road was blocked by American officers. I was ordered to stop short so I hit the brakes and they ordered the lieutenant to walk up to them. I didn't know what was going on.

He comes back a little red faced and he says, "Boy, we were almost in big trouble." I said, "Well, why?" He said that we were off limits. Nobody is supposed to be down this road. I said why? He said, "Well, I'm not supposed to say this but, this is the time when the tanker goes down and fills up the gas tank for the water works, for the little generator down there. It's a big tank and it takes the Vietnamese a while to drain it everyday at this time." And I looked at him. He said, "That's why we have water. They told me that before we got there, during Tet and before, the waterworks was blown up virtually all the time."

The waterworks was an easy target, and it was difficult to put back together. It was a water purification plant and pumping station, and they had this arrangement and we were never without water. Someone had made a deal with the other side, with the "enemy."

That trade arrangement for gasoline was fresh in my mind when later in the spring, I was put on ration for gasoline for the jeep. And I said, "What the hell is going on?" The motor pool sergeant said, "We're low on fuel." And one morning I came and I was refused. He said, "You have to have emergency status paperwork to get even a gallon."

It got to the point where they were going to cut off the heaters for our showers, and the water was pretty damn cold. So I kept asking, "What's going on?" Well, they can't get the tankers up Mang Yang Pass (a very steep stretch of switch back that we called Ambush Alley). The Viet Cong have got .50 calibers hunkered into the ledges and they just riddle 'em as they snake past. And they can't do enough by helicopter. The Viet Cong totally destroyed the pipeline again and again and again. It was busted up along the pass, so they couldn't get the fuel up.

I remember this one morning I go out and I say, "How much gas can I get." And the sergeant in the motor pool says, "How much do you want?" I said, "I'd like to get a full tank for a change." He says, "Go ahead." I said, "Wait a minute. Yesterday I could barely get five gallons. What's going on?" He says, "I don't know. All I know is I got plenty of gas today." So I had some free time, and with this whole thing about Ben Ho Lake in my mind, I drove down to Pleiku City. And I saw a whole string of brand new bright shiny 10,000-gallon tankers parked in the middle of the city. In sharp contrast to the OD color of Army tankers, these were a flashy yellow and bore the Shell emblem. You couldn't miss them! Apparently they had all just come up through Ambush Alley and I didn't see any scratches or bullet holes.

There was a little reading room on the base. I came across this copy of a book titled *The Betrayal*. It was hot off the press in either 1967 or 1968. And it talked about far worse things than I had seen. The author, Colonel Corson, was disgusted with the dirty dealings and unnecessary deaths of Americans. I learned from his book why there were so many defective artillery shells or short rounds. The military contractor was allowed to cut back on quality control. A short round totally destroyed the NCO barracks beside our hooch. Had it happened minutes earlier, the death toll could have been high.

One thing that upset me right from the start was we had special training on the M-16 there, to try and keep it from jamming. We were told in Vietnam you can't put more than 18 rounds in a clip or it will surely jam. And you had to use a special type of grease and you had to keep it up all the time, and then it would still very often jam. Some of the guys wanted to get AK-47s, which were readily available. All the civilians carried them. John Henry carried one, could get you any number of AK-47s. We were not allowed to carry an AK-47. It was illegal. You were forced to carry an M-16 and only an M-16 otherwise they would have been chucked. It was an inferior weapon and half the fire power. Hundreds of little details like this built up over time.

As a draftee I was slated to do a two-year hitch. What happened was the military came out with this new ruling that if you had put in x number of days in the war zone and you only had five months left when you left the war zone, you could be discharged upon return. Now, I was so frazzled by this time. I hated the military by the spring of 1969, with a passion. I felt that if I were stateside in the military I would spend it in the brig for sure, or worse. I doubted that I could have lasted five more months in the military. So I did the paperwork and extended my tour, and all I needed was something like three weeks, barely a month. The paperwork went through. Everything was cool, which meant that when I completed that extension I was done with the military.

I got verification that I'd been accepted. Everything was cool, and then I got the word that everybody else is going stateside. My whole unit is disbanded. I said, what's happening to the equipment? Oh, this is it. The Army is getting out of the high voltage lineman business. I said, what do you think they'll have me doing? You'll have to report to so and so. That's when I learned that my secondary MOS was combat engineer.

This miserable, cold, numbers-juggling sergeant that I reported to wants me to work on explosives. I said, "Excuse me, but I haven't had any training on explosive devices." He says, "It's not that hard. You'll learn. Now get out there on the front line and report to so and so."

Now an incident had happened maybe two months before that was one of those powerful experiences, one that has bugged me for many years since I returned. I was asked by the officer in charge if I would mind going with a survey team and making sure that they did the survey right, and that they weren't playing around. He was a real stickler for good straight pole lines, and so on. We were going to run a new line at the logistics depot. The end pole was right on the perimeter. There was only one extension of the logistics depot, and that ran along the bomb pits for the 500-pounders and other major explosives. When I got there my job was to put a stake where we wanted the surveying team to begin, and then I had to pace out—I think it was 70 paces—and put another stake.

When I got to the perimeter and was pounding in the stake I noticed three guys between the rolls of concertina. They were between the second and third roll out. I was so engrossed in what I was doing and I had a bit of a time limit, but I remember chatting with them. It turned out they were setting explosives. There were three of them. So I said, "Well, have fun. Stay cool." And I set my sights and I paced off the 200 feet and there was a hell of an explosion. We were right near the perimeter and the bomb pits, and at first we didn't know what was going on, whether it was the start of an attack, incoming, or what the hell was going on. So we dove under the jeep. There were several of us there.

Then I realized that it was the guys that I'd just been talking with. After assessing the situation, with no more explosions, we could hear somebody crying for help. So we went back up to the wire. Two of them were pretty obviously dead, but this one large guy, the biggest guy of the group, something had shielded the upper part of him. He was blood red from the waist down, and his voice was like a little boy. He was crying like a broken record for help.

He's out in a minefield and we don't know what to do. We were waiting for the people from the camp and they got there as quickly as they could, but they said there's only one sergeant who knows where the damn mines are and we can't find him. They couldn't get out to this guy. Then a military ambulance team arrived, and they put planks, which was a pretty brave thing to do, they put several planks on top of the concertina coils and crawled out. One went out on his belly to pull this guy, try to pull him across. We had to leave, so I don't know what happened in the end. It took so long I doubt that he made it. Now, when this sergeant is sending me to do on-the-job-training with explosives, my first thought is, what really happened there? Was one of those guys doing on-the-job training, someone who didn't have any prior training? So I was in a hell of a panic. This scared the shit out of me.

I went to the CO but he wouldn't do anything. Then I went to a rather interesting first sergeant. He had more clout than the company commander, but he said there was nothing that could be done. I went to everyone I could think of, and I don't know why I went to this specialist four at a typing pool. I must have looked really frazzled. It was just before I was going to be out there fusing perimeter mines and setting trip grenades. He had just come in the office, I think I started out with, "You know, they're trying to kill me. They're having me do on-the-job training with explosives. I haven't had any explosives training before." I said, "Is there anything that could be done to get me out of this?" He very quietly said, "Come back at noon and I'll see what I can do." So I came back, and I'm trying to psych out what's going on here. He had me sign some forms. There were quite a few copies. And I said, "What's going on?" He said, "You're out of it." I said, "Well, how?" He said, "You're going on R&R." I said, "Well, where?" He said, "Singapore." I said, "Well, when?" He said, "You can leave right now." That I did.

I hitchhiked out. I can't remember which airport. I think I had to get all the way down to Cam Ranh Bay for a commercial airliner. I'm the last one walking up to this gate. The time was tight. The officer at the barbed wire entrance asked me for the paperwork. He looks it over carefully and growls, "There are no flights to Singapore." I looked out at that commercial airliner. I said, "Well, where's that flight there going?" It's going to Hawaii. I said, "Well, that's close enough." He looks me in the eye and then I see a big grin. He crosses out Singapore, writes Hawaii, and says "Have a nice trip."

I got several extra days beyond the normal R&R allotment due to an airlines snafu. But now I still had over a week to go, and I was still assigned to this sergeant and the guy didn't care. I was just a number to him. So I did the freak thing. I didn't show up, and said I'm so frazzled I can't tell time anymore. I don't even know my name. I'm short and I'm dangerous. Well, they threatened me with court martial, but I really did a good show. I hid in the barracks, and they sent two MPs to get me, to look for me. I was well hidden and I heard one say to the other, "Well, the guy's short and he probably is dangerous to himself and everybody else. Why don't we just suggest they make him barracks guard." So I finally show up and report and I get my new orders, barracks guard. This was May of 1969.

Nineteen sixty-nine started out well with an R&R in Japan but went down hill from there. Around Tet I was sent to Bong Son, to LZ North English. I was going to be an acting sergeant in charge of a combat engineer team to engineer and install defensive lighting on the Bong Son Bridge. A general had the feeling that the bridge, a vital link on Highway 1, was going to be blown by sappers. There was no lighting; it had failed. They had previously sent two or more groups of engineers out and they couldn't make a go of it. It was a half-mile span or more, and the only generator they had that could do it was a three-phase unit. You needed a background in phase theory to set it up and work with it. I loved science and I was good at theory. The general had put the heat on to get this job done, so I was treated like a celebrity.

I had many officers with their sergeants come, and I never saluted a single one and no one ever called me on it. The officer would say, politely "When do you think you'll be finished?" And I said, "It depends on when I begin. I need supplies." The officer replied, "Tell the sergeant what you need." I looked at the bridge and told him what was needed. He drives off. Another officer would come and ask "How's the bridge project going?" and so on.

I got sucked in. I was given a lot of kudos for even tackling the job and I was treated like royalty, which was a nice switch. I'd been hassled a number of times for not being a good soldier, for sitting on the COs desk, not saluting, that kind of crap. I was never into it. So here I was, treated like royalty.

The problem was, although it was an easy drive to Quy Nhon with those huge supply depots, they couldn't find the material. I'm talking basic electrical supplies. Apparently, they had all disappeared—been sold on the black market. Another guy came with me from Pleiku, a fellow from Texas. He didn't have the theory but he was a mechanical genius, an excellent climber, and we worked well together. Between us we came up with ingenious ways to make things work. We made cable holders out of spikes and scraps, we bow-tied together the copper strands of wire to make connections because there were no split-bolt connectors and so on. It was quite a challenge.

One day we went to check on the generator and try and do some figuring to see how much power we could get out of it. I was deep in thought; the generator was down in a low area with quite a large guard detail, and then you come up a quite steep embankment and you're right at the start of the bridge. The bridge was quite protected. It had a lot of steel. We just got back to the bridge and there was a hell of an explosion near the generator. It was pretty hairy because we were up on the bridge, easy targets. When we calmed down, and the med-evac choppers started coming, we raced back down and they took out quite a few people. Some of the wounded were being worked on right there. I believe it was a "friendly" Vietnamese who had set up a booby trap.

The day we arrived at LZ North English I had to report to the commanding officer, a major as I recall. That night when I went for a beer with the group that I was going to be in charge of, and we were getting to know each other well. It turns out these guys were pretty hard-core. They had lost a lot of their friends. They were pretty ugly when on duty. They were pretty mellow with me, pretty decent, young kids, younger than I. They told me how upset they were about the commanding officer killing a group of Vietnamese children out in the dump that was just outside the defensive berm around that LZ. They told me that a Spec 4 was given the order to shoot the kids, and he just said somebody's been out in the sun too long. So he ignored it. This officer, I was told, was being ferried out in a chopper when he saw the kids in the dump he had the chopper hover and he killed them all, quite a number of children. And as hardened as these guys were, they were still very upset about this incident. I didn't realize just how hardened these guys were until one morning we got ambushed on the way to the bridge. Fortunately nobody was hit. These guys were good. These guys put down a hail of fire, I mean, their reflexes were so incredibly fast and they didn't duck. They just put down a hail of fire and suppressed the fire coming from behind the railroad berm and we were going at a pretty good clip, but it was a heavily loaded five-ton at full throttle. We drove for miles and the next village that we came to, the trucks stopped. I don't think anybody was signaling. I didn't hear any orders given. I'm sure there were none given. They leaped out and they blew up, tore apart, everything on the same side of the street of that village as the shooting came from many miles up the road. Every single hut was set on fire. They fired every round of ammo they carried, including all M-60 grenades. The two of us from Pleiku were the only ones with any ammunition left and we never fired a shot. There was no fire coming from that village. This was retaliation. Apparently this was standard operating procedure.

This incident bothered me a lot; it still plagues me. Over beers that night back inside the LZ I asked this kid. I'll never forget his expression, he was really taken aback, like nobody would ask, you're not supposed to ask a question like that. "Why did you try to kill those unarmed people, those civilians?" His response: "Well we had to teach them a lesson." I think he was just grasping for a rationalization. I don't think anyone had asked that question. It's just that rage and that adrenalin, from being under an attack, and they had lost a lot of their friends, and they hated Vietnamese. They only did it on that side of the street. It wasn't totally random shooting. But I had a hard time with that.

That experience and the explosion near the generator—as I got shorter it seemed there was more and more happening, and I was in worse situations. Bong Son was my toughest assignment. We were awakened the night before I left, in the middle of the night, to be on alert and not to make a sound or to fire any shots because an enemy unit that was going through the area was so big there wasn't enough firepower to stop them. If they decided to take us out they could have. That's what we were told. This was all whispered. I was pretty happy to leave.

The day I left, I was being driven to the little airport, the tiny strip, and they were flying me back to Pleiku. I was in the officer's jeep. His driver drove me out. The radio was on, and the guys I'd been working with they were calling in for support and it sounded desperate. They were pinned down by some big guns and if support didn't come they were goners, the whole group I had worked with. I asked where they were. The driver said they had taken a left and were just up the road, and we were heading right and we're going to go like hell and get you out of here.

Here we are today, bogged down in yet another immoral war. I see the same patterns, the same lies, the same misinformation, the same mindset surrounding the Iraq fiasco. Again I see working class folk doing the dirty work and the dying. Again, privileged sons and daughters and the draft dodger Chicken Hawks who send them to Iraq are raking in the profits. Worst of all—and this is the most depressing for me—I see these poor suckers and their parents getting hooked on the "hero" hype just like we did. How many of the 100,000 Iraqis killed and maimed in this illegal war are children, women, and old men? In Vietnam, nearly 60 percent of the carnage was inflicted on defenseless civilians. Two million more still suffer the horrible effects of Agent Orange. What will be the long-term effects of depleted uranium on Iraqis and our own returnees? When other countries commit such atrocities, we call their leaders and soldiers war criminals. This kind of craziness is a repeating pattern. I'm absolutely sure of it. I've seen and heard too much. I've witnessed it myself. The most incredible thing to me is why, for example, did World War II vets lie? Except for those rare ones who must have felt like odd fish because they were saying something that no one would believe because everybody else was saying something else. I think they first lied to themselves about the atrocities they committed. They were blinded, couldn't see 'em for what they were.

I have talked to former soldiers in Hitler's army. I've talked to several people here in Madison who were in Pol Pot's army, Pol Pot's murderers. These were very deep and no bullshit sessions face to face. They were still trying to deal with how they could have done what they did. They didn't realize they were doing it at the time. I don't think those kids in Bong Son really thought about what they were doing. I think they were blinded by the hype and acting mostly unconsciously. No orders needed, it just happens, these were all basically decent guys. Over a beer or something they're kids just like you are. I've counseled vets, and what I've seen is nothing compared to what some of these very hurting individuals saw and experienced. When they tell it straight, it's like they can't quite wrap their mind around it. It didn't seem that bad at the time. It's when the nightmares come back and it connects with emotion that it all starts to unravel. At that point there's no longer denial, just the big questions like how could I have been a part of that and maybe even felt good about it at the time?

What I've been doing for a number of years, I started developing a course that would really deal with the core causes of war and strife and how to get from there to peace. I started by working with large groups of street people at Interfaith House in Chicago. Some of the street people were vets and all were veterans of ghetto warfare. The course was mandatory if they wanted to stay at Interfaith, so they had to take this course that I was developing. I would counsel in conjunction with the course. They had to take the course as a background to counseling. I wasn't doing normal psychology or counseling, you know, where you do it piecemeal. This was kind of a holistic thing, and they had other volunteers and staff who were filling in too. Social workers, psychologists, and therapists worked with them as well. It was a situation where they were being honest for the first time in their lives. These people had been hustlers on the streets, hustling to live. But here they were trying to turn that around because they had people who cared about them and showed it. They came clean with their addictions, with some pretty horrible stuff that they were part of. About 65 percent of them did not return to the street.

With some of the veterans, I realized that part of their craziness was war related. It was more war related than street related, and they understood my experience. I would just say what I observed in the war zone while easing into the conversation and then they would take it from there. I didn't see anything special, but I did see it. I perceived what was in front of my eyes. Maybe that's because of the brave people who told the truth, like my high school teacher. I mean he had nothing to gain by telling me this terrible story. He was about to die. I don't know if he knew it, and he's telling someone who's a good listener something that's been tearing him apart. Even

LONG SHADOWS

though I couldn't wrap my mind around it, I did believe him. And so how come some can see it and others don't? He was a young kid. He wasn't one of the vicious torturers but he observed it, and they all kept quiet. And I don't know if he said it to anyone else but to me.

He was a caring individual, extremely good teacher, brilliant, and sensitive enough to be bothered by it. I think that war experience was part of his alcoholism. I think it weighed on him heavily. And he was going under. I was too young to realize how bad off he was, and like I say, a few days later ... it was listed as an accident, but I feel it was a suicide.

He had lost his job as a teacher because of alcoholism. He had started an electrical business and after I finished high school I worked for him, but I told him that I probably wouldn't be working much longer if he didn't straighten up because he was ruining the business. There were a lot of contributing things. I still don't know exactly why he told me that and so close to his death.

It took some months after I came back in 1969 before I became an active protester. The moratorium came up in the fall of 1969. I was at Eastern Connecticut State University in Willimantic, Connecticut. I remember carrying a sign, not because I particularly cared about what was on the sign but to protect from flying objects. We had people threatening to drive their cars through our march line. They were furious. They viewed us as traitors for protesting the "holy war" against Communism. This was the end of 1969. I felt like I was back in another war zone. It was kind of weird.

That's when I began to realize the greater courage that it takes to go unarmed and be a peacemaker and a protester. I didn't have a lot of fear while I had all that heavy gear and weaponry. I had some very tense moments. I've never known fear quite as bad, but it was like one incident in Vietnam that was so terrifying. Much of the time I had this rather typical feeling it was not going to be me. It was a good feeling. It just didn't bother me. But without any protection and with people that angry, now I have even greater respect for Martin Luther King. It takes a special courage and I wanted to be part of that.

My role models are Tolstoy and his connection with Gandhi, and Muriel Lester, who studied under Gandhi and converted Richard Deats to nonviolence. He was executive director of FOR, the Fellowship of Reconciliation. I headed a Chicago chapter of FOR for several years, so I worked with Richard Deats from a distance and I feel this kind of transmission of the torch from some very important peacemakers. Many FOR people worked alongside Dr. King from early on.

The Jewish theologian Martin Buber has made a big difference in my way of thinking about others and the world. I was into literature. My first major was classical literature and I ended up studying Holocaust literature, and the brave witnesses like Primo Levi, Emmanuel Levinaus, T. Borowsky the Polish writer, Viktor Frankl, and others. Their experiences dealing with the situation, and what they were part of and what they wish they had done or not done, helped me deal with guilt and distress that I felt for having been kind of a just go-along-to-get-along type. You know, trying to look out for my own ass instead of taking a proactive stand and just letting the chips fall where they may, instead of going along and even getting sucked in like when I got all these kudos for engineering the Bong Son Bridge lighting. Feeling kind of good about that, and then having to deal with what that really meant later. Not a good feeling.

As I look back on the entire war experience there is only one thing, one incident, where I still feel I did something right. It was a wild night of partying in the barracks on Engineer Hill near Pleiku and it was getting very late. Most of us were a bit drunk or stoned. A group of black soldiers from another barracks congregated at one end of our barracks. They had become very loud with their music and belligerent about it when asked to turn it down. I was asked by several people to go and talk with them. These were big guys. I'm almost six feet tall, but I had to look way up when asking them to tone it down so we could get some sleep. They refused and when I came back and conveyed that message, there was an angry verbal response from everyone at our end of the barracks.

I decided to trip off the main electrical circuit breaker located on our end of the barracks to shut things down. But one of the black soldiers found the breaker panel with a flashlight, restored power, and the music was cranked up even higher. Then they loudly threatened serious bodily harm to anyone who dared turn it off again. It was then that I saw and heard ammo clips being inserted into weapons. The black soldiers had left their weapons back at their own barracks.

My gut told me something ugly was about to happen. I told the other soldier in our cubicle that I was about to shut them down again, and that he'd better seriously pretend to be asleep in order to avoid retribution. The main electrical cable went along the back wall of the barracks behind our bunks. I cut into it with a pocket knife and the blade welded into the copper wire with a big explosion, but the music was so loud no one could pinpoint where the explosion came from. Then I jumped into the bunk and began to snore loudly. Moments later a black soldier was training a flashlight around our cubicle and then on my face, a few tense minutes later he moved on and the party was over.

Weeks later in Hawaii on R&R I started to relate this incident to a member of the provost marshal's staff. In astonishment he blurted out details of another incident so similar that he thought I was a witness to the case he was currently investigating. In that incident more than a dozen unarmed black soldiers were shot to death at one end of a barracks by white soldiers at the other end. He asked me not to tell anyone about this because only those with top secret clearance ratings were supposed to know the details of this mass killing. I felt quite certain that I had saved some lives that night.

I'm equally certain that weeks later, on the way back from the war, a black man saved my life. I was emotionally devastated by the war, and he picked up on it and was worried about my safety. He was the second cook on an east bound train out of Tacoma, Washington. Almost out of money, the ticket I had purchased ended in western Montana. When I told him that I'd be hitchhiking back to Connecticut from there, he expressed grave concern. At dawn, just before reaching that Montana station, he woke me up and hid me away in the cook's quarters. He brought food and water, too. All he asked of me in return was "pass it on." I've tried to do that, especially while working with street people in Chicago. I still keep trying to do that.

I think a spiritual component is critical to peace. It's a way of seeing. It's a way of visioning self, other, and world that brings out the peace from the inside so that it's not an angry or violent stand for peace. Instead, it's real peace that comes from the depths when you yourself are at peace. You're better able to make peace outside. That's what I find in the great peacemakers. It comes right down to this power of being, and peace being a virtue, as Spinoza rightly said. It's not the absence of war. It's a virtue. It's a power, an inner power, a state of mind or being that is one of benevolence and confidence. Violence is the method of the weak and fearful. When we're strong and we're confident and we're connected, we wouldn't gravitate toward violence. We'd be able to steer clear of it.

DON McKEATING

Vietnam

I was raised to be strongly anti-Communist. My formative years were during the Cold War. My father loved Joe McCarthy. I was led to believe that if the "atheistic international Communist conspiracy" was victorious, we would be sent to Siberia. My father was abusive and a chronic gambler, and so, early on, I learned that "might does not make right," and learned to be self-reliant at a tender age.

When I was drafted, I was actually proud to be able to serve in the military. I thought the military was a noble institution. I believed in duty and heroism. I felt that military service was a rite of passage as a man and an obligation as a citizen, and, in my particular case, the means to get out of a bad situation, a ticket out of poverty and abuse. However, I was surprised that they would take me, because I was born with a club foot, which kept my left leg in a cast until I was three years old, resulting in my right foot being a full size larger than my left, and my right leg stronger than my left.

When I got to basic training at Fort Leonard Wood, Missouri, in June 1967, I had quite a shock. We were referred to as "dick heads," told we were stupid, and could have gone to Canada. I was being treated worse than I thought anyone in prison or in a Communist dictatorship would have been treated. The drill instructors would say things like, "There's a thread loose on your uniform." I'd look down and see there wasn't, but I was made to do push-ups until I would agree that there was indeed a thread loose on my uniform. The drill instructors would repeatedly shout, "What's the spirit of the bayonet?" and we would have to shout back: "Kill, kill, kill!" as we made jabbing motions with our bayonets. I could see that military discipline does not build character; it destroys character. I quickly decided not to make a career of the Army.

I'm a klutz. Late in basic training, we were marching and doing a complicated drill, known as the nine-count manual of arms, in which the rifle is transferred from one shoulder to the other, and back again. I made a mistake, and I was hit in the back of my head (I was wearing a helmet) and knocked to the ground. Everyone marched over me as if I wasn't there, like nothing happened, without missing a step. I could see that the military had no respect for human life, human dignity, or what is right or wrong. Their purpose was solely to produce blind obedience. The ideal soldier is a robot to them. I began to question if it was possible to be both a good soldier and a decent human being. I was beginning to realize that I am a non-conformist, and despised the military mentality.

My foot problems made basic training particularly difficult for me. My boots didn't fit properly because of the size difference in my feet, so the skin of my left heel was worn off during a 25-mile march. I was hospitalized and missed so much of basic training I would have had to start basic training over again, if I had missed one more day.

In spite of how miserable I was, and in spite of my disenchantment with the Army, my strong desire not to disgrace myself and my family, and my belief in the fight against "Communist aggression" continued to give me the strength to hang on. I had not yet decided if the end justifies the means, but I had not yet experienced war!

Fortunately, I graduated with my unit and was sent to Fort Sill, Oklahoma, for training as a rocket launcher crewman. The conditions were much more reasonable at Fort Sill. What little free time we had was usually spent at the G.I. bars, in nearby Lawton.

After basic training I was assigned to a missile battalion in West Germany. The duty was all spit and polish, dress rehearsal. The only time I felt like a real soldier was in February 1968, when we spent almost the entire month sleeping outdoors in the snow, on maneuvers, near the Czechoslovakian border. The Soviets had invaded Czechoslovakia.

Overall, I was pleased to be in West Germany. I avoided the G.I. bars and frequented student hangouts, where I enjoyed stimulating conversations about the war and issues of the day, and was exposed to "pinko peacenik ideas," which is probably why certain places were off limits.

Fed up with endless inspections, drills, and pointless busy work, I decided that if I had to be in the Army, I wanted to be a real soldier and experience combat, despite the that fact I have never condoned violence, and have never felt the need to have a scalp hanging from my belt. I find hunting to be abhorrent. However, my naive spirit of adventure and my belief that the war was necessary convinced me to volunteer for duty in Vietnam. My timing was perfect; I had a little more than one year left, just enough time for a full tour in Vietnam.

There were no missile units in Vietnam, so I was difficult to assign. I was without orders for almost a month. I just hung out, or "ghosted" as we called it, pulled K.P., and was temporarily assigned to the American Combat Center instructing trainees how to avoid booby traps—which was fun! Eventually, I was sent to a self-propelled field artillery unit with the Americal Division at a firebase near Chu Lai. I was assigned to the Fire Direction Center, which was composed largely of officers and college grads. I was in over my head. The duty was highly technical, I had no training in fire direction, and was only a high school graduate.

Our firing missions were typically at night, almost all night at times. We fired hundreds of rounds. Each round required complex mathematical calculations. It was very difficult to sleep. We were not given any ear protection. I put cigarette filters in my ears, to soften the noise of the guns. My ears have been ringing ever since. I still have a hearing loss and am considered 20 percent disabled by the VA.

During the first few days with my unit the laundry detail truck came roaring back to camp from the nearby village. One of the two men assigned to the laundry detail had been shot in the testicles while visiting a whorehouse. At the same time, our beer and soda ration was dropped by parachute. Our battery commander gave the people of the village a short time to evacuate, and then ordered direct fire on the village while the men drank beer and cheered. It was a surreal scene. I just stood there dumbfounded, wondering if vengeance was a proper military objective.

When the Bob Hope show came to Vietnam in 1968, I went with half of our people. The next day, while the other half of our unit went to the show, our base was overrun by North Vietnamese sappers. Ours was one of many firebases that were attacked that night. It was total chaos, explosions everywhere. The ground shook. Everyone was frantic, shooting indiscriminately, sometimes at each other. People were killed. I never fired a shot. I had never fired an M-16 rifle before. I was trained on an M-14 rifle, but I never saw a target, and had no desire to become one.

The battle lasted until dawn, when the fog cleared and a helicopter gunship named Puff the Magic Dragon arrived on the scene and pounded the perimeter with Vulcan cannon and minigun fire.

That morning we assessed our damage. Three of our four artillery pieces had been destroyed. We found 150 unexploded Chinese hand grenades on the grounds, and the body of a North Vietnamese Army (NVA) sapper who had blue eyes and was over six feet tall. He must have been part French. The fact that he was a human being, not a nameless, faceless "gook" was apparent as we looked at the photographs of his family. The one person that I knew that was killed in our unit had been scheduled to go home two weeks later.

We were soon ordered to blow up our own firebase and build another near Tra Bong, in Montagnard territory. We were ambushed and hit a landmine along the way. A young lieutenant who had just become a father was killed.

Our ponchos were our only shelter while building the new firebase. It was the monsoon season. We filled sandbags all day and did firing missions all night. It was exhausting.

One day while it was my turn to command the gunners, we received a very excited radio transmission from a reconnaissance team. They had found an NVA (North Vietnamese Army) hospital on a hillside, and requested artillery fire. Everyone in the fire direction bunker seemed to share their excitement except me. I was facing the biggest moral dilemma of my life. It looked like I might be faced with an illegal order and, judging from the enthusiastic reactions of my colleagues, I was on my own, and was low man on the totem pole. As I sat at the microphone the fire direction crew took their positions, and the brass crowded around me as the gunners scrambled into position at the guns. It was show time!

As I sat there trying to gather my courage, the specter of being court-martialed and life in a military prison weighed heavily on my mind. When the movement around me stopped, the atmosphere of tension in the silence seemed to be building to a crescendo. I broke the silence, and told the commanding officer that "firing on the hospital, would be against the Geneva Convention," and he quickly replied, "Okay, get out of the chair," which I did. Another guy sat down and directed a barrage of artillery fire on the hospital.

I will always feel fortunate that I had the presence of mind and the courage not to have taken part in a war crime and not to have that blood on my hands. However, I will never know what I would have done if I had been seriously pressured. I will never know if there were any repercussions from my refusal to direct artillery fire on the hospital. I soon had other problems.

During a routine firing mission, around 3 or 4 in the morning, I made a mathematical error, which put an artillery barrage on the wrong location, and somebody caught the mistake. We checked the map, which had pins that indicated our troop positions, as well as intended targets. My calculations resulted in an artillery barrage on a cross roads where a company of Marines was positioned for an ambush.

I was immediately relieved of duty and placed in custody. It was a long night. At dawn, it was determined that the Marines screwed up also. They had given us the wrong coordinates; nobody was there. If they had been, it would have been the biggest "friendly fire" incident of the war. That still haunts me.

A horrifying image that I will never forget occurred at an Army field hospital, where I was treated for a broken leg I sustained by being run over by an ambulance. A three-year-old Vietnamese girl had been brought in. Her eyelids had been cut off with a razor blade by the Viet Cong or North Vietnamese Army as a lesson to her village not to cooperate with the Americans. The issue of whether or not the end justifies the means was finally settled in my mind.

While recovering from my broken leg, I was assigned to intelligence. My duties were simply to read intelligence reports concerning the villages of I Corps, and classify them as government controlled, contested, or enemy controlled. According to the reports, it appeared that most of the villages were contested, except obvious places like Da Nang. They were furious! I heard the ranking intelligence officer yell, "This is not what we want. Get him out of here."

Not fully recovered from my broken leg, I was assigned to reconnaissance, a job I enjoyed. I was way up in the air, in a tower, by myself, scanning the jungle, with a "starlight scope" looking for the flashes of enemy rockets. When I saw a flash, I zeroed in on the location and called in the grid coordinates to the fire direction center, who directed artillery fire on the enemy's position. It was my first night job. My sergeant declared: "Anyone who likes that job has got to be a doper!" I was then searched for drugs on a regular basis.

I became seriously sick in my eleventh month. I had a severe case of jaundice. It was believed to be caused by an allergic reaction to medication we took on a daily basis to prevent malaria. I was sent to Camp Zama Hospital near Tokyo where I quickly recovered. My Japanese doctor took me on a tour of Tokyo. The Japanese people were very gracious. I enjoyed experiencing the culture.

When I recovered I had too little time left in the Army to be reassigned. It was May 1969, and my time was up in June. I had been counting down the days to my discharge since my first day in basic training. The words of Dr. Martin Luther King Jr. come to mind: "Free at last, free at last. Thank God almighty, I'm free at last." I regarded military service to be slavery. I still do. The draft, by definition is involuntary servitude. Yet as happy as I was to be free of the Army, I felt guilty, leaving Vietnam before the war was over.

Contrary to popular belief, many of us on the ground in Vietnam were not disillusioned by the Tet offensive. It appeared that, like the Germans in the Ardennes Offensive of World War II (Battle of the Bulge), the Viet Cong had thrown everything they had at us in one last desperate counterattack. I was certain that we would soon have victory. We had overwhelming military superiority, and we had not yet invaded North Vietnam, which I anticipated would happen and would have supported at the time. However, the argument over the shape of the conference table at the Paris peace talks in 1968 was very demoralizing.

My first exposure to anti-war protestors was at the San Francisco Airport on my way home in May 1969. I had been discharged, but was still in uniform and subject to military discipline while traveling with personnel of various branches of the military. The protestors, who were kept at a safe distance, shouted insults as we passed. I heard the phrase "baby killers" and saw people spit in our direction. There is some denial today concerning the behavior of protestors during the Vietnam War. Perhaps embarrassment over the mistakes of the past has kept us from repeating them.

My support for the Vietnam War never affected my respect for the sincere pacifists and civil rights activists who formed the anti-war movement, but by 1969 the movement had grown to bandwagon proportions. The tone changed, as its ranks swelled with draft age baby boomers. It had become more of an anti-draft movement. Idealism and respectable dissent had been eclipsed by violent protest, the war often used merely as an excuse for rebellious youth looking for excitement. This age group has been known to engage in mob violence over such trivial reasons as victories by their favorite baseball or football teams or to celebrate Halloween.

At the time I never suspected that at least some of the violence and destruction attributed to the anti-war movement was actually an effort to disrupt and discredit the movement by government provocateurs. Cointelpro had not yet been exposed. We must never again permit hooligans or provocateurs to sabotage our efforts and discredit the peace movement.

Shortly after returning home from Vietnam, I was encouraged to join the American Legion by my father. The local post commander was a close friend of his. My application was rejected because Vietnam was not yet considered a war, and according to the post commander, many of the members who were World War II and Korean War veterans considered Vietnam veterans to be "undesirables, only interested in drugs and sex." Now the American Legion is constantly after me to join.

As I started college in the fall of 1969, returning veterans faced a hostile social climate. Many of us wore our field jackets or "boony hats," which made us very visible. Our presence must have been a constant reminder of the unpopular war and of the draft. We formed a veterans club, which was a non-political, social-support group like an informal fraternity. We used Greek letters for "X-GI" as our symbol. I was probably the most conservative one of the bunch. I still believed in the war because I believed in the Domino Theory, that our defeat by the Communists in one arena would lead inevitably to further conflicts. It was maddening to me that the war dragged on unnecessarily. I wanted it to end as much as anyone, but for it to end with victory, so lives would not have been lost in vain.

Having been drafted as a teenager, the three months I had been out of the Army and back from Vietnam was not a sufficient time for me to adjust to civilian life as a responsible adult. I felt like a soldier on leave, and drank and partied to excess. Adjusting to academic life was even more difficult. I was interested in history, the arts, and social sciences but had not yet chosen a career. I had not developed sufficient study habits in high school. My family moved so frequently that I often attended more than one school per year. I was not ready for college.

I attended college on the G.I. Bill and worked nights, full time, in hospital security in order to support myself. I had frequent contact with the police as they dealt with the victims of accidents and violent crime in the emergency room, and I was favorably impressed by their work.

A full class load and a full-time job proved to be too much, so I dropped out of college, but continued my education, sporadically, for many years. Choosing a career in law enforcement was largely in response to the tumultuous political and social climate of the time. I was every bit as alienated by the antics and attitudes of anti-war protesters as I was by my experience in the military. I deeply resented being stereotyped as a "baby killing war criminal" by people I stereotyped as "pampered, spoiled brat, college kids."

Not yet disenchanted with the system, I saw the rule of law as the only alternative to "might makes right," and law enforcement as my only opportunity to work for peace and justice and against privilege. My perception has changed, but my values have not. I later became an activist in the cause of peace and justice for the same reasons I became a peace officer, and was both for much of my career.

I was attracted to police work because of the reforms in law enforcement resulting from the fiasco at the 1968 Democratic Convention in Chicago. Police departments were abandoning the military model, softening their image, and actively seeking applicants with a social worker's perspective. For instance, the police in Madison, Wisconsin, advertised itself as "the other peace corps."

I started out in a small town. I believed the urban legend that small towns were friendly and that rural people were wholesome and honest. I also thought the law was the law, and a cop was a cop, and so I felt a small town would be a good place to learn the basics. Eventually, I could join a larger department.

The chief of police was a retired Chicago police officer who quickly earned my confidence and became my mentor. My training consisted of riding on the midnight shift for two weeks with the man I would replace who told me: "This is a tough town to work in. Only a J. Edgar Hoover or a Barney Fife can make it as a cop in this town."

The chief who hired me soon retired. It was quickly evident how important he had been in keeping the lid on. The bars were soon permitted to remain open until 4 a.m. I vividly recall the image of bikers urinating in front of a biker bar around 7 a.m. one Sunday as people were going to church across the street. The new chief issued an order forbidding his officers to enter any tavern without being called by the tavern. The town quickly earned the reputation as being wide open, attracting a criminal element—including motorcycle gangs who filled the bars and trashed the town.

There was no public outcry. The tavern owners were making money and almost everyone was related. I was learning a hard lesson that had already become an adage in police circles: Communities receive the quality of law enforcement they demand. It had become obvious to me that the only reason the town I worked for had its own token police department was to keep outside agencies out.

I finally understood what my predecessor had been getting at. I was a threat because I was not a Barney Fife, and I was in jeopardy because I was just a rookie—and certainly no J. Edgar Hoover. Facing my inability to deal successfully with the corruption around me, I quit.

In spite of my demoralizing experience, I decided to continue to pursue a career in law enforcement, but only with a respectable police department. My wife was working for the post office, so I was able to return to college and received an associate degree in police science, graduating with high honors, which improved my resume. My efforts to enforce the law with integrity in the midst of corruption had not gone unnoticed. I was told that when the suggestion was made that I be asked to return to my old job, the mayor said: "Don McKeating is the most honest man I ever met. We can't have him here."

It was fortunate my reputation transcended the stigma of having worked for a police department that was not trusted, because I was hired by the sheriff's department in the same county. I remained there the rest of my police career, working for a total of six different sheriffs.

Still, I had no illusions when I began my career with the sheriff's police. Bitter experience had weakened my faith in the system. While some people enter law enforcement because they actually believe in justice, I knew that police officers run the full spectrum, from noble to criminal, and that the great majority fall somewhere in-between.

I was initially assigned to the county jail, where I became familiar with some of the cast of characters I would be dealing with on the street. I was then sent to the police academy, and was finally assigned to the patrol division on the midnight shift.

Working alone as a sheriff's deputy, patrolling vast areas with a high degree of autonomy, had great appeal for me. I also received much more respect and cooperation as a sheriff's deputy than I had working for a small town police department. There was more than a little truth in the saying, "It's better to be a county Mountie than a local yokel."

The war on drugs coincided with my entire career and, in my opinion, there is no better example of a cure that is worse than the disease. It has made proper law enforcement, which depends on the trust and cooperation of the public, very difficult. I had no enthusiasm for the enforcement of laws concerning victimless crime or regulatory matters, such as traffic laws. I never anticipated that the majority of people that I would be arresting on warrants would be for nonpayment of medical bills.

By the late 1970s, police work was changing, locally and nationally. The military model was returning. Applicants with a social worker's perspective were no longer welcome. Even very small police departments were purchasing automatic weapons and forming SWAT teams through federal grants.

The prime rate was becoming more important than the crime rate: Pressure to write tickets in order to bring in revenue became so flagrant that ticket quotas were declared illegal by the Supreme Court. I was becoming very disenchanted with the job and the entire system. I had seen the rule of law circumvented too many times by power, influence, and politics. Internal politics became so treacherous that staying out of trouble and pleasing one's superiors were the top priorities of many of my colleagues, at the expense of public safety.

The 1978 Academy Award winning film *The Deer Hunter* was an epiphany for me. Unfortunately, the film is remembered for the Russian roulette scenes. However, I found that the film dealt very eloquently with how well-intentioned, working-class people are manipulated into fighting wars they have no stake in. The message is timeless. The last scene in which the friends of the deceased soldier who died in Vietnam sincerely sang "God Bless America" finally connected the dots for me. I had become a born-again radical.

By mid-career I was getting very resentful of the negative impact being a police officer had on my life. Even today, in retirement, I have met very few people who can relate to me as an individual and not as a symbol.

Knowing how it feels to be maliciously stereotyped, I have great empathy for members of oppressed minority groups. Ironically, many of those who would never consider making a racial slur have no qualms about subjecting police officers they've never met to similar indignities, without provocation.

Besides the danger, the stress, working weekends, holidays, around-the-clock rotating shifts, and going to court sleepless, the interference with one's personal life was even more objectionable. For middle-class wages I was legally considered to be a public figure with little recourse to slander, libel, or invasion of my privacy. I was also expected to be a role model and could be fired for bringing discredit to the department.

Fed up with police work, I changed directions in my education and took many classes in the arts, art history, and a course in interior design in hope of changing careers. I became a real estate agent in the early 1990s and worked part time with the intention of working full time in real estate when I retired from police work. Real estate gave me a greater degree of financial independence and the opportunity to deal with people under more pleasant circumstances.

In 1986, police in Illinois were finally granted collective bargaining rights, the right to be involved in politics while off duty, and the right to serve on a jury. Seeing an opportunity for reform, I helped establish the first police union in Illinois (other than Chicago, which had collective bargaining rights under home rule since the 1970s).

I was working in a very conservative county, and for a very autocratic sheriff who adamantly opposed unionization and made it clear that he considered the establishment of a union on his watch to be a grave personal insult. For the same reasons, it was both the best and worst time to unionize.

Those of us who organized the union did so at great risk. We were all mid-career. I was financially dependent on my job. I had not yet obtained my real estate license. No one involved in founding the union was ever promoted again. We were under constant scrutiny. Our photographs were shown to anyone making complaints in an attempt to solicit misconduct charges against us.

Not all my colleagues supported the union. Some of those seeking promotion, and many of those in cushy assignments as detectives or in drug enforcement, rejected the union. Some refused to join the union because they believed unions are a Communist plot. I was very familiar with that attitude because I had been raised with it.

I now saw through Cold War propaganda and realized that the real issue is capitalist exploitation and imperialism. I no longer accepted the myth that we were defending freedom and democracy against Communism and tyranny. Our government is frequently on the wrong side of the struggle for freedom and justice, and has a long track record of helping dictators crush liberation movements.

I also rejected the cherished notion that our soldiers fight and die to protect our freedom, and for the flag. Most of our wars have been wars of conquest. I know of no one who ever fought or died for the flag. Our freedom was most often fought for on our streets.

The union more clearly defined the schism that has probably always existed in police work between those whose loyalty is to the people and the Constitution, and those whose loyalty is to the man who signs their check. So we now have the "good old boys" versus the "do-gooders," and the "company men" versus the "union men" added to the mix. The so-called "blue wall of silence" is a myth. The various types of cops hate each other.

Once the union was established I negotiated contracts and represented officers in discipline cases. I was introduced to the ACLU by a jailer who later became an attorney and was disciplined for studying law on his break by a supervisor who read *Playboy*, *Penthouse*, and a book titled *Cowboys and Real Heroes* on duty. Information I obtained from the ACLU was very helpful in defending officers in discipline cases, so I joined and have been a card carrying member ever since.

The Gulf War was my first opportunity to take a stand against war, which I finally realized is "might makes right" in the extreme. I felt that the Gulf War was totally contrived, and was dismayed at how quickly and easily war hysteria was whipped up. The news media was in obvious collusion with the first Bush administration, and presented the war and our military in the most favorable light, and turned one of our typical dictator allies into another Hitler.

Living and working in a very conservative area provided little opportunity to protest the war, but I spoke out against the war at every opportunity. While getting off duty one morning I saw a large demonstration in the town square. There were at least 500 pro-war demonstrators and about six to eight anti-war protestors standing across the street. I quickly went home, changed clothes, and came back to take part in my first anti-war protest, but they had left. Another morning our televised police training featured two dogs ripping apart an Iraqi flag, which everyone found amusing except me. I walked out in protest.

It seems that ever since Rambo made it cool to be a Vietnam vet, phonies and problem people looking for notoriety began to surface. Some veterans made a career of complaining about Vietnam, yet supported the Gulf War, and were proud to have their sons and daughters serve in it. I refused to jump on that bandwagon.

Being a cop is like owning a boat, they say: "The happiest days in a boat owner's life are the day he buys the boat and the day he sells it." The pension and early retirement are by far the best things about police work.

I was eligible to retire at age 50, so I made sure I was financially ready when the time came. My pension was averaged over my last four years, so I ended my real estate practice and devoted all my spare time to building my pension through overtime and extra details during my last four years in police work.

While working the courthouse security detail, I was assigned to keep order in a courtroom where trouble was expected. There were only two trials. The first trial was a fraud case in which a con artist allegedly swindled about a dozen senior citizens out of their life savings. The second trial concerned a retired school principal who allegedly fondled a teenage boy 15 years earlier.

To my everlasting astonishment, the con artist's trial proceeded without incident, but the school principal's trial was almost derailed by a group of frenzied, apparently sexually repressed women of various ages who packed the courtroom. The knowledge that soon I would no longer be a pawn in this nonfunctional system was a great relief to me.

Realizing that I would soon be out of their reach, some high ranking officers actually tried to frame me a few weeks before I retired. My views on gun control and the death penalty had become an issue. They said it was rumored that I had stated, "I would never use my gun under any circumstances, not even to defend my fellow officers." I was ordered to state whether or not I had made the statement, and if I had not, state whether or not I agreed with it.

They had laid a trap for me. They knew I hadn't made the statement, because it was later revealed that they concocted it, but if they had been able to get me to agree with it, they could fire me, and I would have lost my pension. They had violated my rights. I consulted with a lawyer, the same one who years earlier was the jailer who had been disciplined for studying law on his breaks. He told me nothing could be done because I couldn't show that I had been actually harmed.

I moved to Madison with the intention of becoming an activist in the cause of peace and justice. I had discovered Madison in 1991. I had read an article about Madison's liberal politics and high quality of life in the *Chicago Tribune*, so my wife and I decided to see for ourselves. One afternoon in October, on the spur of the moment, we drove to Madison. We parked on the capital square and walked down State Street. By the time we reached Radical Rye Restaurant, we were already planning to move. We could immediately recognize and appreciate the sense of social freedom in Madison that was lacking where we were living in Illinois. It was like another country.

We went back to Madison whenever my wife and I had days off together. I had a sense of peace and relief in Madison that I never experienced in Illinois. So we purchased a condominium in Madison in 1995 that we used as a second home until I retired in 1997. We moved to Madison the same day.

I found socialism to be the only system that honestly and effectively deals with economic and social justice. However, I had not joined a socialist organization until I moved to Madison. I was a member of a student-oriented socialist group on the University of Wisconsin campus for a short time. Some of the members were uncomfortable with my background in police work, and I was uncomfortable with the group conformity, so I moved on to another socialist group, and joined the Green party.

One morning, while checking my mail in the lobby of my building, I heard people singing the "Star Spangled Banner." I asked one of my neighbors what was going on, and she said: "Didn't you hear? Our country is under attack. Two planes have crashed into the twin towers in New York City." It was September 11, 2001.

My worldview did not change on that day. I still saw terrorism as a crime, but I had a strong premonition that Bush would use the events of September 11 as an excuse for war in order to boost his sagging popularity. I had no idea that the

Bush administration would be as damaging to the welfare of our nation and to world peace as it has been.

Shortly after September 11, I had the good fortune to meet many of Madison's greatest activists, such as Jack Bariszonzi, Clarence Kailin, and Rae Vogeler. I was certainly at the right place at the right time because I was able to take part in founding the Madison Area Peace Coalition (MAPC).

As a member of MAPC, I drafted the Resolution to Defend the Bill of Rights and Civil Liberties in collaboration with a student group in response to the Patriot Act, which the Madison Common Council adopted in October 2002.

Realizing that the credibility of the voice of veterans was lacking in the chorus that makes up the local peace movement, I organized and was the first president of the Madison Chapter of Veterans for Peace, and named the chapter in honor of long-time activist and Spanish Civil War veteran Clarence Kailin. It was my intent to create an organization of activists who happen to be veterans, and not a self-serving support group.

In anticipation of reinstatement of the draft, I have received training through the Friends Society [Quakers] in counseling conscientious objectors and am a member of the Wisconsin Draft Counseling Network.

In October 2004, I was nominated for Peace Maker of the Year by the Wisconsin Network for Peace and Justice. In 2005, I worked on the highly successful advisory referendum campaign in Madison to "Bring the Troops Home." One of the most rewarding aspects of working for peace and justice has been the opportunity it has given me to know some very fine people whom I otherwise may never have met.

The current peace movement seems to be more inclusive and less divisive than the Vietnam era movement, when the silly notion that no one over the age of thirty could be trusted was popular. We are now closer to being the change we wish to achieve. We owe it to the many activists who preceded us not to permit the Bush regeim to continue to roll back the progress in economic and social justice and in world peace that our predecessors worked for generations to achieve. We have a call to action that cannot be ignored!

JEFFREY KNUPP

Vietnam

I was born and raised in the western part of Pennsylvania in a smallish town called Warren. My father was a World War II veteran who has two purple hearts, wounded shortly after the St. Lo breakthrough in July of 1944, and then again during the Ardennes in December of '44. Christmas Eve, no less, of 1944.

During the Vietnam era, I was actually fortunate enough to have a college deferment for four years and went to St. Olaf College in Northfield, Minnesota, from 1964 to 1968, majoring in liberal arts with a slant toward history and theater. I wasn't going into teaching or medicine, dentistry, or the seminary, which a lot of students from St. Olaf do, in Lutheran seminary.

When Johnson ended all graduate school deferments in February of 1968 I was basically dead meat with choices to make, because as soon as I graduated in June, my draft board reclassified me as 1A. This was before the draft lottery and before the end of the draft with Nixon. I basically had three months that summer before I was gone. During my time at St. Olaf, I probably started off like a lot of the younger students from the high school class of 1964 thinking this is all fine— Vietnam, it's the thing to do. Of course as time went on, I became more and more anti-war, not vehemently so but I certainly began to see the war in a different light.

An irony to this was in Kildahl Hall my freshman year at St. Olaf in Room 319, and both of the guys in Room 320, which was the room right next to mine, left school during their sophomore year because of grades. One was killed at Khe Sanh with the Marines as a Navy medic, Winston Parker, who was highly decorated. That was in early May of 1968.

His roommate, David Denny, was killed with the Army in January of 1968 over there. So there's two guys just gone, right there. And I had more of a pervasive attitude about being against this war.

To get back to western Pennsylvania, very much the area where the *Deer Hunter* movie was made, there was this atmosphere that even in 1968, a majority of the folks back there thought this was still the right thing to do.

So I had decisions to make. I knew I was going to get yanked in. There were options. At the time it wasn't even like living in a mid-size city like Madison, where there was a lot of anti-war stuff. The problem in a town that size that was heavily industrial based at that time, was that your friends and neighbors that wanted you drafted had a tendency to take it out on your family and your parents if you didn't toe the line.

I felt that the decision for me to make was to just get this over with, and I refused to volunteer for three years or go into a different branch of the service or whatever because I just said I'm not going to give them one more year, one extra day, of my time if I can avoid it.

Basically I ended up going in and actually joined the regular Army, but only for two years because I thought there might be an opportunity to do something other than combat infantry—which I found out was a huge lie by the recruiters, because you were going to do just what the draftee did. Thinking that option was better, I listened to the recruiter. I shouldn't have. I was actually regular Army, but I might as well have been drafted. The alternative wasn't there. The two-year deal was simply that.

I will always remember going through the games of basic training thinking: college degree, I'm older than some of these guys, this'll be okay. I got my orders right out of Fort Dix in November of 1968 to go to Tigerland, Fort Polk. All I remember asking the drill sergeant was, "What does this mean?" He was a black guy. He says, "It means you're going to the 'Nam as an infantryman," just like every other draftee.

At the time, the peace negotiations were going on. So then they came up with the idea, well, maybe you'd like to go to Shake-and-Bake School at Fort Benning, Georgia. It's a chance to become an NCO. Of course what it means is you're a squad leader. You're really in deep shit. But, I thought, well it's another six months. You never know. Maybe this crap will be done, which it turned out it certainly wasn't. Anyway, I went to Shake-and-Bake, came out an E-5, and was headed for Vietnam in early September of 1969, where I ended up with the 1st Division, the 1st of the 4th Quarter Cav Mechanized based out of Lai Khe, but mainly out in the field running highway 13 and Ben Cat, that area.

Right into the crap right away. Fortunately for me, it was a mechanized unit and I wasn't out in the field immediately as a squad leader or humping trails, which probably was to my advantage. As soon as I got over there I realized, compared to guys that had been there even two months or three months, I didn't know anything. It would have been a tough situation.

I had been in country only about four days before I realized it was the most totally ridiculous situation I'd ever been in. We were doing our in-country training. I remember a Vietnamese woman who looked to be in her 70s, very wizened and somehow she wound up down at the end of the range we were working on just out of Lai Khe. We had to stop the whole thing and she was down there with a water buffalo and a cart loaded with wood. I remember the lieutenant running the exercise having to take six guys down—heavily armed—just to check this 70-year-old woman out. Nobody knew what was underneath this wood in the cart, and blah, blah, blah.

A bunch of guys on the range just wanted to shoot anyway and ask questions later since it was training range. We were pretty heavily armed. They went down and checked it out and I could just tell right away that she was scared shitless. There was a bunch of new guys in country that were scared shitless. It was like, this is what it's gonna be for a year because you don't know who's who.

It became obvious right away that we weren't doing a very good job of winning the hearts and minds, which is what we were supposed to be doing, because I'm sure that woman left that day scared to death, pissed off at Americans, and if she had younger relatives in her family or whatever, I'm sure it's very possible they may have been Viet Cong sympathizers. By that point in the war, we were into Nixon and his secret plan to end the war, which wasn't any secret plan at all. It became so obvious after a couple of days that this was total waste, just total.

I was actually only in Vietnam about a month and two weeks to the best of my recollection. I could look it up on my file. The reason was that after I got there my dad had some mental health problems that I believe were brought on by the strain of World War II. He was very sick before I left with depression and suicidal tendencies.

It was tough because the Army is real big on doing things after the fact but not beforehand. They'll never act to take any preventive measures to help somebody out. I had worked through a few channels to try to let them know before I went to Vietnam that my dad was in very bad shape and it was a mental thing. Of course, mental things are, "Yeah, right," you know. That's about the answer you get.

Literally what happened while I was over there was my father rolled himself up into a ball and willed himself to die, and died in a local hospital from no natural known causes other than he literally went into a very deep coma, self-induced, to the best of their knowledge. It wasn't the misuse of any drugs they had given him, or any of the prior shock treatments that he had had to go through. He was just so sick as a World War II veteran that had been through heavy, heavy combat from D-Day right through to the final fall of Germany.

In fact he was scheduled, with all he'd been through, to go to Japan if they hadn't dropped the bomb. Even with two kids he was damn near called up for Korea, even though he'd been drafted in World War II. We were at a point in Korea where they were so out of trained troops that they were actually talking about bringing back combat infantrymen from World War II who had been draftees and hadn't even stayed in the Army, recalling them. That never happened, but there was always this pervasive atmosphere hanging over the head in our family.

My dad was good about it. He didn't talk a lot about World War II. He did talk every Christmas Eve about the Zippo lighter that saved his life. He had a Zippo lighter in his left breast pocket that has a chunk of German shrapnel in it as big as the tip of my thumb. He always talked about how that saved his life. A lot of his squad was killed later that night after he'd been evacuated. It was not a good time.

I would talk to my father before I left for Vietnam about how in his mind, he was so "lucky" to have fought in Europe. And I would say to him, "Well, what the hell do you mean, Dad, about lucky to be in Europe?" He says, "I couldn't have stood the Pacific." And I said, "Well, why not?" And he said: "Well, you just don't understand. I have this terrible fear of jungle warfare and these Japanese are not Christian, they're Asians and they don't treat prisoners like the Germans do." As if there was a big difference. He was literally scared shitless that I would end up in a jungle war against an Asian. And it all came to pass. All of it.

The poor guy. My mother always said, "I married him in 1942 before he went off to Camp Atterbury where he did his basic in World War II, and when he got back in late 1945 he wasn't the same guy." Wounded twice. Worked the last 23–24 years of his life as a mail carrier, but …

Western Pennsylvania had a lot of hunting culture, deer hunting. My dad was totally against that. I cannot recall him ever, ever in the 23–24 years that I knew him, ever picking up a gun. He was really pissed off at me when I went out and hunted with my friends, because it was the thing to do in high school. It was a social thing. I'd just as soon stay back at the hunting camp and cook as far as I was concerned. But it was the idea of even being out there. He never said no. He never forbade it. But I could always tell there was a feeling of dejection, of just playing around with weapons for killing purposes.

I guess if I'd belonged to a ski club he wouldn't have minded that a bit. But there was a difference.

I was out in the field north of Ben Cat when the Red Cross called and said my father had died. I thought maybe it was a heart attack because of the stress. And then when I got back home, I found out exactly what it was.

I firmly believe that he decided that he knew enough about the Army having been in it in World War II, that if he died, I could get back on a compassionate reassignment and not go back to this shit. And that's exactly what happened. There were tons of people willing to help out after the fact, including the Army.

I remember his psychiatrist telling me, "Write up that you're not fit to go back to combat. One guy in the family has, to my mind, already been through two wars, and died because of it of ancillary circumstances. So that's enough for me."

I have very sharp feelings about this entire experience. I'm not totally anti-war. There are times that I think that it's necessary. In fact, I'm not even quite sure that what we were doing in Afghanistan was totally wrong after 9/11.

But the thing that just tripped my trigger is this Iraq thing because it's just a total waste. It was bad intelligence. It was, in my mind, all about money and power and who wields it and who's going to do what. There hasn't been anything since the start of Iraq to change my mind one iota about the fact that it is all economic. It was just the wrong thing at the wrong time. It's one of the stupidest things we've ever done. It's a waste.

I'll back our troops to the nth degree when they're in deep shit, which they are, but I cannot stand the policies of the chicken hawks who sent them there. By and large it's 95 percent people who never served in the military themselves. If they did they were never in combat. They never had sons or daughters in combat. It's people who don't know what it's really like.

I was probably totally apolitical for 20 years after Vietnam. Of course, over those years we weren't involved in any major scale operations. We pulled some things, Iran-Contra among others.

I got out three months early to come here to UW. I was out of the Army and three days later I was here for summer school, going to grad school. I came here in June of 1970 and have never left.

I remember being blown out of my bed the morning Sterling Hall was bombed. I was only about three blocks from there rooming with another guy who was a Vietnam vet. I remember getting shaken almost right out of the bed. Our windows cracked or blew out from it. He got up and he said: "Jesus Christ, that was a fucking bomb. It sounded like a B-52 strike." And I said, "Something's gone up."

We crawl out, get some clothes on, start wandering up the street. Of course then all hell was breaking loose. So that's Sterling Hall to me.

I felt the draft board was fair in our community, but I knew there were a lot of people getting away with things. Warren at one time had more millionaires per population, by ratio, than any city in the United States. We had not one Sylvania plant but two of them, heavy industry. National Forge, which made all the big heavy howitzers for World War II, and some battle ship guns, was 10 miles down the road. Nobody was out of a job in Warren in the 1950s and 1960s unless they didn't want one. It was heavily Republican with the working base being Democrat.

All I know is a lot of kids did their job. A lot of them from Warren didn't come back from Vietnam. To be fair, a lot of the sons of the people with money served as officers over there too. There was the same pressure on sons of the rich in Warren, the rich Republicans, to do their duty too because it was such a small town. Even from the business owners: "I did it in World War II, you're going to do it." It was that mentality which sent us into it. And their kids didn't get out of it either.

There were some that did. There were a lot of them that went into teaching. And to be fair, a lot of these kids were going into teaching from September of 1964 when they were freshmen, and Tonkin was only three weeks earlier. I can't hold that against them either. It's what they wanted to do.

It's odd. As Republican as Warren was at the time, we were all at that age heavily influenced by Kennedy. And Kennedy had his problems expanding Vietnam, which Johnson took over.

My primary emphasis was on American history at St. Olaf College and we didn't have a large Asian Studies department. There were the usual sit-ins. The entire Students for a Democratic Society on campus was maybe eight people. Though it was a Lutheran school, it certainly wasn't as conservative as you think it might be. We lost a lot of people from St. Olaf in that war too, in Vietnam.

We respected our teachers in high school, which is another reason why in that small town atmosphere a lot of people ended up in the service. A lot of them got the National Guard slots too. Except for really young teachers, almost every role model you had from the male side of the aisle in teaching was a World War II or Korea veteran. They just had certain ways of approaching things in your history classes.

I just stayed apolitical for about 24 years. I mean I had my feelings on it but … . I worked in history primarily. I taught for a couple of years here in Madison and ended up in state government. Looking back, I regret not having gone into theater. I would love to have had my masters in that, to be able to teach at the college level right now, which I'm fully qualified to do. I've directed plays at Edgewood College and worked with students.

I did a lot of work with the Madison Scouts Drum Corps here. That was really fun. Madison was very off-the-wall while Vietnam was still going on. Like I said, I got here in the summer of 1970, and I had been big in drum and bugle corps. I marched in Pennsylvania. Loved it. Here again was this atmosphere of the American Legion and everything. You get inculcated with it. We came here to Madison and the scouts were hilarious because they were literally one of the drum and bulge corps that broke up the Veterans of Foreign Wars hold on the national championships by going to competitions and not toeing the line with inspections, which were held separately from the regular competition. They wore shorthair wigs. Then they'd come out at the night show with hair down the middle of their back and everything. Or Afros out to here with little scout caps on. And the VFW guy running it would just be going nuts. They didn't look like that in the morning at inspection.

In 1971 we had a year where we had skipping and dancing and running and jumping in the show. This guy that ran the VFW show was going crazy. Well, the long shot was all the other corps went with Madison. They said goodbye to the VFW. And that's when Drum Corps International got started.

We were in a Fourth of July parade in La Crosse in 1971. The corps was marching in the parade. Guys had hair down the back or the big Afros or whatever. So, we're going down the street and they provided convertibles for the staff guys to ride in behind. We all jump into this convertible behind the corps. The corps is marching down the street of La Crosse and the good citizens of La Crosse: "That corps ought to be ashamed of itself. Look at the hair on those kids. What a bunch of freaks. Blah, blah, blah."

Well, here comes the staff looking the same way. There were five staff members in that convertible. Every one of us had seen combat in Vietnam. Two of them had been wounded in

Vietnam. Appearance versus reality? We're just sitting there smiling and waving. Every single one of us. One had lived with the Montanards for a year. These were the best serving guys you could ever have, and now they were back and just saying, "The hell with it. We're going to live our lives." Here's the people in La Crosse yelling at us on the Fourth of July, you know.

I was very involved with the Madison Scouts for so many years, which became more artistic. The further we went along with that, the more I liked it because it got less and less military. The artistic thing now, it's like a Broadway show or a philharmonic concert or modern dance or whatever. It's not a march around.

Everybody back in my hometown from the generation I grew up in, they know what happened. There's very few people that will argue with me anymore. I still get the usual e-mail chains from some of these people about, back Bush and this and that. I write back saying, "You know where I stand. And you know where you ought to stand. You were used in Vietnam."

The coroner said my father's death was by pneumonia from deep coma, but there was no stroke. There was no misuse of drugs. They couldn't find any residuals from the shock treatments that they had given him. They couldn't find anything. He literally, literally rolled up. My mother was convinced too until the day she died. She said, "The minute you left for Vietnam your dad was going to do something to get you back." And he did it.

I'll tell you what really pissed me off was they sent a guy from Veterans Affairs to come to the graveside and do a few things. My dad, I don't think he wanted any military type, no Legion, no this and that. He wouldn't join any organizations like that. No VFW. So the guy mumbled a few words and everything, didn't do a very good job of it.

The next day, because Xeroxes were so new then and I needed to get some of this paperwork copied for my application to be reassigned to the States, a compassionate reassignment, I went to the VA office because I knew they had a Xerox. The guy goes, "That'll be $1.45." I looked at the guy and, that's when I finally snapped, I said: "You fucking son-of-a-bitch. I'm just back here to go to my dad's funeral who was wounded twice in World War II. I need something done. I come in here and you're gonna charge me?"

"Well, it's our policy."

And I said, "You take your fucking policy and shove it up your fucking ass." And I walked out of there. I never heard from the guy again.

JOEL GARB *Vietnam*

I was born in 1945 in a little town called Benton Harbor, Michigan, across the lake from Chicago. I'm still struck by a remark a friend of mine made, a colleague that joined the military along with me, who after seeing *Doctor Zhivago*, he always remembered the line that said, "Happy men don't join." So, speaking for a lot of us, I had been an unhappy adolescent; I was in my early 20s, I was working in a factory, and like a lot of us, not very happy with my parents. I felt like my life wasn't going anywhere and couldn't see any way to get it moving. I decided to join the Army even though by that time I was relatively certain that the war was wrong. And yet there was so much official propaganda that I felt like I should go see for myself.

Not having much common sense, I didn't realize that you can't really see a lot from the perspective of a soldier in a war. You can't see a lot about the causes and reasons for a war when you're in a war. And yet I was fortunate enough to actually meet a Vietnamese man, a colonel, who had been involved in Vietnam's politics since he completed high school and joined the Viet Minh in 1944 or 1945. And so I learned a lot about Vietnam, and the things that he told me reinforced what I already thought, that it was wrong to be there and that we were acting criminally, that our country was acting criminally, and that we soldiers were acting criminally.

I met him in Saigon because I was working in a renal dialysis ward in a hospital and he came into the ward one day. He was in a coma, and we treated him, and then as he got well I started talking with him. He spoke English well. And then I started visiting him at his home in Saigon after he left the hospital, and got a great education both about the Vietnamese and about the war.

I arrived in Vietnam toward the end of 1968, and I was in Kontum, which was in the central highlands, for nine months. I joined to be in the medics and then at some point I realized that I wasn't very ambulatory. So I tried in every way I could to get out of the medics and got into a training program for practical nurses.

I had some dreams about becoming an M.D. when I got out of the service. So someone had recommended that there was this renal ward where I could actually be doing some medical work. When I was in Kontum, I was in a dispensary and was not doing a lot of medical work, which was probably fortunate. So then I went to Saigon for another nine months to work in the renal ward with a month at home.

When I was in Kontum I also was very lucky. Nearby there was an ARVN hospital. They had the only x-ray machine within about 20 miles, so if people needed x-rays we could take them over and get x-rayed there. I met a PFC in the ARVN army who had been wounded and was now working in the hospital as a clerk because he had some education. I bought a Honda 50, and on Sundays we would go out to the Montagnard villages all around Kontum and see what they were doing.

We found that they were weaving. The women would sit on the ground and they would attach the cloth that they were weaving to the side of these houses that they had, one-room houses on stilts off the ground as if they were in a low-lying area and being protected from floods. It was a very long process for them to weave, so we had this idea. His name was Pham Khue and he had studied as an engineer, so we decided that he would build a loom, a pedal-operated loom. So he designed it and had it built in Kontum.

But they weren't very interested in the loom. It went to a refugee camp near the city and it actually had its own room. They didn't care for it that much. What they did like though, were some little gismos that Pham Khue had made where you could rapidly wind the thread that they would use for the cloth. They thought that was great. They could get it all wound up, a sort of spindle.

I don't know what the fabric was made out of. It might have been cotton. It seemed like it was cotton when I felt it, a rough cotton. Almost like burlap, that heaviness and coarseness, but not that scratchiness.

Pham Khue and I developed a good relationship. Then there was one weekend that he took me out drinking with his friends. And he got very drunk. They all got very drunk. I wasn't much of a drinker. They were singing. We were in downtown Kontum and they were singing and it got late. He and I drove back on the Honda. He kept the Honda during the week. And he dropped me off and he was drunk and he went up to the guard at the gate and was trying to explain to him, you know, that it was okay, that I wasn't AWOL. He drove away drunk on the Honda.

I was very lucky to have been able to meet them right after all the attempts by the Army, starting in basic training, to turn us against all Vietnamese, that they were all "gooks" and not to be trusted, you couldn't tell the "friends" from the "enemies," right? When we got to this small company in

Kontum, a helicopter company, and we had the hooch maids, or the hooch girls, none of them were really maids, that came and did our laundry and swept out our little Quonset huts and so on. But we weren't supposed to be friendly with them. Maybe they were scoping us out, looking for the weak points, you know, while they were out cleaning our clothes.

But I didn't feel that way. I, some would say naively, embraced all of them. And I think that's one thing that distinguishes people that are in Veterans for Peace is that we do have a sense that we're the same as others. We do not appreciate, what's the word, this dehumanization of the so-called enemy or the people that are different from us.

I don't know where that idea comes from. But when I was quite young, five or so, our family went to a restaurant in the afternoon. I remember it very well. It was a hot afternoon. My brother and I were outside waiting to get a table, and he was stepping on ants. And I got very upset. This was my older brother, and I wouldn't let him step on the ants. I pushed him away. I remember pushing him away. Then he stopped. And my mother said that, I believe in reference to Ghandi, that some great men would have acted as I had acted.

And then I remember one time when I was walking with my mother, and of course, I'm Jewish, and I was always as long as I can remember, cognizant of the Holocaust, even when I was five. At one point, still very young, I had said to my mother, "All Germans are germs. Germans are germs."

And my mother said, referring to the husband and wife who worked for my father and who had worked for my grandfather in their clothing store. The clothing store was handed down from my grandfather to my father, and this couple had worked for both of them for 40 or 50 years. And my mother said, "Well, Sam and Mathilda are Germans."

That really hit me how wrong I was, how stupid and wrong I was.

So I'm not sure but I've always had an interest. Also, I remember a book that I used to have on stories that took place in the South Seas, in Asia, near the water, stories that took place on islands and on boats, about pirates and about people stranded on islands with natives on the islands and so on. I was just fascinated by that, fascinated by other people and what they were doing, fascinated and attracted, wishing myself to be stranded in some tropical country with strange people and learning about strange things and other ways of living.

Vietnam sort of fulfilled that wish. When I joined the service I wanted to do two things, to go to San Francisco and to go to Vietnam. I went to the nursing school in San Francisco for a year and then went off to Vietnam.

I have a lot of pictures of Do Thi Thup, the woman that took care of the dispensary and did our clothes and swept out the dispensary. I would often sit outside with her at noon and she would share her ramen with me and tell me about herself. Her sister worked there. Sometimes on Sundays Pham Khue and I would go visit them and meet her sister's husband and their kids and their mother, the grandmother, and see how they were living and what they were doing. They were great to us.

I had some very good friends in the military in Vietnam. When I got to Kontum, it was sort of a punishment for me somehow because of the way I was perceived when I was at the practical nurse school. I was perceived as being anti-war, and not very pleased with the service. But I believe I was a good student. I was very into the practical nurse training, what we were learning. I was not into the military. I had a little apartment, a room, off the base. I was, along with a number of others, interested in the music and the subculture, the hippie subculture in San Francisco.

Then when I was in Kontum, as I say, Kontum was the least safe spot they could send someone who was in the 17th Aviation Group. It was like the worst place. Some stayed in Na Trang. Some stayed in Pleiku. And I was sent to Kontum, which in Pleiku they referred to as "rocket alley" since there were a lot of rockets lobbed at us.

That's all by way of saying that when I got to the company, I was then sent to the motor pool to work on the ambulance as a further punishment. Who else works in the motor pool? The blacks work in the motor pool. So my first friends there was the community of blacks in the company that worked in the motor pool.

Joel Garb

One day a guy stopped by who was the head of the shop for fixing the engines for the helicopters. This guy was sort of a mechanical genius. They never trained him to fix the engines, but he became the head of the engine shop. He stopped by one day because one of my punishments was to cut 50-gallon drums in half for the shitters.

They gave me an axe to do this with, so I was having a little trouble doing that and he stopped by. Then we hauled all the drums over to where he worked and he cut 'em with an acetylene torch. Then he and I became good friends, and I met others. There was sort of a little community of us that didn't spend our evenings where all the alcohol was served, it wasn't really a PX but there was an area where the officers had a bar and there was a bar for the enlisted, the club.

There were some of us that listened to different sorts of music and did other things.

Also in Saigon, in the hospital, there were even more people that were not interested in attending the clubs, and who were sort of interested in what was going on in Saigon for its own sake. And the nurses were very nice. There was more of a sort of stateside social life in Saigon. That was great and I made some great friends. Unfortunately most of whom I never heard from. But I have kept in contact with the colonel. I was in contact with Pham Khue for quite a while and then we lost contact.

I think back today, there's been this book on Madison during the war that's been serialized lately in the paper here. Somebody came up to me at work. There was a big picture of one of the confrontations between the police and the protesters, and this person showed me that and said, "Well, you were probably there, weren't you." My response is I wish I had had the sense at that time to be there. I didn't. I was not sensitive to the peace movement or the protest movement either back here in the Midwest or when I was out on the coast in San Francisco.

The closest proximity that I had to the conflict was visiting Berkeley one day with a friend of mine from the base. The street, Telegraph Avenue, was if you can imagine, empty of people except the two of us walking down and window-shopping. A large man in police uniform and helmet came up to us and said, "You're going to have to leave or I'm going to arrest you."

We were just looking in the window in the record shop. And we were in the military. Of course, we didn't want to get arrested since we were in the military. There had been some problems apparently and it was very tense in Berkeley in mid-1968. I'm not exactly sure when that was. We headed back to the military base. The base was on the Presidio. It was the most beautiful place you could be. The barracks were right on the water. You'd go out. The water was 30 feet from the rear door of the barracks. To the left about a mile away, plain as day, was the Golden Gate Bridge.

When I got out of the service, I went home to Benton Harbor and became sort of a recluse in my father's basement. Still no sense of protest against the war or even that it was going on, not even watching TV, maybe watching a little of the news. I went to numerous schools, went in and out of different schools, and finally met my wife a few years later. We went to India and came back, and then I was able to settle down and do school. I got a bachelor's degree in philosophy and history 13 years after I graduated from high school and worked in the VA in Ann Arbor as a practical nurse on the psych ward for two years.

I went to law school thinking that somehow I could be helpful to the world as a lawyer and practiced law for six years. I wasn't very helpful to the world as a lawyer, and found it very unfulfilling. There are lawyers who seem to be more helpful to the world than other lawyers. Whether I won a case or lost a case, it wasn't fulfilling. If you lose, it's not really fulfilling and if you win, all you've done is countered what some other lawyer was trying to do. They probably shouldn't have been doing it anyway. There probably should have been a better way to do things than that. A lot of it is just fighting with lawyers.

Gave that up and went to study philosophy as a graduate student. That brings us up to 1990 when my wife and I came to Eau Claire. She got a job in Eau Claire where my brother was. So we went up to Eau Claire, which was like being in exile for me. That's also when I, in 1990, discovered Bourdieu, the French sociologist. I was always interested in human nature and the questions why are we the way are and how are we the way we are, and started reading Bourdieu at that point. That's what I thought I would learn from philosophy, but I realized that I wouldn't during my master's program. I became sort of fed up with it. So I intensely studied Bourdieu for about 12 years. And then he died a year and a half ago. It stunned me. I sort of quit reading.

The business with 9/11 and Afghanistan and Bush and so on. I filled that void with activism. I'd never been an activist before. I've never been very social. I was a bookworm, I would say, uninvolved with communities. The activism started out one Friday at noon when I saw the group at the library mall protesting the Palestinian situation. I went over and I told them that I really agreed. I was just picking up some food. They said, well come and join us. Tom Benish said, "Come and join us." So I did. Then Don [McKeating] said, "I'm forming this group." Before that I hated to join things. The only thing had I joined was the Army.

It's different to have sympathies and to try to live in an isolated way, according to certain principles. That's different than associating with like-minded others and trying to be a presence and to have an effect. To manifest your sensibilities publicly, that's a whole different game.

You're not trained that way but in the theory of warriors, there's sort of an esprit. I would say that I was in no way a warrior. The notion of a warrior seems a little bit ludicrous about anyone that I knew, even people that had killed. Except for the colonel I spoke of who was trained to be a warrior, I don't know any warriors. But the idea of esprit, there was a lot of esprit. There was a lot of esprit at basic training. They didn't tell us about it but there was this sense of camaraderie and closeness. In Vietnam the same, among the little group, even among the guys in the motor pool there was a cohesiveness, definitely in the medical corps in Saigon, a lot of teamwork.

That was one thing that was great there, that I will never forget and I have rarely if ever seen since leaving the service, it was the teamwork and to be in a team in the medical corps in the hospital. There was great teamwork. Whether it would be making beds, you'd have a ward with 40 beds and 30 of them had people in them. Two guys could finish all those beds with 30 people in them in a couple of hours working together and knowing how. You know, you've got to roll the person one way and make one side, roll the sheet under them, and roll them the other way, and give them their baths and so on. Just the teamwork, it does have some relationship with esprit.

If it's true that there is esprit among warriors, that was about the closest I ever got to being a warrior was being involved in that esprit, making beds or up on the renal ward— more complicated things that needed a lot of team work. You were always right there, virtually without saying anything. You were always right there ready for the next step, ready to help someone with the next step.

I guess the other point is this happened even though I was rarely in danger. Or if I was in danger, I didn't know I was in danger, or think I was in danger. When we used to get rockets I figured they weren't aimed at me. They probably weren't going to hit me either. I didn't take them personally.

This idea of being a part of a community has all been confirmed more by going to the national Veterans for Peace convention and meeting a host of people there who were interested in what we're interested in and finding out about them, and how important face-to-face relationships are, which I did not realize until these days.

Probably in some way, because my relationships with my parents were so strained, that probably was one reason that I might not have been that interested in relationships with others. My relationships were with many dead white men that wrote books about philosophy and history, or my relationship with Bourdieu who was sort of a guru for me, but whom I never anticipated meeting. For six years, when I wasn't working—and even when I was working—most of my life, I spent thinking about him, and thinking about his works and how they could be applied to war, to the issue of war.

There are no conclusions as yet, but I wanted to do what I called "a sociology of war." I had in mind how to try to do that. But I have never been in a position to do what I needed to do, which was to be in a position to do surveys and to interview people about these issues. I do have sort of an outline of where I would start with three issues. The first issue is our direct sort of relationship with war which I think, in this case, our attitudes about war can be mapped along a sort of dichotomy between the horror of war and the glory and honor of war. This is the working hypothesis: Our own attitudes about war fall somewhere along this dichotomy, and that there are all sorts of cultural artifacts that relate to different positions along this dichotomy about the glory of war or the horror of war.

Saving Private Ryan sort of covers the whole field in a way. In the beginning it's like the landing at Normandy. You get a sense of the fear. They're coming on these sort-of-barges where the front drops down and you're in the boat and you feel the fear. The front of the boat opens up and machine gun fire kills like two-thirds of all the people. They can't even get off the boat. They're all killed right on the boat. There's this 15-minute scene of the soldiers trying to get onto the land. It is so frightening. You can hear it. The bullets are whizzing by and people are dying and you feel the horror of war. You're scared. You're in your seat in the theater and you're scared and you're horrified.

And then the rest of the movie is the glory of war, first of all how the Army bureaucracy is so efficient that it realizes that two of the three sons of Mrs. Ryan are dead and that the third son is out there somewhere and that we'll go out and save the third son. There's the efficiency of the government bureaucracy. Then the word comes down, and they get a group together to go out and look for Private Ryan on this grand mission. They get to a little town. There's the bridge in town and they have to hold the bridge while they're looking for Private Ryan. So they find him and then they defend the bridge, and so on, and it's the glory of war.

So that's the first pillar that I see, and the second pillar is the relationship with authority, which is very hard. But I keep it in my mind by thinking back to the Vietnam War when we were told in the mid-1960s that the government has all the information, and we should just go along with the government.

The unspoken text is that they're not going to do wrong by us. They're protecting our interests and so on, so this sort of docility, docileness in the face of authority. I think that's part of the reason that even though I thought intellectually that it was pretty evident that we were wrong to be in Vietnam and that we were acting in a murderous way, I sort of also, because I was a recipient of the government propaganda and sort of docile in my own way, I thought that I'll go over to Vietnam and I'll settle this question myself empirically by seeing whether we were wrong or right to go there. Actually, we've gotten this same thing a little bit lately with the Iraq war.

The third thing that I think we need to understand about ourselves better is the modes and the reproduction of modes of dehumanization, how we in so many ways, at least I think, in so many stupid ways all day long, reduce others to something less than the whole human being deserving of the utmost respect that our closest loved ones deserve, and also reduce non-humans and the environment itself to something less than the utmost respect that it deserves and has a right to. The archetype of this is when we were all trained to think of the Vietnamese as "gooks." Racism is one mode of dehumanization but there are stereotypes, and just a whole culture of reduction of the human to the less than human, to dehumanize, that needs to be understood. According to Bourdieu, for all these things, we need to understand the social conditions and the social structure and the hierarchies of domination that lead us to view the world in these various ways.

I would call it the "sociology of war." That sort of captures it. I've had these ideas in mind since 1996. But now being with Veterans for Peace, and of course WORT-FM, the radio station here in Madison, has played such a great role in educating us and helping us to understand. Now I think it needs to be Sociology of War and Peace, or Sociology of Peace and War. Why are we so weak on peace, and weak on the ways of peace? We know so little about peace. I know so little about peace.

That's one of the things that's startling about Mike Boehm is how much he knows about peace. I guess I heard him on

WORT, but it never struck me so much as when he showed his slide show about Vietnam, about going to Vietnam and working on the Peace Park with the Vietnamese, and working with them in a non-hierarchical way as best he could, of reaching them and dedicating himself to reaching them in so many ways. There is so much to be learned from that. Maybe a lot of it for him is unconscious. He says he's just doing it out of his intuition. There is just so much in there about peace and how to change the world in a peaceful way toward peace.

I fear the future. I fear the way things are going, but I don't have much of an imagination about the future. My wife is very frustrated with me because I'm unable to plan for my retirement. I have a hard time thinking about the future.

I have a hard time with the future. I do better with the past. But "hope" is a problem. For instance, I try to be involved in the Palestinian issues in town, another group, Palestinians and Jews and others that are interested in helping, in being helpful in some way. But there are times when it seems so hopeless. I have been with that group, and listening to them speak, especially the Palestinians, I've said if there isn't hope, what are we doing here? I'm wasting my time if there's absolutely no hope.

For me, it is impossible. I don't have the inner strength to proceed if I don't have hope. I'm not hopeful for myself. I'm not expecting some sort of rewards for myself in the near or maybe even in the distant future. But if there isn't going to be some positive resolution to these issues, if I can't believe that we are involved in setting a course and helping that course and furthering the course, it would be very hard for me to go on.

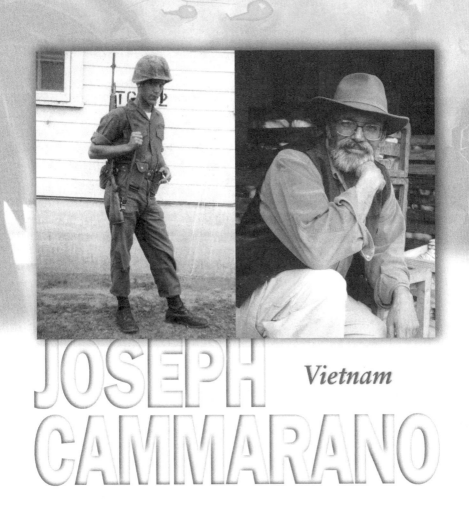

JOSEPH
Vietnam
CAMMARANO

I was born October 18, 1949, so that made me the prime age, of course. I'm originally from Jersey City, New Jersey. My parents moved to the early suburbs in East Brunswick, New Jersey. When I moved out there it was quite rural.

I come from a large, extended family. On my father's side there was himself and he had four brothers. They were all in the service during World War II. My father was not. He was the young one. He was born in 1928, but got drafted, believe it or not, after the war. He got drafted in 1946 and they sent him over to Saipan to clean up and to get the Japanese out of the caves. My father actually saw action in Saipan because of the holdouts, the Japanese soldiers who refused to believe that there was a surrender.

I grew up on my father's side where everyone was in the military and everyone felt there was an obligation to be in the military. My uncle Peter, he was in the Army. My uncle Dominic was in the Army. He was a cook. He was in Normandy. My uncle Neil, he stayed in the state, and I believe he was also a cook. He was stationed in Fort Dix, New Jersey.

Now, on my mother's side of the family, there was my uncle Nicky, he was the oldest. He stayed home because he was the oldest. And there was my uncle Johnny, he was a bombardier navigator. Then there was my uncle Freddy, who was in the Navy. He was a submariner. And my uncle Victor was a truck driver. And my uncle Johnny, who was a tail gunner on a B-29. Everyone survived, by the way. Everyone survived.

One thing that I remember talking to my uncles before I went over, they all told me the same thing. All you need to do is think about coming back, whether you pray, whether you meditate, or whatever. My uncle Freddy was into meditation. My uncle Freddy, I guess he spent a lot of time in the Orient. And it was Buddhism, I guess. This was back in the 1940s. When he got out, Freddy went to school on the G.I. Bill and became a professor of mathematics over at St. John's University in New York.

On my father's side, Freddy was the youngest. My grandmother and grandfather on my father's side started having children right after World War I. And the same thing with my mother's side. Which is an interesting point. During World War I, my grandfather on my mother's side, Michael, got drafted here in this country. And my grandmother went down to city hall, down to the draft board, and said, "You can't take my husband. He's not a citizen yet. Why are you taking my husband? He has a family to raise." She actually had to pay money to get him out. She was able to pay money to get him out of being drafted. Really funny.

I think she paid off the right people, you know. Somehow the papers got lost. She was Italian.

My grandfather and grandmother on my mother's side of the family came over in the early teens. My grandfather on my father's side came over probably about 1906, 1907. Maybe even earlier. My grandmother came over probably about the same time. But what's interesting is that my father's parents did not meet in Italy. They met in New York. My grandmother was working in a shirtwaist factory, and my grandfather, Neil, was a seat weaver for the New York Central.

Back in those days, the commuter trains, the seats were rush and cane. What he would do is he'd repair the rush seats and things of that nature. He got a hold of some guy who said, all right, you want to learn how to weave seats, and he did. My mom's father was a baker.

I think it's important to bring up the fact that everyone fought during World War II. My uncle Herbie—I forgot about my uncle Herbie. He fought in Korea. He fought in Inchon. He was a Marine. He went through some serious shit. And when I went into the Marine Corps, he thought I was absolutely out of my mind. But he said, okay, as long as you're going in, that's the best outfit to be in. At least you'll survive or have a chance. I says, well, I'm going to be working on airplanes. And he started laughing, and he said it doesn't matter. The Marine Corps credo is "Every Marine is a rifleman." Which I found out the hard way.

Actually I got drafted. I got my notice for a physical, so I thought to myself, spend two years in the Army or who knows how long. What they're gonna do is give me a rifle and send me to the swamp and that's it. Probably I'll get wasted. I thought to myself, okay, I've got an idea. I'll just join the Air Force.

I went down to the Air Force recruiter's office in New Brunswick, New Jersey, which was located at the post office. I had never heard of this, but apparently a lot of people had the same idea I did. I was told by the recruiter that there was up to a six-month waiting list. I said, "What?" In that area in New Jersey there was up to a six-month waiting list. I talked to the recruiter. He says, you could go down to Trenton. Maybe you could go down to Seaside Heights or something where there aren't a lot of people, or maybe they have a larger quota or something like that. I said all right. I was leaving. I look up and

I see this sign. "Ask about Marine Corps Air Wing." I thought to myself, Air Force/Air Wing, what the hell is the difference.

Before I go further I got to say that I was in college. This was in 1968. I had like a low C, almost a high D average. I was the perfect age, 18 going on 19. At that time they were taking 18-year-olds. But that was a lot of my fault. I was goofing off. I never thought I'd get drafted. I was too young. Because a lot of the guys I knew were 19 and 20 and 21 were getting drafted. All of a sudden, that particular block. I got that notice and I didn't tell my parents.

I went through a serious moral dilemma. I remember sitting on the stoop. I remember having the notice that I have to report to the physical, and also the greeting from the president, the whole thing. I was tapping it on my knee, and going, "Well, you know. I could take off. Not a problem." I had two friends of mine who actually did. They both went up to Canada. They did not go to the east coast of Canada. These guys went out to Vancouver, way out there. They got hooked up with some people out there.

I sent them a telegram. I went through the channels. I sent them a brief telegram. Came back within a day, real fast. I'm still thinking about this, but then you know what came through my mind? It was all my uncles and everybody. And not only that, I thought about my mother and father. Regardless of what my feelings were, I know this might sound like a cop out, but it's not. I didn't want my uncles or anybody saying I was a coward, even though it didn't matter to me. I could give a damn. It didn't matter. I knew how I felt. That's one of the reasons why I did sign up.

I felt if I take off, I know my uncles; a lot of them were flag wavers. A couple of them weren't. The ones who had seen combat weren't, which is very interesting. They weren't the flag wavers. But my uncle Victor, who was kind of behind the lines, well, uncle Victor and my uncle Neil, he was kind of indifferent about it. Now that I think back, even though I was worried about the other uncles, I think the one that I was really worried about was my uncle Victor. Because later on in life he became this big VFW commander and then he went to the Am

Vets, blah, blah, blah, blah, blah. But my uncle Johnny who was a tail gunner, he didn't talk much about it you know. My uncle Freddy, who was a submariner, what he talked about was religion and he talked about reading all the time down in that torpedo room. And my uncle Dominic, I didn't know really all that well, but he used to tell me everybody got fed well. Even my uncle Neil, when I think about it, he says I used to pull all kinds of shenanigans, and was always in trouble, which is understandable.

As far as my father is concerned, it would have hurt him if I had just taken off, because even though they weren't flag wavers, I think they still had a very viable connection to the patriotic experience, so to speak. They felt they did their duty. I did have a couple of cousins who went into the National Guard and went into the Reserves, but still they were in something. Even though they copped out that way. But with me, I really didn't have a whole lot of time.

I was looking up at the sign again about the air wing. I said that would be kind of cool. I says, I don't really want to get stuck on a patrol boat, but if I get in the Marine Corps, if I work on airplanes, maybe I'll be on a nice air base or something, so I went and I signed. Back in those days, in order for a male to sign a contract you had to be 21 years old. If you were a girl you could be 18. I don't know why, but I know my father had to sign for me. He had to sponsor me. He had to sign for me. I remember Pop had to sign, also my mom too. I signed up in February and I was supposed to go in March 3, 1968.

During that time a bunch of us went out partying and we got drunker than hell. So I'm down in New Brunswick in the train station. We were just singing and everything and a couple of police officers came over. They told us to go home and this and that. And I just: "I ain't going anywhere." The cops take out the billy club. Boom. Raps me on the side. Knocks me down, and says, "Now you stay down." Anyway, I got arrested.

Here I am three days before I'm supposed to go in, right? Three days before I'm supposed to go down to boot camp in South Carolina, and I have to go to Newark, New Jersey, and fill out some forms and do some other things. I don't know if we were going to get sworn in that day or what. I'm not sure. There was this staff sergeant. He was asking me all these questions. And all of a sudden he gets to this question.

"Have you ever been arrested?" I look at him and I went, "Well, what do you mean by arrested?" He says, "Just what I said, arrested." I says, "Does being drunk and disorderly count as being arrested?" He says, "Of course it does! When did this happen?" I says, "Oh, about two weeks ago." So he goes, "You got arrested two weeks ago for being drunk?" I says, "Yeah. We were partying." I didn't say partying, I said my friends took me out and we were drinking and stuff.

He says, "Well, because of this you have to go in to New York and fill out some more forms." Come to find out years later I could of got out of it all because I was arrested. Like the whole Alice's Restaurant thing, you know.

I finally got sworn in and I was sent to Paris Island March 4, 1968. I got out of boot camp May 7 or May 9. Then I went home for 10 days leave, then to ITR—infantry training regiment—where they taught you how to seriously shoot the weapons and the different types of weapons, the squad tactics, et cetera.

After ITR, where they taught us how to shoot the guns and throw the grenades, for a lot of us it was just fun stuff. I know it sounds sick and weird, but after being regimented and the discipline was so tight in boot camp, in ITR we were Marines now, actual Marines. We were not recruits. I made PFC. They made me squad leader. I got myself my first stripe.

After that was over they sent us right to our schools. I was sent to Memphis, Tennessee, which was actually Naval Air Training Technical Center, Millington. In the Marine Corps, we received all our technical training with the Navy because essentially the Marine Corps is part of the Navy, so everything we did was done under Navy guidelines, which wasn't bad. Millington wasn't bad.

I started my schooling, which was avionics fundamentals, where they taught you the fundamentals of aviation electronics, radios, navigation equipment and so on. That lasted from August of 1968 until January of 1969.

Then I went to a communication and navigations systems course. That was another two months, January and February. I graduated and they sent me down to Cherry Point, North Carolina. That's when I got my second stripe. I scored high in school. I liked working on radios. I liked working on airplanes.

The airplanes I started working on were the A6As, a low-level attack bomber, two-seater, made by Grumman on Long Island. It was called the Intruder, looked like a flying tadpole, a baseball bat with a fuel probe on the other end.

Because I was only in North Carolina I used to swoop up a lot. I used to swoop from North Carolina up to New Jersey. It used to take us probably about 10 hours. We'd run a hundred, a hundred and ten (miles per hour) on the turnpike. At the time I had a 1957 Chevy station wagon. It wasn't a Nomad, but I had a 283 and a three-speed off the column. I'd fit about eight or nine guys in there, and I'd charge them like $10 a head. At that time it was good money. I'd swoop on up. Take them to Port Authority. Collect five bucks. Okay, be here. We're going back on Sunday. You know what time to be here. Boom. We'd be back in time for muster Monday morning, eyes bleeding all over our faces, and the top: "You fuckers swooped again, huh?" We were known as the super swoopers. I had that on the back of the car, "Super Swooper."

Things were going nice, and all of a sudden December 1969, sitting in the office, I was up for sergeant. And this guy comes down. He says, "Hey, Mr. Cammarano, the gunny wants to see you. You're gonna get a surprise."

We go upstairs and the gunnery sergeant, one of the nicest men you ever want to meet in your life, very bright, very intelligent, I really like this guy. He looked over at me, he says, "I got a surprise for you." I says, "What kind of surprise?" He says, "You are going to the Asian vacation." I says, "What?" He says, "You are going to Vietnam."

Vietnam, come on, man. I thought I'd escaped the Nam. He says, "You ain't escaping shit, pal."

So we go home on leave. That was 1969. We go home. We only had 10 days, but I had to cut it short because I couldn't handle it. I went home for about six days, seven days. I had a hard time, holidays coming up, you know. I had a hard time. I really did.

I told my mother, I says, "Ma, there's a good possibility I won't go to the Nam so be cool on this. Because I'm an air winger now, and we got an air base in Irikuni, Japan, and we send airplanes over all the time. I might even be stationed in Okinawa."

We flew to Hawaii and then went to Okinawa, picked up all our jungle utilities and an M-16. I had never seen an M-16 before, because when I went through we were training with M-14s, they were rifles. Now we had these little toys, Mattel things.

Come to find out we were going to go to Irikuni, but we were only going to stop off in Irikuni for maybe three days, four days, pick up some equipment, and then bring the equipment to Da Nang. They told me that I was going to Da Nang. I said, "Da Nang. Why can't I stay here?" And they said, "Well, you just made sergeant, and we need somebody to take over the shop over there."

I says, why? "Well, because they had a rocket attack a couple of days ago, and blew the shop up and we need somebody." So they flew me over, but instead of going to Da Nang, I went to Chu Lai. I was in Chu Lai, which is probably about 60 clicks south of Da Nang. We had some birds in Chu Lai, some birds up Da Nang. We were bouncing back and forth. Sometimes you'd take a chopper up. Sometimes we'd hop in a jeep or something.

I spent New Year's of 1969/1970 in Chu Lai, which was just horrifying because they hit us with everything. Bam, bam, bam, they hit us. And we hit them. That was my introduction. But it only lasted like a half hour, and then I found out that they had been hitting us every day and night.

We worked on airplanes. We performed missions. What they were doing was they were flying into North Vietnam and bombing trucks. Here these pilots were getting air medals for knocking out trucks. Terrific. But there were times when we would also do close air support for some operations that the

Army was doing and that the Marine Corps was doing and things of that nature.

I was there for probably about three months, four months. Then we got orders to go over to Irikuni because they were going to disband the squadron. They were going to send it back to the states. I was ecstatic. I figured, oh, terrific. So I talked to the top, our top there, and I says, "Hey, you guys aren't going to keep me here are you?" And he says, "No, I don't think so." I says, "Really, are you guys going to keep me here, because if you are, I don't really want to, you know, I've kind of had it."

They would walk rockets down the runway, and they'd hit the field dump every so often. Or there would be a sapper come in and things like that. More than anything it just grated on my nerves.

We go to Irikuni and I got reunited with a lot of my friends, and the first thing I did was I bought myself a little Honda 90. I still carry a picture of that. This is one of the most important parts of my life. You know, I was 20 years old. Shows black and white photo from wallet. And that Mickey Mouse T-shirt I bought in California when we went to Disneyland. That was the first thing I did. I bought myself a little Honda 90, and we traveled a lot. We traveled Japan. We had a marvelous time. We went to Expo '70, which was the world's fair over in Osaka.

While I was stationed down in North Carolina, I was sent to schools. I was sent to various Navy schools to learn how to work on certain equipment like the total communications package, a package called the electronics countermeasures package. What essentially electronics countermeasures does it sends out erroneous signals to bait the enemy's radar, and to essentially confuse the enemy's radar.

When I was over there, okay, the second time I went over, they sent me back to Da Nang. All of a sudden these two officers came in. One was a captain. I'll never forget his name. His name was Captain Royce. And this other captain, I don't remember his name. Real tall man. Big handlebar mustache, real cowboy. They asked me if I wanted to volunteer for a special mission, and I said, "what's the mission?" I don't usually volunteer for anything. I'd been over there since March and I only got about seven, eight months left. I didn't want to get in anything really weird, you know.

Captain Royce essentially lined it out for me. What it was was we were gonna take four Prowlers. There was an abandoned French airstrip that was located on Marble Mountain. Seabees and combat engineers were going to go in there and they were going to lay down some temporary runway. Anyway, I agreed. I thought it might be kind of fascinating to actually be in the jungle where it was really nice. I figured we'd be with the Seabees. These guys were crazy. They had machine guns on their bulldozers and stuff; they'd take care of us. I didn't care.

We were also supposed to have a reduced grunt company, two-platoon grunt company. A rifle platoon and a heavy weapons platoon. I figured, why not. We only have five birds, and we'll go up there and we'll take care of everything.

I have to be quite honest with you. I usually have three versions of the time that I spent up there. I have what I like to refer to as my mom version, the version I told my mother. Then I also have a version that I tell, you know, when we're sitting around a bunch of guys and we're talking about experiences, but sometimes I leave some stuff out. Sometimes I might add something in order to kind of smooth something else over. Then there's the truth. It took me a long time to accept it, the absolute truth, of what really happened up there.

What I'm gonna do is I'm gonna try to go as far as I can.

We go up there and we fly in. We got these big huge sky cranes, and we flew the trailers in. There were Seabees up there and there were some engineers. But there was only like two squads of grunts because they couldn't afford 'em, and they were getting hit all the time.

I'm up there. I'm going, what the fuck's going on? Royce is up there. He's like the CO, sort of. We were not supposed to wear any chevrons. This was supposed to be a clandestine operation. Wait a minute. Am I going to get paid for this? What's going on here? Is this a CIA operation? What the fuck is this?

He says, "No, no, it's legit. We're bombing Hanoi."

I says, "We're doing what?" Oh yeah, we're bombing the shit out of fuckin' Hanoi, and these five birds have been equipped with everything, all the state-of-the-art equipment and also some other stuff too.

Well, these tech reps from HP (Hewlett Packard), and from Grumman McDonald were there. We couldn't go into this one particular sealed unit. What the hell's going on here? What is happening? Where is the support we are supposed to fuckin' get? There's just nothing here. What's going on?

They said, there's been a few incidents that have occurred up here. You're in a very hostile area. I says, oh, we're in a really hostile area obviously, man. We were right smack dab in fuckin' Indian country is where we were. And here I am, I've got myself and five other techs in my department, and then Russo, he's got his hydraulic guys, and he's scared shitless. Where are the grunts?

They sent us over a couple more squads. I went over to this one kid, and he was a salty fucker, you know. He was real short. He had like 20 days left. He says, "Oh, so you the fuckin' NCO?" I says, "No man, I'm just avionics." I says, "Listen, why don't you come inside, let's get high, let's talk." I says, "Here, fill me out please. Just help me out here. I had no idea this was going to be happening."

He says, "Yeah, you probably didn't." He says, "Either way I'm fuckin' short, man. I'm real short."

So we get things going. About two weeks, three weeks go by. It seemed like eternity, but it was probably like two weeks, three weeks. The operating engineers, these guys were just hot. They were good. They were really good dudes, and they hung out with us. They stayed in our trailers and our bunkers. We dug in big time. We were getting hit quite a bit. And we had to run our own patrols.

I'm not a grunt. I'm a technician. I'm a "communications/navigations system technician." But it got to the point where I dug in. I always had a defense position. Every so often, there was this one kid who was a hydraulics technician who was from Texas, he was a cowboy, and his buddy, Roscoe or whatever we called him, I forgot whatever his buddy's name was.

There was a lull one afternoon, the vill(age) was probably maybe three clicks away and we'd go out there and do a patrol. We'd go different ways all the time.

We go in there and there was little orphanage in there where we were hanging out. I would go in and mess around with the kids. But I had a real bad feeling this day. A real bad feeling. Bad, bad, bad feeling. Bad feeling.

I told everybody, okay, stay close. We'll just make a circuit. I was with this kid and Roscoe, I says, don't go anywhere. Don't cross any bridges. Don't do nothing. Well, they didn't listen to me. They started walking across this bridge, next thing you know, boom. It was rigged. They went up like a cannon. Next thing you know, all hell breaks loose.

We get down. The orphanage, right. Somebody opened up on the orphanage. I had no idea who it was. Somebody nailed six kids. We don't know if it was us, if it was them. We weren't even sure if there was any "them." Three of the kids got wasted. Three of the kids were wounded bad, so we took care of them, called in a chopper. There wasn't anything said. The people in the vill, they didn't say a word—which is weird, man, so weird. And I knew, I had that feeling.

When we got back, I made a report. There was a staff sergeant from Da Nang that came up. I told him exactly what happened. He says, "Well, was there any fire coming in?" I says, "I don't know. There might have been some coming in from the ridgeline."

He says, "Okay, there was AK fire coming in from the ridgeline." I says, "I don't know." He says, "There was AK fire coming in from the ridgeline." Okay, whatever, but I don't know if there was. All I know is that there were booby traps on the bridge. There were booby traps over by where they had their latrines. That was it. We didn't lose anybody over there, but they did. I don't know what happened where, what, and why. He says, okay, fine, it was just something that happened.

That really bothered the piss out of me. Bad, really bad. Bad, bad, bad. But we still got the airplanes flying. We still did the missions. Then one day, probably going into our fifth week, sixth week. We got hit. They just walked everything down and just destroyed the piss out of the runway. I mean just blasted everything. Hit our fuel dump. We had these big bladders out there. They hit the bladders. We had two trucks out there that they didn't get.

Went out there. Started hosing everything down. All of a sudden I heard this screaming. Two guys were caught in the fire. I ran in there. Otis ran in there. We took these guys out, and I wasn't good for a week. I mean, the whole thing. All I could see was this guy's skin just peeling off. Really, really bothered me, man. It bothered me. Just bothered me, because all of a sudden the war was comin' home. It was a real war. I wasn't just an avionics technician any more. I mean I just didn't walk around with a headset and an apex wrench and a screwdriver stringing fuckin' wires. People were dying, man.

I figured, all right, calm down. So I started writing a friend of mine. I started just writing some stories and writing just anything. I started listening to music. I had a harmonica. I started playing my harp. We'd do stuff. We'd get high, you know. We'd talk. We'd do coffee, you know. My mom sent me some care packages, and I'd make stuff in the helmet, you know. I'd make spaghetti, and stuff in the helmet.

We heard that there was going to be a pretty big operation going down. Oh, I forgot. I'm getting way ahead of myself. After the fire, they came back and they moved us to the other side of the airstrip. The other side is where all the barracks were, all the old French barracks and everything.

There was rats and there was snakes and some guy said he saw a tiger, and I wouldn't doubt it, you know. We got rid of all that shit. We set fire to a lot of stuff, and shot rats. That in itself was horrifying, and then there's these big goddam snakes, these big boa constrictors. And I just wanted to let 'em go. This one guy insisted he wanted to catch one. He couldn't. It was like, well, suppose they strangle us? I says, listen man, these cats aren't gonna come by us. Believe me. The ones we gotta worry about are those little viper suckers, man.

Everybody was so tense. Everybody was just on edge constantly because we were wing wipers, man. We're not grunts. We're wing wipers. There was an outfit that came up, there was a Marine Corps combat engineer outfit that was down in

Chu Lai and they had just gotten in country because what they were doing was they were dismantling a lot of stuff because—we were kind of part of a pull-out or whatever. So they sent them up there and they saw this nice runway. A lot of our shops were left.

They didn't really nail our shops much, you know, bullet holes and stuff like that, a couple grenades here and there. But we got a lot of it inside the old stone French warehouses—the stonework was beautiful. The stuff was locked in (gestures showing how the stones were laid) ... beautiful. Looking at it and thinking you know, when I get back to the world, man, I'm gonna do this kind of shit. I wanna do this.

About a week later, the Army had this operation going down. They were probably about 12 clicks away. They came even closer, like two clicks. And they were coming in and out and doing all these things. ... We had heard a lot of firing going on. And then what was left of 242 they left a couple birds in Da Nang. Apparently 242 went up there and worked out and helped these Army guys out. They needed this real close air support.

Then about three, four days, five days, a week after their operation, probably about a week, I just needed to get away. Everything was closing in. We had three birds that were up. We had two birds that were down, and we were working on parts. I decided I was going to take me a little stroll. I kinda knew the area, so I went over and I talked to Royster, and I talked to the top, too. I said, "Hey gunny, I'm gonna take a stroll." He says, "All right be careful now." I said, "I just gotta get away." And it was interesting, because the gunny kind of looked at me and he says, "Be cool." He says, "I think I know, you just need to spend a little time." And I says, "Yeah. I know what's happening. Maybe I'll ask Royster to come with me." He says, "Yeah, that's a good idea."

Royster and I go out, maybe about a half a mile out. And Royster says, "I'm gonna go in. You gonna be all right?" I says, "Yeah. I'm just gonna hang here, hang out, relax." He says, "All right." He goes back, probably about half a mile. I could see the base.

I got up and I started walking. I see this snake. The snake kind of twisted around. I wonder where he's going. (Pause.) All of a sudden I smell something I had never smelled before, the most horrible stench in the world. And there was like this little hedgerow. I'll never forget the flowers, little white flowers, and purple flowers. And flies. What the hell! I went there, and there was ... later on I found that there was eight bodies ... eight bodies. G.I.s. Lined up. Mutilated. Private parts stuffed in their mouth.

I mean really bad. I lost it. Totally. Going back, and I lost it. From that point until the time I was in Japan I don't remember anything. I was told that I just came back screaming ... screaming. And then I just sat down, and that was it. That was it. I don't remember any of that. And that was it. And I never went back. They sent me home. I never went back. They sent me to the states. They sent me to Bethesda, Maryland, for a while. They sent me down to Cherry Point where I became an instructor. And then I was discharged.

That's the truth. My mother's story is a lie. A lot of people don't know about that. I'll tell you. I feel comfortable with you. I told a few people, people I needed to tell. That's the truth. That's what happened. That's it. That was it. That was it.

I don't know where they came from, who they were. But that snake sent me to them. Later on I dreamt about that snake and whenever there's any danger in my life, I see a snake in my mind's eye or in my dreams. I'm not frightened of it. It was a snake. It was a small boa constrictor. I see those flowers too. I see the flowers.

DG: What weird paradoxes.

JC: What's that, the flowers and the snake?

DG: And then what you saw, what was there.

JC: Yeah. They were lined up just like cordwood. Afterward I'm thinking they shouldn't have been there. None of us should have been there. They shouldn't have been there. I mean, in more ways than one they shouldn't have been there.

DG: How long did you have to stay there on that mountain?

JC: They never told us. They never told us how long the mission was.

DG: But I mean, after this happened?

JC: Oh, I was gone. I don't even remember ... okay, here's what happened. After this happened, apparently, I mean, I was just comatose and they sent me to Japan right away. Well, actually they sent me to Da Nang and they left me in Da Nang from what I understand for a day and they sent me right over to Japan and from Japan they sent me over to Bethesda.

That was it. That fast. Bam, bam, bam. The thing of it was they didn't even fuck around. They didn't fuck around with me. They didn't fuck around with me at all. I think a lot of it was because of the top. I think Royce too, I think Jim Royce, Captain Jim Royce. He had a lot to do with it too. Like, just get this man out of here.

Well that's my story.

DG: Want to quit there?

JC: Oh, yeah. I'm done.

PAUL McMAHON

Vietnam

I was born December 21, 1945, the darkest day of the year, right after World War II. My father was a soldier in the U.S. Army in World War II. I had an older brother who was born during the war. My mother was an English war bride. I was born approximately six months after the war ended, which took me several years to figure out, so I couldn't claim I was born during the war like my brother.

My mother immigrated when I was three months old to the U.S., to Wisconsin where my father was originally from in Columbia County, met up with my father … came all that way

209

on her own with a three-month-old and a two-year-old. My brother is two years older. It must have been love.

I was born in Kingston-on-Thames, which is really today almost contiguous with London. It's a southwest suburb of London, part of the greater London metropolitan area now, but it's in the County of Surrey. That's important I think in terms of my feelings about a lot of things, my half-English background.

The British and my mother were, I would probably say, the greatest influences growing up in my life, and taught me to be proud of my English heritage. It's a funny thing. My father was a very hard-working, 70-hour a week person, two jobs all his life. So I didn't see him a whole lot. My mother, sort of in the classic 1950s style, raised the children. I had four siblings so there were five of us. She always took great pride in being an English citizen, even though she became a naturalized American citizen. She always had the view that she was still an English citizen. She just instilled this pride, I think particularly in my older brother and me, in being English-born and sort of in a sense English-bred, even though not really.

So I had this pride. It was a unique thing. We all look for things when we're kids that make us special, and I was proud I was born in England. I had an English heritage, and I sort of believed in the English Empire, even though it may have had its dark side, as being peacemakers and diplomats in the world. That's something that, mythical or not, was always out there for me.

I was an American kid growing up in a small American farm community of 800. I lived for baseball and I liked all the things American, but I had this piece of me that I never forgot. I think my mother played on it, quite honestly. And so someplace along the line when I was a kid, I started to develop this sense to serve others.

It might have been from an Errol Flynn movie, it may have been generational, and it may have been that and a small town and my family having a Democratic tradition. My father was a union Democrat. Service was a big thing. So I formed this idea very early that I was going to become part of some sort of diplomatic service, even without really understanding what that was. I was probably 12 or 14, somewhere in there. Ultimately that translated into thinking I wanted to get an education in political science or government or international relations and maybe join the state department. That didn't bear itself out, but I think this idea of service and peaceful resolution of conflicts was born very early.

I was also, quite honestly, the classic conflict avoider. I was the peacemaker within my family among my siblings and also, probably between my parents, who had some very rough times in their marriage. Probably something I didn't want to be but I was.

I went through grade school and high school. The idea of going on to college was never questioned. It was sort of expected. I did a lot of things that were "expected," you know, this conforming. If you believe in the birth order thing, I was second, and the first child is the conforming one, and the second tends to be more of a rebel or something, although I was only two years younger than my brother. At any rate, both of us just assumed that we were supposed to do this.

I don't think I would have said, "Do I want to be something else? Do I want to be a photographer, for example?" Now, looking back, I think there were other choices. But that was pretty uniform I think in the 1960s, most of us had this expectation that if you did okay or better than okay in high school that you really should think about something like that.

I, of course, went to school. I didn't go to the Madison campus. I went to UW-Platteville with intentions of transferring. As it turns out, I stayed there four years. I graduated in 1968. This is important in terms of the chaos that was starting to form on American campuses, in American society, mainly college campuses, among young people in 1968.

I was amazingly uninformed about the war. I was pro-Johnson. I was pro the war on poverty, but not in an impassioned kind of way. I don't think that the mental attitude and the political maturity formed for a long time. That's one of the things that, looking back, strikes me, those years of 18, 20, 22, 24 … why did things take so long to form in one's mind? That's because one is young and stupid or inexperienced. Sometimes when you're 30 or 40, you're better able to see these things, or 50, or beyond.

I graduated in 1968 and I went on a full fellowship, which was far beyond my dreams, to Georgetown University, majoring in international relations in Washington, D.C., ironically right in the heart of the whole problem. Talking about how things change, I was drafted in late October or early November 1968, I got a letter from my local Dane County draft board saying the usual thing, whatever it said.

I was completely shocked. It had never occurred to me. I had a student deferment all those years, and had worked hard to be a good student. I never thought about the fact that that ended. At that time, I think the selective service policy was they didn't have grad student deferments. I read of—I want to say Lon Cheney—Dick Cheney who I think was in graduate school in 1966, as I recall, and it made the point: "Why didn't he go?" He was married. He was doing some other things and also there was a grad student deferment at that time. It mentioned in there that it changed. Well, I wasn't aware that it changed. If I was, I had forgotten about it.

I was shocked to get the letter from the president of the United States saying, "I need you." My dislike of Nixon was fairly intense by that point. Nixon wasn't elected technically until November 1968. So I actually, in a panic, wrote back to my draft board, and said, could I stay at least for the semester. They granted that, but that was it. Then I went into sort of a funk. I'm not sure that grad school was for me, and I think I was coming to the conclusion at that point that diplomatic service, foreign service, all of that state department service was really not what I was about. Not because I wasn't service oriented and other-people oriented. I think I was starting to believe that this had been built too much on a mythical thing, as opposed to carefully reasoned from the ground up. Maybe it would be like saying, "I want to be an artist." It probably wouldn't be the same way because I think if you went to be trained as an artist and do art work in college and grad school, you would actually produce work that said, "Yes you have a future in this," as opposed to the artificiality of studying government and political science, and it may or may not have any connection to what you really would do.

At any rate, if there was a balloon there, it certainly popped. So I came back. I actually dropped out of grad school in about December. I just said, "I'm not doing this." I spent a month touring around D.C. and having a good time. I think my parents, who probably never knew that, would have been appalled, except they were not paying for any of it. Then I came back to Wisconsin in January and I was inducted in February of 1969.

I didn't want to go to Vietnam. I knew that much about the war at that point. So instead of taking my two-year draft commitment, I enlisted for an extra year to get trained in the field of intelligence, which was also sort of romantically interesting to me. MI6, MI5, to use the British equivalents of the FBI and the CIA, spy novels, all of that stuff. I didn't want to be a spy, but I thought that was interesting stuff.

Frankly, it was a lot more interesting than the dry stuff of diplomacy. Intrigue is always more interesting than hard work around a table. So I actually gave them another year, which I thought was a huge mistake in retrospect, except that it may have saved my life in Vietnam—because instead of being a grunt, I was in intelligence, and went through intelligence school. Ultimately I got shipped there anyway, but I wasn't with a combat unit. I was with an MI (military intelligence) group.

The reason I say all this is that a good friend of mine from high school with a parallel track, who got drafted that same fall, and went to Luther College in Iowa, went over. He did the two years. He was assigned to a combat unit and was seriously wounded. So I just say there is no reason why I wouldn't have followed that same direction. Maybe giving the extra year saved my life just by not putting me in that sort of situation.

You know recruiters. I was living in Washington, so I went down to Baltimore—or up to Baltimore—to a place called Fort Holabird. At the time, I didn't have any idea what it was and later I would find out a lot because I was eventually stationed there. But I took the sort of "Are you a Communist?" test. I was interviewed by a counter-intelligence type to see if I was worthy of that profession. He asked about my feelings about Marx and Lenin. Really! I kid you not! "How much do you know about it? What do you think about it?" Sort of this implied loyalty stuff. And I should have said, "I'm a damn Brit. What do I care. We protected Marx when he came to London to write his work."

I played it straight because I didn't want to screw up the possibility. What I had hoped was I would be assigned to an intelligence group in Germany, or even better yet, in England. I'd have time on leave or two weeks leave every year, I could go around Europe. I could see my mother's family in England. I was totally focused on that. But did he make any guarantees? No. I thought, "I have a minor in French. I have an English background. I was strong in languages. I'll play the odds."

Well, I was strong in languages so they sent me to Vietnamese language school. And I went to Vietnam anyway. That's just the way it worked out. There's a little twist there too. This is the "great green machine, right?" I spent two years in training to do one year of real work. This was the irony. You would never train somebody for two years to work one year for a firm. But I spent essentially one year with basic training, intelligence school, which was six months, a long time at Fort Holabird. Then I was sent for 47 weeks to the Defense Language Institute in El Paso, Texas, which is right next to Fort Bliss. I went to Vietnamese language school for 47 weeks.

There was another thing. You could go to Fort Myers, Virginia, outside of D.C., which everybody wanted. Or you could be sent to the Presidio in San Francisco. Or you could be sent to the desert. We sort of thought we were Christ-like because we wandered in the desert for 47 weeks. And we didn't care.

I spent all that time to be shipped overseas for one year, so my attitude was pretty poor all the time we were in El Paso. The group I was with, I had actually been with many of those fellows, they were all men, no women, through six months at Fort Holabird in Baltimore. Some did get shipped to Europe. Some got shipped to Hawaii. People went to different, really neat places. I'd say probably 15 of us out of the 30 in my intelligence class got sent to El Paso, Texas, to sit there from January until December in 1970 to study language day in and day out, which is the worst way to teach a person a language.

Week in, week out, learning how to use all of the military terminology in Vietnamese, for "battalion" and "machine gun" or whatever, and all these artificial situations. We were the poorest students. We were taught by Vietnamese civilians or Vietnamese military who were on assignment to the Pentagon or the Defense Department, and we were barely able to say, "Why are we here studying the language to go over to your country when you're here, if it's such a great war, teaching while on leave from your own military situation?" So our attitude was bad, bad, bad.

We all passed the final test. We were all certified as Vietnamese speaking. If you speak to someone who is not a native English speaker and they've had stilted training—take for example our good Vietnamese friends who, let's say, learned English at the University of Saigon for a year and came over here. Our ability to understand their English would be as difficult as their ability to understand my Vietnamese after 47 weeks.

We all passed the test and there really was only one out of the 30 of us who could speak it. He was an exceptional person who just decided because he was an odd duck, and kind of a brilliant guy, he was going to learn it no matter what. He didn't care about the military part of it.

We all went over there and we got dispersed into the country. I went into Saigon. I think it was Long Binh, which set me off right away in terms of the conditions and how the Vietnamese were treated by the military. We got dispersed from Long Binh and we all wanted to stay with the 525th Military Intelligence group, military intelligence in Saigon. We knew a few people there we had seen in intelligence school and we thought maybe we would just get lucky and stay.

You get assigned to one of the four military regions. I got sent to the furthest north, which was in Da Nang, the old French port city of Tourainne. When we got up there we said, "Well, maybe we can at least stay in Da Nang, which is a beautiful city on the edge of the ocean."

From there, I got sent to the furthest northern point which was just 20 miles below the DMZ, a place called Quang Tri

City. We were closer to Hanoi by a long shot than we were to Saigon.

In retrospect, it was just as well that we were away from the brass and the whole military shtick because nobody up there really hassled any of us. It's just like the infantrymen that were out in the field. They had enough to deal with. No one was going to hassle them about anything military. Just save your skin for a year and then get out. When I went up there, I was assigned to a small intelligence team of three people working with three or four Vietnamese counterparts every day in an office, which was a little old rice warehouse.

We took in intelligence reports from agents, Vietnamese agents in the field. Because there was a captain and a lieutenant, and we had a couple of sergeants, and they had more officers, it had to balance. This was a save-face thing. It was sort of like in diplomacy. What's the shape of the table? Let's spend six months talking about the shape of the table in Paris, right?

They credentialed me as a first lieutenant because they needed one more officer. So my entire time up there I was a first lieutenant, even though I was an E-5 hard stripe, buck sergeant. I drew officer's duty. I ate in the officer's mess. I hung out in the officer's club, which means one drinking place versus another. I was documented because this was all to save face. My best friend who I went to intelligence school with, himself an E-5 sergeant, he had to call me "sir" the whole time. There were only a handful of people who were in on it. But I had to carry this cover the whole time. My big fear was that I was going to run into somebody who talked about, "How did you become an officer? Was it ROTC? Did you go to OCS, or how else did you do it?" I never wanted to talk about any of this because I thought it would blow my cover. I was extremely uncomfortable. It never happened. It came close once or twice. That was just one more stressor.

I was paid as a sergeant. I wasn't an officer. The funny thing is when I left country and I went back to the States, or on R&R as soon as I left Da Nang and went south to Saigon, I had to make sure I switched. I couldn't wear officer's garb. I did run into somebody in Saigon once when I was wearing enlisted stripes. And I had to deal with that. What do you do?

You sort of make up a story. It was just part of the folly of Vietnam, my personal folly of Vietnam. I told an officer years later when I working for the Department of Veteran Affairs. The guy was a light colonel in the Reserves. He didn't believe me. He didn't believe they ever did anything like that. I said, fine. You don't have to believe me. I was just laughing about it. He couldn't admit they would do something like that.

I was advised that I had to keep this under cover. I didn't know about this until I got to Da Nang and they said, "We're going to send you up and we're going to make you look like a first lieutenant." They gave me false IDs. I had my picture on all that stuff. It wasn't like you had to present a card. I had to sort of play that game for a year. Actually, my roommate was a lieutenant senior grade, a Naval intelligence guy, and a really nice guy. I got along with him fine. I lived up there all the time and he never knew. My roommate never knew. I always wondered what he would think if he knew. He's director of admissions at Coe College in New England now.

It was only told to me that it was to keep the politics of the intelligence group "straight." The Vietnamese, I think they had a major, a captain, and a lieutenant, and a couple of enlisted. We had to have the same ranks. We sat across the room from each other in this dingy little one-light-bulb place. We had a captain. They needed a lieutenant. It was sort of that political balance. Nobody outside that group knew it, so it was truly only in that room. It never made any sense to me, and I thought it was a bunch of nonsense.

When I left Da Nang and went south, I immediately took that off. There was an attitude, like you don't have the right to wear that so make sure you take it off. Never mind the fact that you've got to put up with all of this. I pulled duty officer. To me it was just part of the total nonsense of the war, one small aspect of it.

After 47 weeks in Vietnamese language school, our attitudes were poisoned I guess you'd say. The feeling down there was, what are they going to do, send us to Vietnam? In fact, we had one guy down there who joined the University of Texas-El Paso peace group. He was brilliant about this. He was in law school when he got drafted. He joined the peace group and became the treasurer. And they didn't do anything. Several of us went to a couple of peace gatherings. We were in the Sun Bowl actually with one anti-war thing once but it was just speeches and a couple hundred students and a few of us. It was no huge rally walking down the street. I mean this was El Paso, Texas. This is Fort Bliss. This is retired military. It's red, white, and blue as it can be.

But he became the local treasurer for the University of Texas El Paso peace group. When it came to going to Vietnam, they pulled him out of the line early, and said we need to talk. We need to interview you. They didn't want to send him because they didn't trust him. He accomplished his whole purpose. He never went. And I thought, why didn't I do that?

We were disillusioned there. In January 1971, we spent two weeks in Oakland waiting to ship because at that time Nixon was making sounds about reducing troop strength. We thought we were going to get turned around and shipped elsewhere. I think we missed some of that first level of activity by a couple of months. We were held there and finally left and went to Long Binh. It was a God-awful place.

Everyone who flies to that side of the world, it's an awful way. You're better off going on a steamer or something. You fly into Long Binh and you see these long facilities. I remember the latrines. They're corrugated roofs and wood sides. But how long has the army been there? Since 1964 or 1965. This is 1971. They had never put a sewer system there. They're still using latrines and people are burning the waste. The local, indigenous population, the Vietnamese, are hired to do this. I couldn't think of anything that could be more demeaning, tremendously demeaning, that they hire them to burn this waste. I thought the water facilities were terrible.

The war back in those days, they were saying was $1 million a day. Sounds like a pittance compared to $87 billion for Iraq. All this money and they couldn't actually put in some infrastructure. These latrines were 24 seats on a side. Huge, huge, massive numbers of troops went in there.

I think we were so far from the flag pole, meaning Saigon, or even Da Nang, that I think there was disillusionment. There was demoralization in the sense of how many days have I got left here to put up with this. But there was no resistance in the sense of can we do anything about this? I think that the most depressing thing was you knew the first day you were up there, you were actually going to be there forever. I mean 320 days sounds like an eternity. I think there was a lot of that feeling. But the other thing I would say was living with the officers and being restricted to that side, I don't know that I got a true flavor.

One end of the compound was officers. There were sort of common buildings in the middle. The other end of the compound was enlisted. I think that would have had a whole different flavor. I had a privileged situation in that I didn't fraternize with enlisted people. I was paid the same as they were. In a sense, I was shielded from that. I used to talk daily to my best friend who had been over there six months. I had been to intelligence school with him. He was a fellow from Philadelphia. I think he was suffering from major depression and disillusionment but I couldn't rap with him, to use the current term. I didn't go to the enlisted club to have a drink with him. I couldn't do any of that. There was a barrier between us. That was something I couldn't do a thing about.

If I had complained and said take me out of this silly uniform, let me wear my sergeant's stripes, even if they had said so, they would have had to ship me someplace else because I would have been burned there. I made it a point to always treat the enlisted as well as I could. In fact, I was doing bunker duty one night with a fellow. I was the officer on duty and there was enlisted in there, sort of a radio guy. We were talking and he said to me, you know, you don't seem like an officer. And I said, I don't huh? And I probably said something like why not? And he probably gave me an answer like I was friendlier or talked more openly or whatever. But I didn't have the officer demeanor and I didn't treat him like a jerk. I didn't treat him like an underling. I thought to myself, I suppose I need to be careful. But I resented that I had to put this on all the time.

We weren't part of a combat unit. There were all kinds of people there. Our cover was that we weren't known as military intelligence types at all. There were people who said who are you guys really? They knew we weren't part of a signal group or communications group. I was on the east end of Quang Tri City, and the compound was relatively small, a couple hundred soldiers packed in there. We were totally separate. There was a combat base on the west side going out of town, which was huge. There was some brigade-sized infantry group there. But our little parent group, which was our place to go to show that we were really communications people, our front was at the combat base. Supposedly we were just doing technical support and maintenance or you name it, fixing radios. Nobody ever asked us much about that. And we didn't have any background to fake that.

Going to intelligence school, we were schooled in cover. We were schooled in having a story. We were schooled in having to know enough about that to be able to convincingly say yes, I'm a teacher at the U, for example. I could give you enough of a line that you'd believe me. We didn't have any deep cover like that, just like I didn't have any deep cover on being an officer. I had a little bit.

I wasn't trained as an officer. We did this refresher firing. We went down to a place in the countryside with some of the enlisted. There was an armored personnel carrier down there firing 50-caliber into a berm, a berm being a large mound of earth that would keep the shells from going down range. I almost had my mouth open. I had never been that close to a 50-caliber weapon on an APC to see how terrible it was, the impact. I just could not believe the size of the round and the way it went in there. Now, if I'd been an officer, I would have had familiarity with all of that stuff.

We were also doing practice firing with the grenade launchers. They're like a shotgun. You launch a fragmentation grenade. I wouldn't shoot it. I made sure the enlisted did, got their practice at it. But I didn't have a clue how to aim the thing. I was very uncomfortable standing there. M-16s were fine. M-14s were fine. Those were the standard rifles, but I didn't dare show that I didn't know how to do any of that. In fact one of them said, lieutenant, you want to take a whack at this? They were picking off small trees or bushes or whatever. I said, no, you go ahead.

I wasn't a combat type. I'm a conflict avoider, combat avoider. Just get me out of here. I didn't have any of that training. We spent all of our days deciphering intelligence reports, writing them up, cross-referencing them with field reports that would come in from different groups, and essentially saying there was this action in this area. And then rating the intelligence to say it was C6, meaning we can't verify the source and we have no idea if it's true, to A1, which would mean it's a very reliable source and absolutely verifiable with other cross-referenced information.

We did that day in and day out.

That was sent up our command. It went to our little group out there at the combat base, and they somehow communicated that to Da Nang, who then passed it all the way down to Saigon.

It wasn't tactical intelligence. It was to put together a big intelligence picture. What we were reporting on were Vietnamese, the Vietnamese who had been recruited by the Vietnamese, they used to use the term "agent handler," but they changed it because they didn't want people to understand what it really was. But the Vietnamese officers were people who had recruited woodcutters, rice farmers, people who would be out and about. They paid them and got the information. Wrote it up. Brought it in. It was translated into English. An interpreter sat in the middle. Miss Tu was her name. She knew basic English. She wasn't very good. They wrote their reports. We wrote ours. Ours went up the line eventually to Saigon, and theirs went to wherever they went on a parallel path.

Once in a while you'd hear that our information, along with other information, had helped to convince somebody to send some jets over to hit an area or to God knows what. It was very sanitized. We didn't ever have to think that what we were reporting and sending on was going to hurt somebody.

Out of the clear blue sky I got about a 15-day drop out. A drop is a decrease of service. Because I was going to stay there until February 18, which would have been the end of my three years, around the middle of January I suddenly got a message, which said, "Pack your stuff. Get on the next chopper. You're gone." It was unbelievable to get that information. My roommate, this naval officer, he wasn't even there. I left within an hour or two. Grabbed stuff and just left. I wasn't going to give anybody a second chance to say, wait a minute. You couldn't call home in those days. There weren't any cell phones or that stuff. So I just left in the middle of January. I got out January 18, 1972, after almost three years.

I came back to Madison. I left Long Binh and it was about 95 degrees, equivalent humidity. And I landed in Madison and it was like 10 below zero with snow. That was within a period of four days. We went down country and they just ran us through. They just out-processed us like crazy. Took off from Bien Hoa. Extremely emotional to feel the wheels go up. Everybody felt good. You didn't care if it took a week to fly back. It was just an incredible feeling.

I came back and I was sick about the war by that time. I was sick about the war before I went, but I was never aware like I thought I should have been. The question I asked myself when I was over there was, "Where was I in 1967 and 1968 when students in Madison were marching?" Madison was a hotbed. It didn't permeate the smaller campuses. In fact, I think that's probably true all over the country.

There were spots where things were active. When I was at Holabird in 1969, Nixon's in the White House and we went down from Holabird in Baltimore in the deep fall of 1969 and were part of the, I don't know how big the crowd was, that marched on the mall. Marched all the way down from the Capitol around the White House to the mall … three, four, five hundred thousand? Eight hundred thousand? I don't even know. I've never seen so many people in my life. There were a number of friends in the intelligence school. A number of other people. It helped to galvanize it. Things were going badly. We were in the system. We knew it was wrong. We believed it was wrong. I think when you're with a group of people, you can share your feelings and there's some energy that's built there. There's some synergy. So it really started then.

We had a very enlightened commander in Holabird. I can see the guy's face. I can't remember his name. But I think he was very opposed to the war quite honestly. But he said if you go down there, you go down in civilian clothes. You can't associate yourselves with the military. We were the only guys with meatball haircuts, meathead, whatever you call it, buzz cuts down there, apart from the narcs or the FBI, who were going around taking pictures of everybody. But how much film can you put through a camera when you've got 800,000 people?

We went down there. We had a great time. I'm afraid it was probably too much of a party, but it was like, yes, we're doing something. I remember we marched from Capitol Hill down as close to the White House as we could get. We went out onto the mall. And when we left hours later, they were still marching down. It never ended. Pennsylvania Avenue was just packed all the time. That was wonderful.

That was probably the first demonstration I've ever been in my life that I can remember. We did that, and from that point forward, I guess we couldn't do a lot. But the problem with being in the military and doing something was, it wasn't duty in the sense that I wanted duty to my country and my flag and all that nonsense, but I didn't want to harm the people in my family, my parents, my siblings.

By 1970 when I went to El Paso, I got married. I've been married for nearly 36 years now. I didn't want to do something that fouled up my wife's life as a teacher or any of that. So I had mixed feelings. I wasn't single, unattached, where I could say I don't care.

The thought about Canada had occurred to me when I was at Georgetown. But I thought I couldn't deal with how that was going to mess up a lot of things. I didn't have the courage to do it. I didn't think my parents could deal with that. My father was a veteran. My brother went to Vietnam. He was there in 1968. He spent two years as a draftee and ended up in Vietnam also.

So I didn't feel like I had this sort of right to cop out for political reasons or personal safety. I guess being there for a year and seeing the incredible waste: The waste of personal time; the waste of everyone's time; the waste of materials; the waste of money; ultimately the waste, tremendous waste of lives, and putting up with that for a full year, that just did as much as anything would ever do to galvanize me into believing that you don't ever want to do this again.

I was only there for a year and I rotated out and there were other people still going there. It wasn't like it was over. That was the thing that really hit me when I came back to Oakland. We were being served the traditional steak when you came home, and the guys on KP serving us were waiting for their plane to load up so they could go. It was just incredibly immoral. So really from that point forward, I came home and I guess that's what really changed my whole view of things.

I never went back to grad school. I abandoned the idea of doing something in the diplomatic service, the state department. I was married. I had a child on the way. I said, I need a job. So I spent 10 months looking for a job because the job market was terrible. The irony was, in the short run, I accepted a job with Department of Veterans Affairs here in Wisconsin because they offered me a job. They were the first people to ever offer me a job. And they hired me because they needed a planner, whatever that meant. And I was a Vietnam vet, and I probably looked pretty straight to them. I didn't have long hair.

They had the WISVET outreach program, and they were trying to "help" returning veterans. I thought that was fine. Ultimately I left the agency feeling like, thank you for the favor. You've given me five years of employment. But I'm not interested in being a part of an organization that is always dependent upon having veterans, and waving the flag, and all of that. Because while they did what they could for veterans, and while they were of course against war, they were interlaced with members of the VFW and the American Legion, who were always wearing their garrison hats, waving the flag, and saying God Bless America, right or wrong. And that was completely 180 degrees from what I felt. I really felt that I had to leave, plus there were other things. It was natural to transition away from there.

I was grateful that they gave me some veteran's preference points when they hired me. I was glad to get a job to support my family. But I didn't want to really have anything to do with that.

To this day, I feel like you can never do enough for someone who has lost a leg, an arm, who's been disabled or, worst case, was killed, for their families. You can never do enough to replace that. But as for the rest of us who went there and got out, we need to move on. They need to move on. The veterans' organizations just didn't ever seem to do that. They talk a good line, but I don't think they act it. Otherwise they'd all be part of Veterans for Peace.

I was against the first Gulf War. I'm against this war. I realized I could only do small things in my own way to be against it and to oppose it. That's why I joined Veterans for Peace. It's too big a problem. The issues are too big for one person to feel like they can go in and make a difference.

Margaret Mead, the great sociologist, said, "Never think that one person can't do something to change the world. That's the only way it's ever happened." But it's lots of single people acting in concert. And I think that's what Veterans for Peace is about. That's what going back to Vietnam in 1995 was about. That came out of the blue. Hearing about Mike Boehm and his experiences, things that people have done, and I just really admire those things. For God's sake, at least join this organization trying to do something, no matter how small it is.

My youngest child is 22 years old. She got out of West High here a couple of years ago, and nearly joined the military. I was really conflicted about this. In the first place, I didn't even want her to consider that option, but the other consideration was— it's her life. Now this was pre-Iraq by about a year.

She'd be the first to say she never paid attention. She had too good a time in high school and she didn't keep her grades high enough. She didn't study. She had a good time. She did the minimum. But I felt like it was her life. Just like if someone had said to me, okay you get out of high school, now you do this. Although in those days we were expected to do this. I was very, English background, dutiful, stiff upper lip, all of that stuff.

I said sure, go ahead, not that it was a bad idea. I was loath to tell her no. I would never say you can't do this. You never tell a third child that anyway. They tell you to take a hike. Fortunately, she waited six months. She was going to enlist and do her three years and get the G.I. Bill or whatever they call it nowadays, and all of these other promises. And I told her about how you will get promises and promises and promises, but even if you get the training they promise, it won't necessarily translate to civilian work, real-world work.

She considered all these things but I don't think she actually wanted to put a financial burden on her parents to send her to school. She wanted to make her own way. This is one way she thought she could do it. She'd get credit. She wasn't sure what she wanted to be. She wanted to go into military police work because she was interested all her life in being either a fireperson, or police officer, or her current thing, and I think it'll probably stick, is working for the federal government in the treasury agency or whatever. Law enforcement is really what she's interested in. Justice. That noble 22-year-old idea of, "I want justice for people. I want to catch the bad guys. I want to help the people who are victimized."

Eventually she dealt with recruiters a couple, three times. She went down and she did her testing in Milwaukee. She came to the conclusion, and I hate to say this for all the good people who are in the military trying to do an honest job, she couldn't deal with it anymore. She said, "I can't work with people making promises who don't know their head from a hole in the ground, and who are stupid." These are people really thinking they can sell a used car to anyone. She was brighter than that.

I think all kids are bright enough to see this. I think some kids join for desperate reasons. I think you have to give kids the belief that there's something better. I think you have to encourage them to think, which is what they try to do all the way through school. Whether they succeed or not, I don't know. It's so hard to tell.

I hope they get good teachers who teach them ethics and morality and the wrongness of war, the difficulty of peace, that violence isn't an answer. Just because another country doesn't agree with us or says bold things in the international arena like, "We have weapons and we'll use them on you," doesn't mean that we can use that as a trumped-up excuse to actually invade their country, to break international law.

We have to put faith in these kids, and I have faith in them. I don't want them to join, and I hope if they join they get through it and they get out and they become spokespersons for saying there's a better way to do this. Join the Peace Corps.

Join almost anything if you're service oriented that really helps people in a constructive way.

The military machine is just ... Sure you need a defense system. But I think most people joining either don't think about it, or they think about it for the wrong reasons. We don't need top-gun people. We don't need that kind of thinking to be a strong country. For me, it's always been hard to be a joiner, and to speak out. I think even leafleting at the high school for example, which I did one day, being part of a demonstration, being one to speak to a group of people ... I always find that hard. I have never been able to get past that and to do it.

Coming back from Vietnam in 1995, I only went out once and spoke to my wife's church group about the experience and what it meant to me. If you do it, it's always worth it. It always pays off, and people want to hear. People aren't that different, whether they're Americans or they're English or they're Iraqis or whatever.

When I have this resistance to putting forth the effort, I tell myself that it doesn't always work. But you have to get out there and try to keep doing stuff. As you get older, you've got some of the life experience that counts for something. But you lose your energy. If you could take what you have learned and apply it to 20-year-old energy and passion, what a great combination that would be.

I admire people like Clarence Kailin. Maybe he didn't do some things in his life that he should have done, but he still stands for something. He still does it. I wish I could be fraction of that.

KEITH DANIELS

Vietnam

I was born in Burlington, Wisconsin in 1951, and grew up in a pretty average small, lily-white town, pretty conservative. I did the usual kid things. I was a good athlete in high school, but not what you would call a Grade A student. I had no idea what I wanted to do coming out of high school, but I was a basketball player and I got a ride to a junior college to play basketball. That was the University of Wisconsin–Marshfield. That's where I started forming my political beliefs. Luckily, we had a basketball coach that was pretty left-leaning. We could grow our hair long. We did any number of things that way. We experimented with pot at that time.

229

After playing basketball there for two years I transferred down here to Madison. Prior to that, my friends and I would come down for weekends. That was 1969 to 1970 for the freshman college, and 1970–1971, a time when we all remember what was happening on campus here. That's where I really started forming my anti-war beliefs. Obviously I hadn't gone into the service yet. I was in the streets. I was gassed. A lot of confrontation, that whole aspect was there. I became disillusioned with school a couple of times. Got sick of work.

I remember getting 85 for a draft number, sitting around with my buddies. There were six of us that lived together. I was the only one that got an early number. You got five happy guys and me that night. Then I started working on a C.O. In fact, I had a conscientious objector all but in the bag, and that's when Nixon started pulling out of Vietnam. Still not knowing what I wanted to do at 21-years-old, I decided I didn't want to work in a hospital for two years either, and I upset a few people who had worked hard for me. One was a local priest from my hometown, another, my coach and athletic director. They had all written letters in my behalf. I probably had that C.O. in the bag, they were all saying, especially the priest who had worked with guys before.

Then I decided to join the Navy just because I didn't know what I wanted to do. Because I had enough college credits, I went in as an E-3, not an E-1, so I went in at a higher pay rate. They gave you a choice of either what school you wanted to go to, or the coasts. I said, "I don't care what school you send me to. I want the East Coast. I don't want to go to San Diego where the boys are going to Southeast Asia."

I became basically a secretary in the Navy. I was a yeoman, which deals with officers' personnel records. The last two years I was on an LST. An LST carries Marines. So you got to know a lot of the guys who had actually been through the crap. I was the ship's bookkeeper and the ship's librarian. That was pretty easy. I was in the service from 1973 to 1977. While we were in, the tapes all came out and Nixon resigned. He would have been impeached. Those were the years.

Most of the people going through boot camp were either poor white kids from the hills or inner-city black kids. I was kind of an anomaly. There were a couple of us in my boot camp company that had some college experience and had seen a little more, but basically they were kids, doing what they're told. They didn't have opinions yet for the most part.

It was interesting when I got to the ship that I was on, mainly working more with officers than enlisted men, that was more interesting because these guys were college educated. There were two distinct camps, even on our boat between the officers, pro-war and anti-war. They never said "anti-war," but you could see which guys were leaning which way. There were the ones that were there because they were ROTC and had to do this now for five years to pay for their education.

The guys that I hung with that were enlisted, you always gravitate toward people you like more than people you don't like. The group I hung with had pretty much the attitude we were just putting in our time to get through this. Luckily, we were on the East Coast. Thank God we don't have to go to Southeast Asia.

We went on Caribbean cruises quite a bit to go play war games. We went through the North Atlantic a couple of times, and in 1975 after one of the Israeli–Arab flare ups, we sat in the middle of the Suez Canal for a couple of months. We were the flagship while the minesweepers were clearing the canal of ordnance. That was interesting duty. For one thing, you could get a chunk of hash the size of your fist for a carton of cigarettes.

We were on an LST, 580-feet long, hollow hull, so that in storms it was like a ping-pong ball. That was awful. But the good thing was that with that hollow hull we could get some real shallow-water ports. We had some good liberty ports, small towns and stuff. That was nice. We had 15 officers and about 200 crew, and we could carry 300 Marines and a dozen tanks or trucks. After an earthquake one time in the Dominican Republic, we took Army engineers down to build roads.

I just watched *Two Days in October*, a good film. It was amazing. Some of the G.I.s coming back in that thing saying: "I don't know if what we did was right or wrong, but I know all these protestors, if they'd line 'em up, I'd shoot 'em all."

I got out, went back to school here. Things were so much different in 1977 and 1978 coming back. When I was going to school here before I went in, the humanities courses were where all the energy was. By the time I got out, everyone was business, business, business. Everything was business and science oriented. I don't get it, what changed. The sororities and fraternities were big again, that kind of thing. I got out in 1977 and went back to school in January of 1978, and I couldn't believe how all the energies were going toward business and money, money, money. I studied mainly English and I was in the school of journalism. I never got my degree. I ended up doing this part-time. I liked being in bars. I'm a social animal. I said I might as well not drink all the time and get paid for it. So I started tending bar and eventually that led to this. I grew up in one too, the Harmony Bar—that's where the name comes from. That was the name of my dad's business when I was a kid.

I was anti-war even enlisting in the Navy. There were a few steps in getting the C.O. I went before a board of a couple of little old ladies. I think there was one guy in uniform there. I don't remember that much about it other than these letters that Father Mason wrote because he was a family friend too. Growing up it was like having seven brothers. He was the oldest. When I wasn't at my house growing up, I was at the rectory. He went before the board too. He was a very eloquent man. He was a Jesse Jackson–type speaker. Then when it came time to actually take C.O. status, the risk of combat seemed nonexistent if you got on the right coast.

My parents were totally blue collar. They were Democrats when I was growing up. That's one thing, growing up even in the mid to late 1960s and you're watching TV and your looking at body bags. My parents were anti-Nixon. My dad voted Democratic his entire life. Being a Democrat at that time was more anti-war than being a Republican. You're with your family, you're watching the news, and you're seeing body bags.

For me it was a right or wrong issue. As a kid, there were no black families in town. But blacks would come from Racine or Kenosha and fish on one side of the river, and we'd fish on the other side. We'd sell them our fish, and people would make comments. At an early age I probably said "nigger" or something. I remember my dad saying, "Don't ever let me hear you say that again." I don't know how he worded it, but he made it clear. And that's a man with a seventh-grade education. He grew up in Kenosha County on a farm, and they lost the farm in the Depression, the family farm.

On either side of my immediate family I was the first one to go in service. There were lots of boys ahead of me too, but a lot of them were farmers. At this time too, they were older, so that they missed Vietnam and were too young for Korea. I have two sisters and a brother. I'm the oldest. When I was 19, I let my hair grow. He wasn't pro-drugs or hippie or anything like that, but my dad and I were so close all our lives, except this one year when we had to go through mom to talk because I was a long-haired hippie.

Presently I view the world as we're the bad guys. Of course there's the Islamic right. There are plenty of idiots out there on all sides, but to think that we're the saviors of the world, you know that's bullshit. This is all about oil. This is all about Bush and his buddies staying rich. I feel for kids. My cousin Mike's oldest just went in the Marine Corps and that scares the hell out of me. I've seen him after boot camp. He's a good kid, but he's "rah rah." He's ready to do what he's told. A Marine can't have questions. He's got to do what he's told and go where he will get killed. His two years' younger brother, 15, has already signed to follow him into the military.

What percentage now is Hispanic in the military? It's huge. You go back to the Roman Empire. Of course they were hiring other people if their citizens didn't want to do it.

I have a very successful bar and grill. We're one of the busiest spots in the city of Madison for what we do. But it's clear, some of the west siders that haven't been here think it's either a gay bar or it's all lefty pinkos. We get that. And I say, "Well, good. That's fine. Keep that image and stay over there."

If you look I've got a picture of Cheney and Bush and it says, "Don't vote fore crazy bastards." I feel that. There's definitely a left-wing attitude here.

You watch presidential elections. The Greens had their election night party here. People use this room for any number of things. I just make it clear that anything that I think is right wing won't be in here. I've been here 15 years. We've got music on the weekends, and great food.

My attitude remains: I totally distrust our government. I think the grassroots things are important. That's why I like doing small things here. I think the only way you get anything changed is locally. That's why I love living in Madison too. That's one thing I loved about our local ballot in 2004. The right wing were Democrats. There was not a Republican on the ballot. I live in a good place. That's very unusual.

I've noticed the national media is starting to actually report the bodies. I believe that a couple of idiots are going to be indicted. Plus I've got a $100 bet with somebody on it. I'm a hopeful person. The glass is half full. It's not half empty. That's just the way I am. Everyone says Clinton was no better. Well I say, yes he was. He was just as money hungry and capitalistic as these guys are, but at least money went to some social programs. It wasn't all just the defense department.

ESTY DINUR

Yom Kippur War (Israel)

I'm a veteran of the Israeli military. I served in 1973 and 1974 in military intelligence.

In Israel everybody—or most everybody—gets drafted, girls and boys. You become 18, you finish high school, and you get drafted.

At that time, the people who weren't being drafted were religious. The same is true today. Also, married women, pregnant women, and mothers didn't—and don't—get drafted. Back in the early 1970s there were very few declared conscientious objectors, or people who found other ways not to join the military. Basically, that was part of your life. Military service was something that was expected of you, and in the last year of high school you were always speculating about what you were going to do in the military. Where you were going, what you would learn, and whether you would have a good experience or not.

There were people who wanted to stay close to home. There were people who wanted to go away. It was really part of what you did as you became a young adult, an old teenager. So that was part of my life too, but I have been very politically active since I was 14. I was a person who was agitating in school, and even organized some demonstrations, and was involved to some degree with political organizations. For me, it all started as a reaction to the militarism of Israeli society.

I realized that I lived in a society that was very, very militaristic, and that everything that we did had to do with that. I really objected to the prevailing militaristic attitude and resisted it. I realized that a lot of the songs that we were learning in school, and a lot of the literature, and a lot of the poetry, it was all about how great it was to die for the motherland. I remember a particular song that we learned in elementary school, where the mother is standing at her son's grave mourning, but then she says: "We will not let our enemy win. We will sacrifice more young men like you." I really resented that.

Later, as I learned and understood what was happening, it also became a resistance to the Israeli occupation of the West Bank, sympathy to the Palestinians, and feelings of what is just and what is unjust.

As my draft date was coming nearer, I was really struggling with my conscience and decided that I wasn't going to get drafted. I spent probably the last six months before my draft date trying to decide how to not get drafted. One option was to marry my boyfriend at the time, which I didn't. Women can choose not to be drafted if they are married. So we decided not to do that, and getting pregnant, we decided not to do that. I was thinking of all kinds of things. I decided I would just declare myself a conscientious objector and spend some time in jail and be done with it.

And then a day before my draft date, the Yom Kippur War erupted. It was the one war that Israel really did not anticipate.

And it was the one war that Israel would have lost if not for American aid. I was 18. I was drafted in September or October and my birthday is in June.

When I was 12, just in time for my Bat-Mitzvah, the Six Day War erupted. The night before it started, I was trying to sleep and there was this endless noise. My parents' house is on a mountain in Haifa, and under it there's this main road going north. There was this incessant noise, which to me sounded like someone was trying to start a motorcycle, but all night. I couldn't see anything but then in the morning when I got up, I realized that it was this endless column of tanks going up north. So that was my first notion that something was happening.

The day before my draft date, I was walking from my parents' house to the apartment I shared with my boyfriend and suddenly there was a siren, and also there was this silence. Of course, it was the eve of Yom Kippur, so it's always silent. But there was this *silence*. There were no people in the street. I can't remember exactly at what point I realized what was happening, that a war had just erupted and there were combat planes going overhead.

For me, it was my third or fourth war, and so I knew the drill. You hear air raid sirens and you just look for the closest bomb shelter. There are no men in the streets anymore. You have to stay home. You tape your windows. The whole thing.

And so there I am, you know, and suddenly again I had to grapple with my conscience. Everything I thought up 'til now has just become irrelevant because everybody's out there fighting to save my life in a sense. I can't just say, "Okay, this is a job that we have to leave to others. I'm a conscientious objector."

In time I came to regret that actually, but at that point that was how I felt. I did go the next day and got drafted. Because I speak English, they took me to military intelligence, which I kind of expected to happen because, depending on what month you are drafted, there are only so many jobs that you can do and it was hinted to me that I would probably be taken to that. I say English because it was a very low-level military intelligence. I was listening to air traffic and to the UN and such.

I mean it's so low level that I can tell you about it. So I was drafted, but first there was basic training which, for females, I'm not sure if it's just a month or if it was just a month because of the war, the aftermath of the war. But because of the war, we didn't really go through much of basic training.

The base where they do the basic training is right next to, I think, the largest military airport in Israel. It's in the center of the country. There were these incredibly huge airplanes that I'd never seen before or since. It was amazing. Day and night. They were landing one after the other. Some of them brought things as big as tanks. Others were bringing all kinds of military equipment, but also things like field rations. That's what we basically did. They put us females to package field rations and to write letters to the male soldiers in the field. This is what we did.

But they also did a little bit of this basic training and I refused to train on guns. I refused to shoot. Any other day, any other time, they would have court martialed me for that. But because of the extraordinary times, they were just like: "Okay. You just go and package field rations." And that's all I did. I didn't learn to shoot until many years later in Wisconsin.

Well, I actually kind of learned before then because, in Israel, in high school, you have military classes once or twice a week. A lot of it has to do with physical education, but then you also have these classes where you have to wear khakis for that particular hour. And you do things like ropes and climbing and jumping off high towers onto a net, which for me was very scary, and all kinds of showing how brave you are. And you also learn how to shoot and how to clean guns and things like that. It's called Gadna, which means "youth corps" basically.

So the basic training was over and they took me to the course of military intelligence and that was three months. And then they sent me to a base down in the Sinai desert. It was an underground base where we were listening to things. I was in several bases, but most of my time I did in Sinai.

What I realized later, after I did my two years and was discharged and, you know, took some time to look back and reflect, is the reason that I came to regret having allowed myself to get drafted is that, you know, you find yourself in a system that is total. You are away from home. Especially in my case, in Sinai, females were there for two weeks, and you went out on a pass and it was a 10 to 12 hour drive, and you were home for a week, and then you went back on the bus to the base for another two weeks. For males, it was three weeks and one week. And so it's really a total system. You are really taken away from the life that you knew. You are in a base and this is the life. The particular base that I was in was large. There were several hundred people there. And so this becomes your life. You really become a cog in the machine. You do your job. You make friends. In my case, since I was a dancer in my younger days, I was on a professional track to be a modern dancer, and so I was giving dance classes on the base. I even had a few male students. People were looking for things to do.

You have sex, drugs, and rock and roll, and the work that you do. It becomes your life. You don't want to screw up on things. You do your work well. Even though my work was very low level and I wasn't out there shooting anyone, but it was the front lines and I was definitely helping the Israeli military machine. We had commando units coming through and going elsewhere. Again, because everybody is drafted and because the military is such a big part of your life, as a female you are raised to think this is who you are going to marry—combat pilots, the combat soldiers. There is a word for them, they are known as "combat."

You know, it's a funny thing, because when I walk around here in the U.S. and I see people in military uniform it disgusts me. When I would go back to Israel, I would look at myself with amazement because I saw these guys in uniform and, you know, this little girl in me was like (sigh), "Look at this guy."

I was in Sinai for the majority of my time, but I also was in three different bases in the Jerusalem area. Some of which were so secret that we didn't wear uniforms.

Males continue to go to reserve service for a month each year after they are discharged. Women, in principle, on paper, do that too, but they never called me again. I don't think they ever called any of my female friends either. I don't know how it is now, but not then.

The Israeli military is really a military of the people, made up of the people. Anyway, there are a lot of people in it who are leftists, who are peaceniks, even high-ranking officers. As you may have heard in the last couple years, a lot of them have come out and said, "This never-ending war of occupation is not right. This is intolerable. We should really start thinking differently."

So I never had to hide my politics in the Israeli military. In fact, when they did assign me to military intelligence, the first day I was there I went to my commanding officer and said to him, "Look, these are my political views. I have some Arab friends. I just want you to know because I don't know if I belong here." And he kind of looked at me with a smile and said, "Well, I'm exactly the same." And then I met a lot of other people who were really very much like me, but we were all there. It's a really strange system because you believe one thing, but you're doing something that goes against your politics and feelings.

What really distinguishes the Israeli army from the American army is that regardless of what you think about Zionism and Israel and all that, the fact is Israel is—even more so *was*—surrounded by hostile countries, and if it was to survive it had to protect itself, whereas the American military has never defended the Americans from any invading army or any enemy.

When I did this reflecting a year or two later, when I was able to look at my military service from some distance, I did think that it was a mistake to have allowed myself to be drafted because of that. I was a cog in the machine. I did help the machine work. I did my work well. They would have had someone else if I wasn't there, but just for myself it was the wrong thing. Since then I've been telling, whenever people asked me, I have been saying to people, "If you believe that war is wrong, you should not join the military because you become part of the system. There's just no way around it."

Right after I left the military I became politically active again, and participated in demonstrations, joined this thing, it was a predecessor really to Women in Black. We were mostly women where every Friday afternoon we would stand in front of the military headquarters in Tel Aviv and demonstrate against the Israeli occupation.

We demonstrated against Ariel Sharon, who was always involved in the military. I think at that time he may have been chief of staff or whatever. I left Israel and then came back, and when I came back he was leading the invasion and occupation of Southern Lebanon. I went back to doing these things, the demonstrations and vigils.

In Israel, like here, there's not too much tolerance for dissension. The way it is manifested is different. We'd be standing in a busy intersection. We'd welcome anyone to talk to us. People drive by and call you names and spit on you and give you death threats. Because we were mostly women, of course the names that they gave us were very sexualized. What they propositioned us with was very sexualized and violent.

In a sense, I just came back to who I am, right back to working for peace and against militarism, first in Israel and eventually here in the United States. We might want to add to the mix that I was married for many years to a Vietnam veteran, a combat Vietnam veteran who was also feeling very strongly antimilitarist and anti-American militaristic policies and working very hard in his own way, which was different from mine, working very hard to educate people and to fight against the American imperialist agenda.

I feel that veterans have the moral obligation to work against militarism and against imperialism and to educate people about these things. Society gives veterans some credence because they have been in the military, they have played these militaristic roles and so they really should speak and educate and be active in the peace movement and beyond, and do it as veterans.

I just happened to hear Don McKeating and Tom Benish speak about starting a chapter of Veterans for Peace. I said, "You know I'm a military veteran too." They said, "Oh, you ought to join." And I said, "I'm interested."

Actually, I was never really a member of a political party. Until fairly recently, I never belonged to any organization, but would attach myself at times to specific organizations because they were doing things that I agreed with. I was doing the lone wolf kind of thing: agitating, arguing, debating, educating, organizing. Whenever there were people who were doing things for an organization, I would work with them. I was kind of a one-woman cell.

I don't talk usually about my spiritual life. I think spirituality is a very personal thing. But I often despair, actually. I often feel like there is no hope. But it is my belief, my faith if you will, I don't like the word because I think it's so misused. I don't like to be put in a category with other people who use these words.

My feeling is that our job here is ... well, I anyway, I'm reaching to the One, right? I'm hoping to end up better than I started. I'm hoping to eventually be able to go to the next stage. My feeling is that we have to do what's right and to do it regardless of the cost, and regardless of the difficulties, and regardless of whether there is hope. This is the struggle.

I've seen some struggles in my life, and some difficulties and hardships. It's hard. It's not fun. But that, I think, is what we are here to do, to go through these tests and trials and tribulations and difficulties and obstacles and keep our eyes on the prize.

The way to that is by doing what's right. And what's right is to do whatever you can, or this is part of what's right. One thing that is right to do is to continue struggling against things that are wrong. I don't want to use the word evil, although that is how I feel about it. To struggle against evil ... it's no fun but we have to do that. And there's a lot of evil in the Israeli and American governments and those who drive their militaries.

Education is incredibly important. At certain points in my life, someone came and opened my eyes to something new and showed me something and taught me things and at times it was really, really hard. I have to give credit to Jeff, my ex-husband, who at one point showed me how, despite everything I've been telling you, I was still so brainwashed about Israel, and so supportive. I was resisting its militaristic bent, and I was fighting against the occupation and what's being done to the Palestinians, and yet in me there was still this naive person who was saying, "Israel is good, and we fight clean, and we don't commit atrocities. We are just fighting for our lives. Even if I disagree with how it is done, I can understand the good reasons why."

It was a process of him showing me that I was really brainwashed. It's very hard to let go of the things that you grew up with and that have been the foundation of who you are all these years. At one point you look at them and you say, "Oh, but this is all false. This is all based on lies. I have to let go of it."

I'm feeling that part of my job is to do that to others. I try to do it gently, but it's got to be done. My way is I'm a communicator, so that's how I do it. I do it through media of various kinds and through talking to people. One rule that I made for myself so many years ago is I talk to anyone who will talk to me. If they identify as Fascists, if they are the biggest Bush supporters, if they are totally stupid in their understanding of political realities, if they are the most ignorant person, as long as they talk to me, I will talk to them.

Let me tell you, I've seen several people just physically run away from me. At one point they're like: "I gotta go!" And they're gone, after we discussed things for a while. And often if it's a man, they will sexualize it eventually.

When I went to the hearing about the Rafah Sister City project, I wasn't planning to talk. But then there was this Israeli woman who was sent by the Israeli government to work with the Madison Jewish Community Council as it's called a *shlichah*, which means an envoy. She had been doing a lot of work in town to garner support for Israel. And some of her work benefitted me because she's been bringing Israeli movies, which are of great interest to me.

She got up to speak. There were only three people who spoke against the sister city project but they were all people who were talking about anti-Semitism and this and that, which is totally a tangent and has very little to do with sistering with Rafah. It's totally irrelevant. She said, well, I'm sure I'm the only Israeli here, and I'm speaking from experience, and here's what I have to say as an Israeli who knows how dangerous these Palestinians are. Everybody looks at me like, you're going to speak, right?

I said okay. I quickly wrote some notes and kind of ad-libbed. One thing I talked about is I, too, am really concerned about anti-Semitism. One thing I did mention is that I'm the daughter of a Holocaust survivor. My father never told his story until about 15 years ago, when he had a nervous break-down. My mother actually dragged him here to the United States to be with me because I'm his first child and only daughter. I have two brothers. And my father and I were always very close. She didn't know that this would happen, but we ended up sitting in my kitchen and I recorded him for three days. He told me his life story. I wrote it down. That was the first time he talked about it.

I realized that here is a case of PTSD, post-traumatic stress disorder. And then I realized that my whole family ... my father comes from a family of 11 ... four of them survived the Holocaust. Seven did not. And also when I say "survived," I have to put a qualifier on that because, while he's lived a very full and in many ways a happy life, obviously the dead were pursuing him until he had that mental breakdown. His sister, who lived in New York, was very much living in the Holocaust; my cousin, her daughter, committed suicide when she was about 20 and she was tripping on LSD and thinking that she was being tortured in a concentration camp.

My other cousin in Israel, she is a psychologist specializing in second-generation Holocaust survivors, my generation. And so we all have been affected by World War II. My mother was in London for the blitz. How did I get talking about that?

So when I spoke in the Rafah hearing, I said I am the daughter of a Holocaust survivor. I was raised among people with numbers tattooed on their forearms. I am very concerned about anti-Semitism. I'm watching it and it's scary to me what's happening, but it's also clear to me that a lot of it has to do with the current policies of the Israeli government. For one thing they are doing such awful things. They are commit-ting such atrocities that people look and say, "Well, the Israelis are evil. The Israelis are bad." It's always easy to say a whole group is doing it, and not look at it and say not all Israelis agree—although way too many Israelis agree with it, in my opinion. But also it gives permission to those who have been anti-Semitic all along but quietly, to come out now and crow. It's very scary.

I said, "If what you're concerned about is anti-Semitism, then you should support initiatives like the sister city because if we can bring peace, it will be a lot harder for anti-Semitism to continue spreading. If you just look at what's good for Israel, forget about the Palestinians for a minute, peace is good."

Since Sharon came to power there have been—I can't remember the number but it's stunning how many—more suicide bombings than there were in the 10 years before that. These last few years have had something like 10 times more suicide bombings than in the 10 years before that because he has come with his iron fist. It's not stopping anything. Violence begets violence, and the more Palestinian blood is shed, the more Israeli blood is shed too. The very same is true for American policies as we can see so clearly in Iraq and Afghanistan right now. The more militaristic you are, the more endangered your population is.

Then again I have kids. I have a responsibility for the kids. I'm scared to death. Both of my kids are of draft age. I told them they needed to think about it. They're not going to the military.

When I was very young, Ariel Sharon was famous because he was the commander of what was known as Unit 101. Unit 101 was going across the border and killing people and coming back. They were doing these nightly raids. And they were our heroes. They were heroes to us. And Sharon was a handsome man when he was young.

Being raised the way I was raised and being an idealistic person, at one point at a very young age before I became political, before I started thinking my own thoughts, I admired Sharon and these guys. They were these macho guys. Another one was called Meir Har Zion, a loner who was killing people all by himself. He was this mythical figure. There was that danger that my idealism would have turned into right-wing idealism. I don't know how or why it didn't happen. I'm so grateful that it didn't happen. It would have been easier if I were right wing, I could be a leader of God knows what awful group or cause.

It didn't happen. I am willing to allow that some people, possibly like Sharon, that they really believe, that they really think that militarism is good, that the iron fist is good, and that the Palestinians are really bad. I'm assuming that Hitler really thought the Jews were, you know, evil, a blight on humanity. I don't understand it, but I think that some people truly think that way. When it comes to the American government, to American presidents, the situation is different. Nobody ever tried to invade the U.S. directly. That is, nobody ever tried to come to rape your mother and steal your sister and slit your throat and all that.

To me, having studied history and looked at patterns, to me it's clear that we're talking, more than anything, about economics. We're talking about making money off of other lands. We're talking empire. Even though it looks different from the empires of the nineteenth century, that is what we're talking really.

Look at who have been the presidents in this country. Look at the government. These are all very, very rich people. By now they have dynasties that stay in these positions. They are people who have never had any idea about what life is like for most people, who don't know anything except that they deserve it and it's theirs. The world belonged to their fathers before them and now it's theirs. The world owes them something, and they are going to take it by hook or by crook. They have no care for the people who are going and getting killed for them. When you look at the current government's feeling for their own citizens, you see them taking away benefits from military veterans even as they send them to get killed. The deficit that they're putting this country in. They feel that it's all theirs. But then again, I was not raised that way. I don't understand or appreciate that way of thinking.

I think a lot of my activism actually came from my father. He was a socialist. I was born on a kibbutz, which was his thing. He was a socialist. He was politically active in a party, in the Labor Party, which is by no means left, but it was more left at the time. But he has changed with the years. He's pretty right wing nowadays. For quite a few years now, we've been trying to avoid talking about politics because I don't see him that much and I don't talk to him that much and I don't want to fight with him. He gets very angry. He's fairly old now, and I don't want to make him angry. I don't want to have fights.

It's very hard because often we'll be having this transatlantic conversation and I'll say something about this idiot Sharon of yours, what the hell does he think he's doing, and he'll start arguing with me and before I know it he's shouting at me. I don't feel good doing that to him.

But my family, generally, they have this attitude of: "Oh, it's just Esty. You know how she is." I just talked to my family last weekend or the weekend before that, and my brother comes to the phone and he says, "Oh, you're so dogmatic in your left-wing politics." I said, "What are you talking about? Where is the dogma?" He wouldn't even go into a discussion with me about that. He just denounced me as dogmatic, and that was it.

I have dual citizenship. It took many years to get the American citizenship, but I think it was more because of economics than my activism. I don't travel to Israel anymore. I just can't stand being there. I meet my parents in Europe or somewhere. I've been traveling with my mother every year now. I do travel, and the last two or three times I've been scared coming back, not sure what to expect. I also was detained for a while in the Vancouver airport by the Canadians when I went last year, apparently because they thought I was a Middle Easterner trying to sneak into their country. They didn't believe anything I told them about who I was. They detained me in the airport for about two hours until finally the guy decided to let me go. I was interrogated. He kept asking the same questions again and again, and trying to get me to make a mistake. It was very unpleasant.

I think the reason I joined Veterans for Peace and the reason I agreed to be the vice president, and the reason I've been trying to make peace within the organization and kind of sticking with it is because veterans have clout. Veterans already know what they're talking about and so they really have to be in the forefront of the peace movement.

I met Jeff on the road. I was on the road for two years, doing first Europe and then the United States. He gave me a ride. I thought I was going with him for a day or two and it ended up a lifelong journey because even though we are divorced now, we still share two kids.

He went to Vietnam. He joined the American military when he was 17. He was a juvenile delinquent kind of guy. He went to trial and the judge gave him a choice of prison or the military. He went to the military, and was sent to Germany. This guy in Germany whose job obviously was to recruit people to Vietnam was telling these guys how great it is in Vietnam. They'll go and they'll get drugs and whores, and so they all decided to go to Vietnam.

So the story is he got there and within a week they sent him to the killing fields. He was in combat for a year. He has Agent Orange and the whole thing, really bad health physically. Like my father, he never really dealt with it. He never talked about it. All these years that I was with him, he always made really easy friends with other combat veterans who were all loners.

He came back from Vietnam and immediately went to Berkeley and started agitating against the war. He was doing things like teaching people hand-to-hand combat kind of things. He also was in demonstrations and was very involved in that whole 1960s anti-Vietnam War movement and has been doing that really in his own way ever since.

His own way was more over the Internet. We got on the Net very early. We started using the Net in 1985, I think. We had what we called People's News Service. We had this publication called *World Perspectives*. We were listening to short-wave radio and transcribing news and providing it on the Net and in a monthly publication. That's before the Net became the Net and that was really the only way to get information from other services. It was a very valuable service because we were listening to the Soviet Union when it was still the Big Enemy and were among the first to hear Gorbachev and understand that the Cold War was over. We listened to Radio

Havana, and the radio of the Salvadoran insurgents, along with radio from the rest of the world. But of course we couldn't make a living out of it. We were working 60 hours a week and not making a living.

So that's what he was doing. To a large degree, he was always putting a fire under me because I have this talent to speak to people and to write, and so he was pushing me to go ahead and do it while he was staying home and taking care of the kids.

I think it's just atrocious the way this country treats veterans. I have to say in Israel at least if you are a disabled veteran, you don't have to worry about where your bread will come from. They take care of you. They take care of your family. Here it's just unbelievable. Knowing what I know about how the government just throws veterans away and doesn't care for them, it totally makes sense that veterans are dying under bridges, that they're living in institutions or under bridges. It's really appalling. On the one hand, I resist this whole thing of militarism. On the other hand, it is so disgusting to watch what they do with these people when they come back. And, of course, Jeff's in prison now for using marijuana to deal with both his PTSD and his agent orange-related chronic pain and degenerative bone disease.

As I look at my life, it has been marked by wars and militarism from before I was born. That is why I feel it is so important for me to do what I can against the current madness, and to educate and agitate and hopefully—it's hard for me to even say, "Try to bring about a better world." Things are just getting worse and worse all the time. Who knows what finally tips the scale and how things suddenly change. I'm seeing nowadays a lot of people, like in demonstrations, before the attack on Iraq. I couldn't believe who was there. People who I've known for years and have always argued with, and to me are probably right-wingers, and suddenly they're there holding signs, marching with us.

Apparently the young people are starting to wake up. That's what my kids tell me. You know, talking about hope, as we were nearing the attack on Iraq and people were becoming very politically active, I felt so grateful and gratified when I suddenly saw my kids, they were organizing among their peers. They were organizing. They were educating. I'd hear them having discussions on the phone and they were explaining to people what was really happening. When they couldn't explain all the way, they'd bring people over to me to talk about that. These kids are now doing what needs to be done among their peers.

DON KLIESE

Cold War Germany

I live in Madison, Wisconsin. I was born on June 26, 1965. I enlisted in the United States Army in March 1984. I decided since I was going to be entering military service, I'd do things you can only do when you're in the military, so I decided to enlist in the infantry. And I'm sure I made the recruiters day. I met his quota for the month I'm sure. He did not try to dissuade me from that in any way, shape, or form.

So I enlisted in the U.S. Army infantry, requested to go over to Germany, and I did my basic and advanced individual training at Fort Benning, Georgia, which is the home of the United States Army infantry. I was there until about August of

1984. I also did extra training there in the Bradley Infantry Fighting Vehicle. That was my military occupational specialty, Bradley Infantry Fighting Vehicle crewman, which is nothing more than a glorified grunt, nothing special.

A Bradley is like a miniature tank, and people probably see them on television. They're using it over in Iraq at this time. It's a 25-ton armored vehicle that combines the concepts of an armored personnel carrier and a tank. It has a 25-millimeter chain gun on it, mounts two anti-tank guided missiles on the side that can be fired. It's got a gunner and a commander in a swivel turret on the top, and they control the 25-millimeter chain gun and a coaxial mounted 7.62-millimeter, (I can't believe I'm remembering all of this) and the anti-tank missiles.

The body of the vehicle is a tracked vehicle like a tank, and it carries an infantry squad—between six to eight individuals and a driver, the fellow who drives it. I was a grunt. I was one of the infantry squad who would, theoretically, when the vehicle entered combat, drop the hatch in back, run out and then the vehicle and the squad would provide support for each other in combat.

After my training at Fort Benning I shipped over to West Germany where I was assigned to the 3rd Infantry Division. I was stationed at Harvey Barracks, which was outside of a little town called Kitzingen in Bavaria. There I was part of the 1st of the 15th Infantry, Bravo Company, which was actually the company that Audie Murphy had served in. ... Audie Murphy of World War II fame who gunned down multitudes of Germans, and of course, whose life ended in alcoholism, and so on. We were indoctrinated with that from the day we got in. We were both "The Rock of the Marne," the division that had stood at the Marne during World War I, and also the company that Audie Murphy had served in.

I was there in Germany for a year and a half, both in a line company, Bravo Company, and also some time in Headquarters Company as a jeep driver for a captain there. I got a little taste of line life and of headquarters life. Peacetime military service was really weird. We spent a lot of time playing at soldiering, breaking equipment in the field, destroying West German property, guarding the border, trying to look tough in front of the East Germans and the Soviets, guarding nuclear weapons bunkers, which we didn't really want to think about.

I was 19 and 20 years old. I didn't have a lot of political analysis or critique at that time of my life, but I would say, overall, I moved in different strata than a lot of people are used to, and I was a little unusual. I come from a privileged white background, and here I was in the infantry. It's a little unusual for an upper-middle-class kid to be part of the infantry as a grunt. Officers, yeah, but a grunt, no.

There was a lot of the poverty draft. It was a volunteer army but there were definitely a lot of black kids, a lot of Latino kids, a lot of poor white—Southern particularly. These people knew that Ronald Reagan's son wasn't going to be there next to them, serving alongside. A lot of them felt a lot of fatalism about being in the Army, that it was their only way out of bad situations, out of poverty. They weren't stupid about that. Maybe they weren't as eloquent about it as someone with a Ph.D., but they knew what the game was. There was a lot of stratification in the army, a lot of class structure. The officers were white overall. Non-combat units were predominantly white. Combat units—infantry, armor, artillery—were a lot more minority and black.

There was a lot of fatalism. We knew we were sacrificial lambs there in what was then West Germany. If there had been a war with the Eastern Bloc, we wouldn't have lasted 15 minutes. We were within missile and jet range of the Soviet bases. We probably never would have even gotten out of the barracks. We would have been gone so fast. It felt like a game in a lot of ways, a game of fatalism.

The German people were very kind to us. They were extraordinarily welcoming, given the situation, especially when Ronald Reagan was threatening to blow up the world, more or less, and we were there as the front line units to do that. They treated us very well. They had to put up with a lot. You know what happens when you have 19- and 20-year-olds away from home for the first time. They can drink as much beer as they want. That's the military's culture: Get drunk as long as you make first formation. It's okay whatever you do.

They'd have to be scraping G.I.s off the sidewalk on Saturday and Sunday mornings.

I didn't interact with the German people as much as I wish I had. I was a 19-year-old away from home for the first time, and I was overwhelmed by everything that was going on around me. But those that I did meet were very kind. They'd have to put up with us driving through their towns with our vehicles and our big armored vehicles, damaging their property. Especially when troops would come over for exercises from America. These guys would be driving these huge tanks, and they weren't used to driving in little German villages, and they'd be smashing things and hitting things. In light of all that, the minor things of smashing someone's front porch, up to the fact that we were waving nuclear weapons around, the Germans were extremely kind to us.

In fact, I had a friend who made much better efforts to reach out, and he met some older gentlemen who had been in the Wehrmacht (German Army) during World War II. I did talk with them once or twice when he would drag me along. And so many Germans could speak English. It's just amazing. You go out there and you fumble along with your German, but they speak to you in very good English.

They always expressed such a deep sadness to see young men such as us primed for war. They had lived it. They lived it in such ways that we could never even begin to comprehend. So many of them were really very sad and angry. They would say to us: "We don't want to see you live what we did, and we're so afraid that's what's going to happen again." That was a very eye-opening experience to talk to those gentlemen.

It's a mixed feeling when you serve in the military. It's that sense of pride of having served, but also a sense of despair about what you did. A lot of them were very eloquent about that.

The unit I was with, we would rotate through border patrol assignments, where we would patrol what was then the inter-German border between East and West Germany. We were what were called rapid reaction forces. We'd actually go out there and walk along the border. And most people had this image of what was then the border between East Germany and West Germany, the East and the West, as an Iron Curtain, big walls and machine guns and mine fields, whatever. Well, yes, that did exist but it existed about 500 to 800 meters east of the border.

The actual border itself was little stones stuck in the ground. Then you had, I guess you would call it a no-man's land between that and the actual fortifications. We would actually walk along those border stones. And East German guards would be walking on the other side about four or five feet apart, we would be like that, walking next to each other. So if you had wanted to you could have reached over and touched an East German, the "enemy," a living representative of the "evil empire." You could have reached over and touched them. Anyway, we're walking along on our side of the border, and there was the aura there of guarding democracy and all that, but you'd start to look. And here was somebody else who was your age, a 19- or 20-year-old kid, walking alongside you. And you're just like: "I'm supposed to want to kill this person?"

Most likely, if we had a chance to sit down in a gasthaus over a beer we'd find out we had more in common than we had differences. The same problems, the same thoughts and dreams, whatever. Beer, girlfriends, some kind of job or school. That was something else that started to make me question all the indoctrination that the military and our culture tries to give us. Here were human beings just like me. Could I really kill one of them? I didn't like to think about that too much. But I did. I think there were other people who thought about that too.

You could not talk to them, at least officially. I don't think anyone ever did that I knew of. If you did, there would have probably been some ramifications depending on who was in charge, from chewing you out up to maybe an Article 15 or something. I don't remember a debriefing or anything. I remember there was sort of a game. We're out here on the front lines and those guys will kill you. They would always claim that the East German guards had their magazines locked and loaded. And we had to carry our ammunition in ammo pouches. We couldn't carry it locked and loaded. I don't know if that was true or not. I think they tried to use techniques to scare us beforehand.

One interesting thing was that the East Germans in particular, I don't remember us doing this, but the East Germans would carry these large cameras, and they would photograph us as we were walking alongside. Not all. Just a few. Our officers would claim that they were using those photographs, that they were sending them back to East German and Soviet intelligence agencies, and they'd use them to try to figure out, to identify who we were, and use it as a way to blackmail us, or try to turn people. I have no idea if that's true or not. This is just the kind of stuff that they'd feed us.

But I think there was also sort of an assumption on our part, on the part of the military, that we would just do it, and that we wouldn't think.

After I was in Germany, then I was stationed in Fort Carson, Colorado for a year before my discharge. Whatever games were played on the, quote–unquote, front lines, I mean peacetime service in the United States was just petty silliness. Think of any kind of corporate silliness you're involved in at a place of employment and multiply it by 10 or 20 times and that's military service in the United States during peace time.

Whatever the military stood for, its propaganda to give you a sense of mission and purpose in life, defending democracy, by the end of my three years, that was gone. That's not what the military was all about. It was a very pathological culture, interested in perpetuating itself. It was based on petty brutality, ego trips. Not to say there weren't some good people in it. I met a lot of really good people that were sort of caught in this. But people are so in lock step. You have these duties in order to survive. You have to do them or else there are punishments.

Also I did some training duty down in Honduras for a while during 1987. I saw some of what was going on with our support for the Contras. I was a jeep driver. I never shot anyone. No one ever shot at me even though I was an infantry soldier, but I saw how we were supporting what were terrorists in the Honduran army. They were just terrorists. We were down there driving around Army National Guard and Army Reserve units, who were supposedly on a humanitarian mission but were actually building bases for these guys. I was driving around with a captain telling them where not to go so that they didn't get in contact with these units.

One of the funny things is these guys would leave equipment behind and claim it was damaged in training, unrecoverable, and guess who'd get it? That was the way the Reagan administration was circumventing a lot of the restrictions. The Contras probably got it, and the Honduran army. I didn't work with them a lot. The U.S. military didn't want us to really talk with them. Most of the time they wouldn't talk with us anyway. But my impression of them was that they were not nice people. They certainly weren't defending liberty and democracy. I don't talk with people a lot about that because I feel a lot of shame that I was involved in that.

Generally, I can sort of rationalize in some ways because in a lot of ways it was like being in the United States. But it's hard for me to talk about that. I felt like I was directly involved in bad things.

We were on training duty. There was the S-2 section, the Intel section I was with in the Fourth ID (infantry division). They'd rotate. Myself, a captain, and a lieutenant. They needed a jeep driver, a specialist to drive their jeep. That's what I did. I was in no covert operations or anything. You could read about what was going on in the *Christian Science Monitor* and the *New York Times* at the time. If you go back, you'll find the articles about what was going on down there, about the Reserve units. They just don't tell you, "These guys were supporting what were then the terrorists against the Nicaraguan people." I didn't know that at the time. I just knew they weren't nice guys. I knew that the people down there were scared to death when they saw people in fatigues. Justifiably so.

I was in Honduras 45 days. That was in early 1987, and then I came back and mustered out. There was a reduction in force levels because Reagan was overspending. They wanted to spend more money on missiles than on troopers, so there was a reduction in force and I took an early out. I got out a month early from my three-year enlistment, and managed to avoid going to the national training center in Fort Irwin, California, which I hear is just hell on earth. I was really glad.

One of the first things you learn in the military: You are going to get lied to early and often. It was really hard for me to reconcile that with what I believed when I went in. I didn't like to think of it too much when I got out. I just knew I didn't want to stay in. I'd never really been a very good soldier, I guess. I did what I could to get by. I drank too much, which is not an uncommon aspect of military life. Then I got out and I just sort of tried to put it behind me. Like, well that's something that I'll just try to forget I was ever a part of. It's a little hard to do that. If you live something for three years.

I guess I really started to feel a change during the first Gulf War in 1991. I was really angry when Bush started sending troops over there because I kept thinking, even though I may not know them directly, those are the kind of guys I served next to who are going to go over there and die so George Bush can get his oil ... Imperial America, not just George Bush, but Imperial America can get its oil. I was really angry. I'd yell at the TV set, but I didn't really do anything about it. I joked about throwing things at the TV set. Then when the war started—and it was another splendid little war—I sort of got sucked up in it like a lot of people ... a great victory, whatever.

The fact that I was angry about it, I wasn't gung ho, I think was one of my eye opening things. I figured that what I'd seen over the three years I was in, also applied to the Gulf. It was another lie.

Then for a number of years, all sorts of things sort of took life over. I didn't think a lot about military service or about peace. I guess I'm one of those people that sort of woke up when there were the Seattle demonstrations against the WTO. I hadn't really been aware there was a peace movement in the United States during the first Gulf War, even though I lived in Madison. I guess that speaks a lot to the control of the media.

I saw people in Seattle standing up for themselves and doing something. I started being more interested in radical politics. I started listening to WORT (listener-sponsored community radio) here. I started to read more about how corporate domination of the world was so tied with military domination of the world. I started to realize the same lies I got in the Army are the same lies I'm getting at the places where I work. Corporate lies and military lies aren't that different. Again, this was very slow. I had no epiphany. I got involved with some people here in Madison and went to some demonstrations and activist things.

I hooked up with the Nader campaign. Some people still hit me over the head for that. One thing I really admired that Ralph Nader was standing for was the abolition of nuclear weapons, because I had guarded them at one time. Whether or not I had thought about it much, now I was thinking about it, what I had been part of and how much of a threat that was to our world. Here was a person who was making a very courageous stand totally outside of mainstream politics and calling for reductions in military forces, that this was making America less secure, not more secure. I really connected with that. Since then I've been much more active in various ways.

It's ebbed and flowed but with what happened on September 11, 2001, and how our government has utilized that to expand the policies that it's held for quite some time, I felt that those of us who served in the military, who have been inside the looking glass and realize that a lot of it is lies and deception ... there is a responsibility to speak out, to tell people that what the Pentagon and CNN and Fox tell you is simply not the whole story. What they tell you is lies. It's more of the same lies.

While those of us who have been in the military and served the machine don't know everything, we've seen it to some extent. We've seen what the machine really does, and that's kill people, destroy lives, destroy cultures, destroy our biosphere, destroy our souls. It's incumbent on us, even if it's in some small way, to stand up and say no. This is not right. This is not what humans are for.

I'm a member of Veterans for Peace, the Clarence Kailin chapter. I'm also involved with the Wisconsin Network for Peace and Justice, and the Madison Area Peace Coalition, and the Green Party. I give greater or lesser amounts of time to one of them, depending on what's going on and try to do what I can.

I was a grunt in the military. I'm sort of a grunt in the peace movement. I feel a little better when I'm doing the more "scut" work, the stuff that a lot of people don't want to do. The office work, getting out hanging door hangers, or making phone calls, putting address labels on newsletters, all the little things that are so important. I work with so many good people who are willing to do that. So that's my basic, the grunt work. I'll vacuum the office or whatever. I did a lot of that during the Nader campaign. I was the official office vacuum guy.

I guess beyond that I'm branching out a little more and trying to work in outreach to everyday people, whatever that means. I'm involved in a lot of door-to-door activities, canvassing, knocking on people's doors and talking to them about their concerns. Right now I'm involved with a number of other people, not just myself, we're planning a door-hanger project for the Madison area where we're going to go to put door hangers on people's doors telling them about what's going on in Iraq, how bad things are, a message they may not be aware of if they look at the front page of the *Wisconsin State Journal*. Providing them with things they can do. If this is something they don't want to be a part of, Not in Our Name, telling them things they can do like contacting activist groups, contacting their representatives, demonstrations, things of that nature. I'm helping with that. I'm helping to be the point of contact for getting the routes set up and people out, getting the literature out so they can go do this. I'm getting a lot of support from all sorts of folks and by building on other social justice campaigns who have done this before.

I'm hoping too we can bring peace groups together. We're trying to get groups involved in this project. Sometimes we sort of stand apart from each other and get territorial. Maybe it's a little pie in the sky, but I think we're stronger when we work together. There are lots of people who are gathering together to help facilitate this, providing different resources. People are enthused. People are talking to each other who weren't talking to each other a couple of months ago. That's good. That's really good because that's where our strength lies, when we're together and we're doing things ourselves. When we can't rely on our supposed elected representatives to effect change, then we need to make that change. I'm finding it really heartening. That's what I'm involved in at this moment.

Somehow it seems like veterans have a little more credibility in the peace movement because we've been there. I don't always agree with that. I think so many other people have experiences and have seen things and encountered things that I have no knowledge of, so why I was silly enough to enlist in the military gives me any more credibility than anybody else, I don't know. I think sometimes we are given more of a platform to speak on in some ways. Sometimes I personally think it sort of negatively affects me in that I can get a little: "Well, I've been there ... ." Certainly I wasn't in Vietnam, which is a lot different from being in West Germany, Colorado, or Honduras.

I'm not perfect. I do have a tendency sometimes to sort of start preaching. My wife rolls her eyes, as many of our wives do. I know making decisions in life can be very difficult and there are a lot of complexities. My frustration as it's connected with peace work and social justice work is that so many people are looking for someone else to save them or lead the way. I'm learning slowly that's not the way it works. I have been guilty of it myself, looking for that savior.

People have to look to themselves and their communities first to effect change. That's the baseline way. To rely on somebody else just isn't going to work. I'm struggling with that right now in my peace work because I'm afraid so much of what we've been doing is going to be subsumed to electoral politics. I'm really afraid that we're going to lose focus. I already see it. We were in Vietnam in 1965. Here we are in Iraq and where has electoral politics gotten us? Republicans are dropping the bombs now. Democrats were in charge at that point. I'm just really afraid of the factionalization.

My analysis is maybe not as informed as some people. What all the terms mean. I sometimes don't even know if people know what they're talking about exactly. I think we need to look at ourselves individually and our communities to bring about change first. How is it that people can't understand that driving their car is directly connected to our invasion of Iraq, informs our response in some way? I don't understand—and I still drive a car. I drove a car over here today.

I think that's the first step. We need to look at ourselves and the way we live our lives, and how that's allowing the institutions that control us to do things. We aid and abet. I'm not saying we all need to leave indoor plumbing and go live in a cave. That's not what I'm saying. I'm saying we need to make those first steps. When we start to effect change that way, then we can move around the politicians and take control of our own lives. I think most people would say, if I made a 25 percent reduction in driving my car, I probably would feel better because I would be walking places, or getting outside, or maybe I could spend more time with my kids. Who wants to be on the highway in traffic at five o'clock?

I know we're caught in complex lives, but maybe we need to start making those changes first instead of looking to some electoral system that hasn't delivered to date. I don't know exactly how to do that. But that's one of my concerns. My hope is that a lot of people are realizing that we need to make changes in ourselves, at least a lot of people that I connect with are realizing that. Kathy Kelly talked about it from *Voices in the Wilderness* when she was here. That was what she said. Our life styles allow these institutions to claim they need to do these things, the military, the government, the corporations. As veterans, we've seen what the lies are. And they become self-perpetuating just to keep these institutions alive.

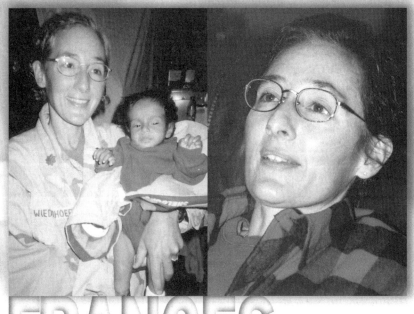

FRANCES WIEDENHOEFT

Desert Storm and Afghanistan

I was born in New London, Wisconsin, July 2, 1960. It's hard for a person to say in just a few words who they really are. I'm a daughter of a Korean War veteran and my grandparents or great grandparents were all immigrants to the United States, with a strong patriotic feeling like: "This is a great country and don't say anything bad about it because there's kind of still this feeling of we're guests here. Like we have to act like this is the most wonderful thing that ever happened to us, and never criticize a single thing this country does. We should feel grateful to be allowed in."

263

That being said, I think almost all of my grandparents fought their whole lives to try and make everything around them better. They were critical of the government of the country, but they always tried to change their environment to make it more fair, better for not only themselves but also everyone around them. In a nutshell, that's how I grew up. My mom's mom was from Metz, France, my mom's dad was from Eastern Europe, and my dad's grandparents were from northern Germany, by the Belgian border.

I had long discussions with my chief nurse when we were in Afghanistan because she's just the most interesting person. She is like in her early 60s, and started serving as a nurse in Vietnam. There aren't that many people who would be willing to talk freely about their opinions in the Army. I don't know why that is. They think that they can't or something, or maybe they have no opinions, I don't know. Anyway, my nurse and I had long discussions about how we got to be where we are, and what pulled us into the military. For her it was very much a feeling like this is the way for me to pay back everything that I have.

For me, I went into the Army because I wanted to go to anesthesia school. That was the only motivation. It was 1989. The Berlin Wall had come down and I thought that we were going to have a thousand years of peace, and it was gonna be okay to join the Army, get my education, and then get out. It just didn't turn out that way.

I went in at the age of 29, already a person with a lot of coping mechanisms. I had a chance to think about the world, which is very different from going in when you're 17, 18, 19, or 20, and the military being a first major experience in your life. I went into the Army and, just like the rest of my life, nothing ever happens quite the way I plan it. Within nine months I was deployed for Desert Storm. That was a bit shocking. We weren't entering a thousand years of peace.

I knew intellectually that we had an economic draft, but that was a totally different experience than seeing it firsthand. Being deployed, my hospital unit was thrown in with a bunch of other hospital units. You know, I've lived all my life in Wisconsin and I met people from other areas and traveled around a little bit, but it was different from working every day with people from some of the poorest parts of the country for whom the choice was going into the Army or live a subsistence life. I'm talking subsistence like a sharecropper-type thing. It was different, and it was a mind-opening experience.

Just going to Afghanistan two years ago is what drove me to join the Veterans for Peace.

I know why I went into the Army, and I got what I went in for. I'm a medical person, so I don't have that experience of feeling bad about things that I've done. I didn't have to kill anyone. I helped a lot of people, so it was somewhat of a positive experience for me, but I saw all these other people, mostly very young people and mostly very immature people, and mostly people who don't have the economic, the emotional, the psychological, or the spiritual reserves to be able to take the experiences they're having and process them in any way that benefits them ... to help them grow and become more happy, fulfilled people in their lives. That's why I joined Veterans for Peace. For their sake.

I could just have my experience and say things were okay for me. I mean there's a lot of stuff I felt hurt by psychologically, you know, like getting bombs dropped feet from the backdoor of my tent, and never knowing if the next one was going to drop right on my head. And seeing little starving babies and children shot full of holes. All those things hurt me, but I have the necessary resources to deal with those things. There are so many people that don't. The people that are in the Army right now are the people with the least resources in our country to be able to take their experience and deal with it in any way at all.

There's even a lot of people from my Wisconsin unit, the youngest people—when we went to Afghanistan, I tried to help them all the time, 24 hours a day, to cope with what is going on around them. But a lot of them are not coping. I just worry about them. Even in Wisconsin, the people that are going into the military are the ones with the least resources to be able to deal with their experiences.

Out of the handful of young medics in the group, there's only one who is back in school and appears to me to be doing okay. He's not drinking excessively; he has motivation to go school and do the things that he went into the Army to do in the first place, to get his education. As far as I know, he's not doing reckless things that are endangering his life.

He's the only one, and I think personally it's because he was sent to this country by his mom from Korea when he was a baby and lived in foster care his whole life. The only reason he has coping mechanisms is because he grew up in a chaotic environment. The rest of them are taking drugs, using alcohol, doing wild and reckless things. Driving around on the country roads at 100 miles an hour, just basically doing things that, in the long run, are going to hurt them. They're not back in school.

One of the kids in the unit, I spent a lot of time with him, to try and help him think about what was going on around him, but then this incident occurred that he just couldn't cope with.

He's not doing any of the things he went into the Army for. He's not in school. The last I heard he was in trouble with the law. It just makes me sad to think that this is what's going on, and I'm sure if that's true for young people in my unit, it's probably true for people across the board.

So for their sake, there's a lot of things that need to be changed.

I went in as a nurse, so they assigned me to whatever unit was closest. At the time, that was the 44th General Hospital, which was down on Park Street here in Madison. We were combined with a Utah unit and a Louisiana unit and some other unit from the South. We went to Germany to the Landstuhl Army Regional Medical Center Hospital, a big hospital where they evacuate all the people to now. The army had been thinking about closing it down. It was just an old decrepit facility and we actually set up tents around the hospital.

I came home from Desert Storm thinking, what are people hearing on this because everyone was like, "Well, what did you do that whole time?" I was gone for eight months. And they were like, "What did you do that whole time, you know, nobody was injured!" It's like, "Oh, you could have fooled me." I mean we had thousands of people come through our hospital in Germany. And they didn't have torn ligaments from playing soccer in the desert. They were blown up and shot up and burned up and every nature of that type of injury. They were U.S. and coalition forces from Kuwait and Iraq.

I was deployed from January of 1991 until August. It was shocking at that time. I knew intellectually I was going to be taking care of the victims of a war, but to actually see it was kind of emotionally overwhelming. We'd get a planeload, we'd get like 300 or 400 patients just deposited onto the hospital. And we'd triage and do surgery on them and send them where they needed to go. I don't know how they are doing, this time, but at that time the triage from the field in Iraq and Kuwait, it wasn't working properly and so they'd send patients that they had just pulled right out of the field with a minimum of care.

They would still have their weapons on them and grenades attached to them and all kinds of stuff. It was so far from the reality of anything anyone heard on this side of the ocean. It was distressing and shocking to me, but I think in some ways when I went to Afghanistan at least I was familiar with.... It's just different. You know, I deal with trauma at University Hospital and I've dealt with abused children as patients and women beat up by their men, and car accidents and injuries can look very similar as far as how it devastates a person's body and mind. But it was different knowing that all these injuries in Desert Storm were caused by one group of people's inhumanity to another group of people.

Desert Storm wasn't short in reality. It was short compared to World War II or the Vietnam War. People think it was like five days long or something. If that were the case, we wouldn't have been getting blown up people in Germany in March if the war was over in January. It's not like I expected the U.S. government would tell the truth to the people. That's unfortunate, though, because I think if more people knew what the reality was of Desert Storm, maybe they wouldn't have been so gung ho to go into Iraq the second time. They would've waited to see if all the other measures that had been put in place would have actually accomplished the same thing in the long run.

When I got back from Desert Storm, I worked like a fiend and went to anesthesia school. I was accepted to go school but I was redeployed, and since I wasn't in school at the time, I had to go. I came back and I went to anesthesia school for two years and graduated, and had a little grandson right away and went to work at the University Hospital.

I did my paybacks to the Army and started trying to get out of the Army when I figured that I was going to get deployed again. It was before we actually went into Afghanistan. To me, I think they had to have been planning something anyway, because I would try to submit paperwork to try to get out of the Army and they wouldn't let me out.

Before 9/11, that's just my opinion, they were planning something because there were people that were trying to get out of the Army and people were trying to retire. It's kind of a sign if they won't let people out, then you know that they must be planning something because they're holding on to all their medical assets.

I didn't have any firm plans. I had six years of paybacks after I graduated, meaning the Army paid for my education so I owed them two years for every year that they paid for my education, two years of Reserve time. Two years for every year or part of a year. I went to school for two years and two weeks, so I had six years of payback.

According to Army practice, if you are a commissioned officer you're in indefinitely because they tell you that you can't leave, you can't resign your commission. I'm a major. As a registered nurse, you can accept a commission as an officer. If you don't have a bachelor's degree, you can't progress past the rank of captain. If you do have a bachelor's degree, you can just keep going. I was a registered nurse. I graduated in 1984. By 2001, when I knew I was going to be done with my pay-backs, I decided that I wanted to get out. But there were a lot of things that went into that.

When I went to Desert Storm, I don't know what caused me to be sick, but I feel like it was the vaccinations. We had a series of ... I think I got 12 vaccinations. My whole deploy-ment, I was so sick. I had high fevers all the time. My joints and my muscles swelled up. Since then I filed a claim to request to have my medical problems be service connected. The thing they always say is why didn't you go and seek medical atten-tion at that time? We were so busy, and no one here fathoms the fact that ... I was working 12 to 24 hours a day taking care of people who were like blown up, burned up, and shot up. My problems seemed minor to me.

I got back and after a while I felt better and I went to school. I've always been a very driven person, and I like to work really hard. Up until the past couple years I used to run a lot. I like running marathons. My personality is to push and push and push myself. I suppose in some ways that's good and in some ways it's not.

I went to school and I felt all right and took my job at the university. I'd feel good for a few months and then I'd just get like drastically sick, high fevers for days and days and days. I had shingles, and I'd have it over and over and over again. I'd just get better and then I'd get it again.

Then I started having these horrible headaches. I went to the doctor and he said, "Oh, well you're a very driven person in a high-stress field. You're obviously an adrenaline junky. You're probably having migraines because you're just the perfect candidate for that." It turned out I had a brain tumor. In 1997, I had surgery to take the brain tumor out. It was a rare kind of tumor. The doctor that took care of me said there was like 32 cases of this kind of tumor in the literature.

He didn't give me bad chances, but he didn't feel the chances of having a perfect surgery and not having any problems afterward were that good. I had the surgery and everything went perfectly. I came out of it and I knew who I was. I had some minor problems. I had a horrible short-term memory problem for about nine months after that. I couldn't go back to work right away because doing anesthesia, you have to remember what you just did. You can't be like: "Let's see, did I give this drug or did I not give this drug?"

I recovered and I did fine. Then the doctor was certain it would come back. There was no case in the literature where that type of tumor hadn't reoccurred within a couple years. But that was seven years ago, eight years ago, and it hasn't. Shortly after that, he didn't feel like I was making a very good recovery. I was still having a lot of fevers and my white blood count was really, really low. So he sent me to this other doctor who discovered I have an illness similar to lupus. In fact, I probably have lupus.

To me there's a lot of evidence—not only with U.S. soldiers but also with British soldiers—that shows that if you take susceptible people and give them multiple vaccinations all at once, especially some of the vaccinations they were giving, that you can induce the state of disease.

Putting that all together, that's why I wanted to get out. I felt like my life is very precious to me. Even though I felt good about everything I had done in the military. I have a stack of letters from patients I took care of during Desert Storm and other soldiers that I served with who said they were so grateful to me and they felt like they couldn't have gotten through that experience without me. It made me feel really good about what I did.

I wanted to get out because I didn't want to ... it would be one thing to go overseas and have a bomb drop on your head and blow up for your country. But I felt like I've been a good server and I want to get out now because I don't want to die like that. I didn't want to get deployed again and have another series of vaccinations and have it make me all that much sicker.

They'll allow a discharge if you're not in an area of critical need. It makes no difference that I'm sick. I can't even get out right now. The whole time I was in Afghanistan, I was taking a high dose of steroids to even keep my body functioning. When I came back my heart was inflamed and I started to have kidney failure. Right now I'm taking strong chemotherapy drugs to suppress my immune system enough to keep all these other systems from going out of whack.

I called up my personnel manager and I said this is what's going on, and said I need a medical discharge. I can't do this.

In August they called me to prepare for another deployment, believe it or not. So I was like, oh no, I can't do this. At the end of August they called me to go to Louisiana to be deployed with my unit to Louisiana, which I would have liked to do if I could have. I'm off work because I can't be working in that germy environment taking this medicine. I have no immune system right now. So I said I just can't do this. I need a medical discharge. And she said, "Well, we'll decide if you get a medical discharge."

I said, "Okay, what do I need to do?" I said, "Send me whatever paperwork I need to fill out." She said, "No, I can't send you that paperwork. Send your medical records and a letter from your doctor and they'll give you a temporary medical leave from your Reserve duties." The rationale behind that is just that they have a critical shortage of anesthesia people, and so, short of death or not being able to move my body at all, I have to stay in. It would be the same if I was a doctor, or I suspect, if I was an MP.

The thing people don't know is that, and I guess they can't go around putting this in the news because it could be dangerous for our country, but almost all of our active duty and Reserve personnel either just came back from Iraq or Afghanistan or are on their way there or are there right now. That should have been obvious when they tried to deploy people to Louisiana after the hurricane. There's hardly anyone here. They had to pull people out of Korea to send them to Iraq. Even the equipment that they have, it's not meant to last forever and they don't keep a supply on hand to keep deployed for year after year. I know that's true for the hospital equipment. When we got to Afghanistan we were missing a lot of important equipment.

We were called up in February of 2003 and initially we were supposed to go to Iraq and put a field hospital in Iraq. I don't know why things changed. I'm not ever sure that the Army has a clear plan or if the reason that things change at the last minute is because of good planning or bad planning. In any case, part of my unit went to Iraq and part of us went to Afghanistan, and part of us didn't go anywhere right away. Some people were taken off active duty after we were at Fort McCoy for a period of time, and then they had to go back on active duty nine months later. We left for Afghanistan in May. We got there and set up at the Bagram Air Base. It's kind of right in the middle of Afghanistan about 20 miles north of Kabul. I guess it's the headquarters of the coalition activities in Afghanistan.

Part of the hospital was set up and running. We took over for the personnel that were there and they went home. We kind of augmented it and enhanced it. I think now they have built an actual structure there since they've decided that we're going to be in Afghanistan for a long time. But at that time it was a deployable medical hospital, which is kind of like a tent hospital.

There was an Afghani woman interpreter with us in the hospital. Her reason for going back to Afghanistan was to reclaim her familial land holdings. Actually, Afghanistan is a minefield. There are more mines per acre than there are people, but I didn't say that to her. I just tried to encourage her and think about how to make things better instead of just thinking about how things were. She had a dream she was going to reclaim her land holdings. She had no men left in her family.

Being a woman in Afghanistan trying to conduct this type of business in and of itself was an undertaking of monumental proportions, but she was going to reclaim her land holdings and resettle all of her women relatives on her familial land. She was still in Bagram when I left and the other female interpreter we had came back. She had been in the U.S. for 15 or 20 years and she had already married and started a family here with another Afghan man. They had three girls and she decided she wasn't going to go back to Afghanistan. She came back to Omaha, Nebraska, where I guess there's a large Afghan American community.

When we were mobilized up to Fort McCoy, we thought we were going to Iraq. I wasn't in favor of that at all, personally. Anything that people in the United States or the United States government felt needed to be done with Iraq, there were measures put in place to try and help and encourage that to happen. I kept thinking about something I had read by some university people in Iran that was written to people in this country saying: "We're not perfectly happy with the regime that we're living under but we don't need your help. Stay away. We'll make our own changes in our own good time and the last thing we want is someone coming over here dropping bombs on our head."

I felt like things were probably very bad in Iraq because my brother had been working and living in Kuwait after Desert Storm for quite a while. He had a lot of Iraqi friends who had escaped from Iraq into Kuwait during that period of time. He had just some horrible stories to tell about why they left. I thought, yeah, probably things are really bad there but I kept thinking about South Africa. Eventually it seems like, from the things I've heard, South Africans were able to make change without any one group bombing the other side and so forth. I know things aren't perfect there now, but it seems like it has a greater potential for improvement for everyone in the country just because one side isn't continually killing off the other side and causing more hard feelings in the family members of the people that survive so they go and kill off the other side, and so forth and so on.

When we were mobilized, I was just hoping that they would call the whole thing off. I know that that's totally unrealistic considering who we had for a president and what his personal motivations were, at least my speculation on his personal motivations. When we found out that some of us were going to be going to Afghanistan, I thought, I'm not sure I'm really opposed to that because for years prior to that I had been getting e-mails from people and hearing from Afghans that had escaped from the country about how horrible things were and how if somebody didn't do something soon, all the women in Afghanistan were going to commit suicide, that's just how desperate the situation was.

Knowing that the Taliban in charge would laugh in the face of any sanctions we gave them because they'd say, "Hey, we must be doing something right. The Americans hate us." So my feelings about going into Afghanistan didn't have anything to do with weapons of mass destruction or if Osama bin Laden was hiding in the mountains. I didn't really know a lot about how things had gone when the Russians invaded Afghanistan and the U.S. was overtly or clandestinely doing things to try and oppose Russia taking over Afghanistan, but feeling like somehow some of the results for the people of Afghanistan had to do with things we did wrong in this country in the first place, I wasn't sure I was opposed to the idea of us being in Afghanistan.

This is like a total aside in some ways because, like I said, my feeling not as bad about going to Afghanistan didn't have anything to do with Osama bin Laden, but my sister was in the

World Trade Center the day that the airplanes flew into it. She survived, but that whole experience for our family and for me personally, my feelings about going to Afghanistan, were all tied up together with that event. It wasn't like a feeling of revenge. It was just like you never know how the things that hurt you in your life are going to get worked out later. I didn't consciously think about it when I thought about going to Afghanistan.

While I was in Afghanistan, for some reason I thought about that day, a lot. It wasn't feelings of anger and resentment but I had a lot of sorrow and pain about that day when we didn't know if my sister had survived. We didn't hear from her. We didn't know where she was. The phone calls ... my brother-in-law called here and talked to Marlys because he was beside himself. He didn't know what to do.

I was at work in the operating room at the UW. Marlys called me. I don't think I've had any feeling of shock that bad in my life. I'm very close to my sister. She's had illnesses. I've had illnesses. But it was so abrupt. I just couldn't think about her being gone. Obviously we had to talk to my parents. Who wants to call them on the phone and say: "Don't worry but ..."

My brother was at work too, so Marlys ended up talking to my folks. We spent a little over 12 hours just in shock, not knowing. It was shocking for everyone in the country. Who would ever think that somebody would do something like that? For us it was different because we were just waiting. More and more reports were coming out, that the devastation was total and that people that were in the building ... it wasn't going to be like mobilized medical teams. There wasn't anyone to treat.

Eventually we heard from her. She was able, her and hundreds of other people, to walk somewhere where they could actually get one cell phone that was working and pass it around or some such thing. She teaches at NYU. The building next to the World Trade Center, they had classes and dormitories in that building.

It wasn't a conscious thing like, "Oh, I want to go to Afghanistan," but while I was there I thought a lot about it. My feelings about everything that was happening were personal and complicated, and I don't know why, but somehow being in Afghanistan and feeling like I was helping Afghan people, in some complicated way, it made me feel better, and all those complicated feelings that were seething inside of me, they were like released.

My feelings about going to Afghanistan? I didn't feel bad about it. I felt like I was a person with coping mechanisms and ways of dealing with things. I didn't want to go to a place that was going to be dangerous and maybe people would be dropping bombs on my head. In some ways, I felt like I already had thought about my own mortality and, in some ways, faced it when I had that brain tumor. You know, when your doctor feels like chances are good that you're not going to survive, you have to start thinking about stuff like that. I didn't feel bad about that personally.

I wasn't harboring good feelings about the Army. The longer I was in, the more I felt there are so many things that are just so wrong. And something happened before we were deployed, which just kind of broke my heart, another reason for joining Veterans for Peace, feeling like this organization is working in some ways to try and improve things for soldiers. If you've been in the Army, you know. It's like in some ways you're trapped. You don't have a lot of choices.

When we were up at Fort McCoy waiting to be deployed, one of our soldiers died. This was a young woman. She was like 22, and there is no reason she should have died. It really broke my heart. It really did. She was one of the young people in the barracks that I had kind of taken under my wing and was trying to look after her and so forth.

Going to Afghanistan, I just wanted to get away from the situation that had surrounded her death and immerse myself in work. A deployment to a combat support hospital is good for that. When we got to Afghanistan, the hospital was sort of set up. The people that we were relieving were the people that had set the hospital up. We thought possibly we'd have a transition period to acclimatize ourselves, maybe get over a little jet lag and familiarize ourselves with our surroundings.

"We're so glad you're here. Okay. Bye." They had their gear packed because they knew we were coming in. They went down to the airfield and proceeded to catch the next plane that was going to take them anywhere out of the combat zone.

Frances Wiedenhoeft
275

Within probably four or five hours we were taking casualties. We started working right away, and slowly over the first few weeks finished setting up the other things that we needed in the hospital, inventorying and figuring out what supplies we had and didn't have. We were taking care of Afghans and Coalition forces and we took care of a lot of children at first. We really had no supplies to take care of children. We had some hard work to do to get that underway.

Our mission was life or limb and eyesight, and so the Afghans could come to our hospital if somebody thought they were in danger of dying or losing a limb or their eyesight. That would most often be the case anyway because anything else they would try to treat in their villages.

I was there about four months.

Supposedly the doctors and the anesthesia personnel are on three-month deployment, and so it's three months every 18 months. That's what it's supposed to be right now. But we had already been at Fort McCoy for several months while they were trying to figure out what they wanted to do with us. Then some of the people that went over had to stay because they didn't have anyone to replace them. Our oral maxillofacial surgeon—there's only five of them in the whole Army Reserve—they put him on active duty, and he'll get off active duty when he dies or the wars are all over.

Two of the anesthesia people that were with me actually ended up staying for four more months. They could have made me stay too, but my chief nurse knew that I was sick and that I wasn't getting better, and she had to select people to stay until the next group of people could come in and be replacements. She selected the other people but they said that they didn't mind staying for my sake. They could have said, we really need to go and maybe the decision would have been made some other way.

I came back in the fall of 2003. I came back and I didn't work for a month between the time I left active duty and the time I went back to work at the University Hospital. I tried to taper myself off the prednisone, which was depressing my immune system to keep everything kind of in line.

Then I started having all kinds of problems with inflammation of my heart, so I went back on it, and got off it. I worked up until the beginning of August. I just tried to struggle along, but my doctor put me on this other really potent immuno-suppressant and I got an infection in my foot, which took eight months to heal up. In the end, I had to go off the immuno-suppressant, which then started all the other problems. I kept trying to see if intermediate measures would take care of things but they haven't. In August I just went to the doctor and he said, you know you really need to take some time off work. So I have been sick ever since I got back. But it wasn't like I was deathly ill the whole time.

I've had an eventful life and these things aren't even the entirety of it. To me, sometimes I look back on my life and I say "Wow." I've lived in my life as much as some people live when they get to be a hundred. In some ways that's because I don't shy away from experiences. And sometimes I do things that in retrospect maybe weren't such a good idea.

I didn't have to join the Army. I could have taken out thousands of dollars worth of student loans, but I took a chance on it and it's been interesting, if nothing else. All the people that I come into contact with have led me to be who I am right now. The people in Afghanistan, it's been a crossroads. For one thing, they're not really a nation in a lot ways, but then most countries aren't. The Afghan people are generous. They're generous, openhearted people. Just being in contact, living with two of the Afghan women translators. We had Afghan doctors working in the hospital as translators. After we became more familiar with their skills, they were allowed to work as doctors too and we would try to help them improve their skills so they could go out and work in Afghan hospitals.

I learned a lot when I was there from being around the Afghan people. To take whatever experience you come upon, a lot of people that were deployed there, bad things would happen. People would shoot at us. Bombs would drop right behind the hospital and stuff like that.

And people like the medics that went out the missions, which I didn't volunteer to do, I didn't have to do, partly because I'm a woman. If I hadn't been a woman, I suppose I would have to have been in the rotation to go out on some of these missions delivering the field care. So in some ways I was spared some of the awful things some of the other people saw out in the field. Although in some ways that's not necessarily true because the awful things came right into the hospital.

Throughout all of that I kept thinking, the Afghans have been living with this, in fact, for most of the younger people, this is all they've ever known. And they're still so open to us and so generous with us. That was my experience. I said, coming back, that I didn't meet any Afghan people that were putting bombs on our heads, that didn't want us there.

All the people I met said to me, "How come you didn't come sooner? This was partly your responsibility. We were fighting with you and for you against the Russians, and everything that's happened since then should have been partly your responsibility." That's what I heard from them. Even given that, all the people that I talked to and people that I heard from, even harboring those resentments, they felt like, "We're glad you're here now." They were so open and generous with their time and their thoughts, and talking to us, any of us who wanted to listen to them.

It's a young country now. Most of the older people either left or died. Even though they've never known anything besides war and desperate poverty and oppression, they were functioning and living their lives to their maximum capacity.

Even the women who had been living under an absolutely brutal oppression, not even able to leave their homes, they were so thoughtful and able to talk about things that I never expected. That they would have been able to evolve themselves as human beings in those circumstances, to be able to talk to us about things, it's part of a whole life's lesson for me: How to meet up with whatever happens to me, and still try and be open and generous and give back what you can.

I'm not saying that being in Afghanistan was the only thing that led me to come to that. People that I met in Desert Storm, some of the other soldiers that I was working with, some of the people from the Louisiana unit, when we would talk about what their lives were like and what led them to join the Army, I was just flabbergasted.

I worked with an LPN who was the only health care provider for like 120 square miles in her bayou down in Louisiana. How we came to that discussion was she could do anything. She could suture, she could give IVs, she could deliver babies. I was like, "How did you learn how to do all of this?"

"Well, Honey, I'm it. People come to me or else, if I can't handle it, we call a helicopter, which may or may not come in time to help them." All these people taught me things in my life, and led me to believe that I'll try and meet whatever I come across to the best of my abilities.

The thousand years of peace was like some crazy idea I was raised with. That's what my dad has always believed in. I don't know what in the world ever led him to believe it. I think that's not part of the human condition right now.

I'll continue to do what I can. Having been in organizations for social change or religious organizations or whatever, they never took the time to examine their own human interactions in the group so they could work for a theoretical good cause without having a good way of dealing with people interpersonally. Having seen that in Veterans for Peace, people committed to trying to use peaceful measures to deal with each other in the group that's working for peace, I think that's a wonderful thing. That's a real foundation.

I don't think there's going to be peace in my lifetime, but I'll continue to do what I can in my life to try and make that come about, starting with how I deal with my family, and then talking to people that I work with.

When I started working at the university, people would make racist jokes and things like that. Every time they'd do something like that I'd confront them, and say: "I don't find that funny, and can't we find a way to be humorous that doesn't put someone else down, and when you tell a joke like that, what is it that you get out of it, what is it that you lose by being able to tell a joke like that?"

After a while they quit telling jokes like that around me. Maybe they do it when I'm not around but maybe they found that they didn't really need to do that anymore. It's like changing my immediate environment and going on beyond that.

To me, our country has a tremendous responsibility to the world because we are wealthy and powerful. In the past 30 years of my life at different points in my life, working with organizations, I realized that we don't need to make our country not be wealthy or powerful to have a good impact on the world.

It will change eventually on its own because no country rules the world forever. There have been empires in this world since the beginning of humankind, and our empire will fall too. But we don't need to make our empire fall to have a better impact on the world as a whole.

There are so many things that need to be changed about how we use our wealth and power in the world. And I actually don't feel like we're going to make our United States of America into a globally benevolent country. It's more like trying to find a better balance, so that overall, hopefully we do more good than harm. Right now I feel like the balance is more harm than good, the way that we use our wealth and power.

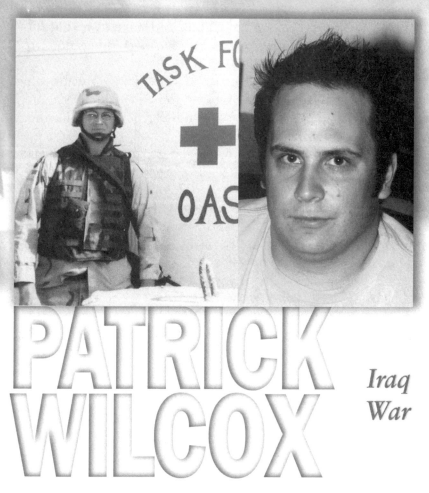

PATRICK WILCOX

Iraq War

I'm 25 years old, and live in Madison. I was born May 23, 1980, in Shakopee, Minnesota—a suburb of Minneapolis. I was born there and moved to Madison with my family about 1985, when I was about 5 years old. I've lived here ever since. I have one brother who's a year and a half younger than I am. I went to school here in Madison, graduated from Madison Memorial in 1998.

I joined the military my senior year of high school when I was 17. Mainly, I didn't have any ambition whatsoever to join the military up until the day I joined. It was never really something I thought about. I always wanted to go to college. That

281

was my intention right after school, and pursue an education degree maybe, I wasn't quite sure, but something along the lines of that.

I got a call from a recruiter and knew I didn't want to go active duty. I wanted something to help me with college and I knew I wanted to start as soon as possible with my education, so I joined the Reserves.

I was trained as both a medic and a pharmacy technician. Pharmacy technician was my primary job in the military. I went to my basic training at Fort Leonard Wood, Missouri, and went to my job training down at Fort Sam Houston in San Antonio, Texas. I got back and actually got a job as a pharmacy tech as a civilian and went to UW–Whitewater for two years as a pre-pharmacy major.

I joined in December of 1997. I actually really enjoyed my time in the Reserves. I enjoyed a lot of the people I met. I still keep in contact with them. If there's one thing I really value and cherish about my time in the service, it's the people I met.

I decided I didn't want to do pharmacy about two years into it. I was accepted to UW pharmacy school, but turned it down. I thought maybe nursing was something I would like to do.

So I left UW–Whitewater and was taking a few classes at MATC and about to transfer to Edgewood College for nursing, when I was called up for the buildup to the war, in February 2003. I was taken from my unit, my unit was actually out of Minneapolis, and I was taken from that unit and put in the 801st Combat Support Hospital in Chicago to fill in for some missing slots.

I went with them as a pharmacy tech. We were mobilized and sent down to Fort Stewart, Georgia, for some training. We spent three months there. Things kind of changed and a lot of people went home. They decided there really wasn't a need for full combat support hospital, which is what I was mobilized with.

I actually volunteered to go overseas with a smaller mission to Kuwait and run a hospital in Kuwait. My intention for doing that was mainly to get my veteran's status for education benefits. I knew my time was running out in the Reserves and

I wasn't quite sure if I wanted to reenlist. I wanted to secure some benefits for when I got out.

As it was advertised to me when I first decided to go to Kuwait, it was a six-month mission. I figured I already lost a couple of semesters of school. Six months would get me back in December and I could start up in the winter again and I would have my veteran's status and everything would be great.

They sent us to Kuwait. We worked in a hospital. It was actually a Kuwaiti hospital. It was like a VA for them. We treated Americans and coalition. I was the NCOIC (non-commissioned officer in charge) of the pharmacy and I also did some triaging because of the medic experience. Since it was kind of a small operation, we all kind of pitched in where we needed to. Besides the heat and things like that, it wasn't a dangerous situation. It wasn't that uncomfortable at all as far as I'm concerned. About three and a half, four months into it we were told that we were going to be extended for an additional three months, so it would be about a nine-month tour. We were all understandably a little upset, but nine months was not a big deal. A few weeks after that, Rumsfeld made the decision that all units were going to be one year boots-on-ground, which would have gone into almost May for our tour of deployment, which was pretty upsetting.

It was a little frustrating to see some disparity in deployment. A lot of reservists were put in these year-long boots-on-ground deployments, and active duty units were going home after six months or seven months. In the beginning, it wasn't as solid as it is now with the deployments. It just depended on what unit you were and if they needed you, you had to stay.

We worked there for about eight months total. The Navy came to replace us. We were ready to go home. We were all packed and our mission was over. We had orders to go home. And on Easter Sunday, 2004, we were extended for another four months, six hours before our flight, and told we were going to be sent to Iraq and be broken up and used as needed pretty much by other brigades and things like that.

Within a matter of days we were packed up and sent up to Iraq. I was sent to 31st Combat Support Hospital in Balad. I worked in the pharmacy and the emergency room there.

My skepticism of why I was there started way before I was sent to Iraq. It started probably a few months after I got in Kuwait and most people thought we were going to be home in six months, and lot of what was happening was going to be wrapped up pretty quickly. Most people believed that they would occupy the country, set up a government, and get out of there pretty quickly. We all definitely were led to believe that we would find all sorts of chemical weapons and everything else.

None of that happened. As the days went by, we were extended and nothing productive was happening anywhere in that region. No weapons, more fighting, more bombs, more deaths on both sides. By the time we got to Iraq, it was a feeling I can't describe, a feeling of helplessness—you had no control whatsoever of what was happening to you or anyone else you knew.

It was around the time those civilian workers were killed and put on display in Fallujah. That pretty much tipped the scale for sending us to Iraq, extending us along with the 1st Armored Division. It was the first time this ever happened in this war. And I think it was the first time a lot of the American public got to see that this administration had absolutely no clue of how to handle what they got themselves in.

They promised all the troops one-year deployments, and they broke their promise. No one will tell you any different. They broke it. I think that left a really bad taste in a lot of people's mouths. As far as I know now, they're not even guaranteeing one year anymore. They're cutting year-and-a-half or two-year orders.

My time in Iraq was not fun. I was moved around from Balad to the Abu Ghraib prison. I spent three months there between Balad and the prison and encountered a lot of different things that really changed how I feel about war and reasons for going to war and really what it costs everyone. It's beyond anything I ever thought. We honestly destroyed an entire country from what I saw. We destroyed an entire country. And we're slowly destroying ours.

Lives have been ruined. So many lives, you can't even count. One thing that struck me is not really the dead, it was more all these injuries that I'd see come in, countless injuries. For every dead person there are 10 or 20 people that would come in injured. They would come in so fast and so often that you'd just think how 5 minutes of your day or 10 minutes, they're there and you probably won't see them—especially in the ER. You see them for 10 or 20 minutes and you won't see them again. Within a few hours they might be in Germany. They might be dead. You don't know.

What struck me was the rest of their lives would be just totally different because of what was happening at that moment. Every 10 minutes I'd see that. Every 10 minutes there'd be someone else coming in. Their lives are changed. It's just unbelievable the numbers. It's so hard to describe and even put into words how I feel about all the destruction.

There are so many ways to measure how a country is destroyed. It's not just that people have died in that country. It's not just the injured people. It's not just all the infrastructure and buildings that have been blown up.

Mentally and spiritually I don't think that country will heal for years, decades even. It's going to take a whole new generation of people to grow up before this is ever healed. No matter what happens from here on out, whether we pull out today or tomorrow, that country will be feeling the effects for 40 or 50 years. I don't even know what we can do to help them move on from this war. You can't bring sons back. We can't bring whatever peace and enjoyment they had out of life before we invaded. We just can't, and that's all there is to it.

When I joined the recruiter really touted a lot of the college benefits because it wasn't as if I was looking for some new life with the military. I knew what I wanted, and I think the recruiter understood that I wanted to use the military as a means of getting an education. He really promoted that, and introduced me to a new profession, a new career that maybe I wasn't even thinking about.

I didn't join the Army to see the world or anything like that. That wasn't an interest of mine at that point. It was mostly college, and in 1997 there really wasn't much of any type of conflict. We thought there were no indications of going to war. Our economy was good and things like that. I really didn't feel any danger with joining.

When I was 17 and even before I was deployed, I was pretty neutral on what was happening. Back in 2003 I probably would have said, "Well, let's wait and see, but let's not discredit everything that's been said for why we should invade Iraq, but let's not jump on the bandwagon and say yes right away."

That's kind of how I felt before I was deployed. I was reserving judgment on how this was all going to shake out. I wasn't sure on really what to believe in terms of what the president was saying and what others were saying. It didn't take long, a matter of months, before things started revealing themselves.

Part of me regrets being so apathetic about it and not questioning it more than I did, just because the lies seem so apparent now. And they weren't that well disguised honestly, I don't think they were. It wouldn't take that much effort to understand what was happening. Unfortunately I didn't know, but I don't think the average 17-year-old can understand the cost of war and what it does. I think most 17-year-olds think more about what it could do to *them* more than what it does to a country or to others in general.

At the hospital in Kuwait we actually treated mostly Americans and coalition. One thing that was a little off I thought was the number of contractors that we treated. It was almost ridiculous, the level of care we were giving them, especially with how much money and resources they already had. For them to drain our resources for our soldiers was a little frustrating.

They used a lot of intimidation and other tactics to get the care they wanted and to get the things they wanted from us. They basically would not take no for an answer in terms of what kind of treatment and how they handled their medical needs. I would say 40 or 50 percent of our patients were contractors. They worked for KBR (Kellogg, Brown, and Root) mostly. There were a few other companies from other countries, Australia, for instance. But I'd say the vast majority was KBR.

They weren't combat casualties, just sick, and their screening process I think is just horrible. There was a 450-pound man that was in our hospital. A military hospital is not equipped to deal with something like that. It just was ridiculous some of the people came in. An amputee came in. It was ridiculous. Their screening process, if there was one, was horrible. For that environment, it's just not right to send someone there when they have chronic medical conditions. All that's going to happen is that they are going to exacerbate it in that kind of heat. It really did put a strain on us.

It was very frustrating for everyone because we were there to treat troops, and we had no problem giving the best care we could to any soldier of any nationality. We treated Italians, Australians, El Salvadorans—just everyone. We treated soldiers from a lot of different countries. We were the only hospital in Kuwait and we treated everyone.

Most of the things we would see were a lot of occupational injuries from heavy equipment and a lot of car accidents and things like that because traffic is bad in Kuwait City. When you're driving five-ton trucks and Humvees in that traffic, a lot of bad things happen. A lot of people were in a hurry to get out of Kuwait or go and get ready and ramp up and go to Iraq. A lot of safety issues would come up. Every once in a while we'd get some friendly fire type of injury, but most of the time it was occupational hazards.

About 10 from my unit ended up going with me to Balad. Other people went to Abu Ghraib. Still others went to Baghdad. Balad was kind of the hub for evacuations and we'd get a lot of that. There was an airstrip there so that's the stop before you go to Germany. Along with combat casualties, we'd take care of a lot of evacuees. They'd come in for a few hours and wait and then get shipped out. We were pretty busy in Balad, especially in April and May when a lot of the fighting intensified. It was pretty bad for a few weeks. The base was mortared four or five times a day, which made things a little stressful. We were right near the perimeter and you could hear them whizzing right over. They would come pretty close a few times. It wasn't the safest place.

It was a totally different type of situation in terms of health care with what we were treating. It was mostly combat injuries. I thought there'd be less than there was, but it was just amazing to see how many Iraqis were being injured. And not just people fighting, but civilians just in the wrong place at the wrong time. Our beds were full of Iraqis. They had no place to go. We couldn't evac them to the hospitals because their hospitals were not equipped to handle what was wrong with them. They would come in faster than we could get them out. Our beds were full. They were full of Iraqis.

Everything you can think of would come in. Every type of injury you can think of would be there with both Americans and Iraqis. We were in tents. There were, I think five wards, two American and three Iraqi wards, and ER and everything else, four or five operating rooms, it was a pretty big hospital. I think it was, if not the biggest hospital, the second biggest hospital in Iraq.

On the average day there would be 30 or 40 Iraqis and probably 20 Americans. The Americans would be in and out pretty fast, so the American census would fluctuate throughout the day. If need be, if the situation was that bad, Americans could be in the ER and out on a plane within six hours. The evacuation was pretty efficient because we were right at an airbase.

At Abu Ghraib we treated prisoners. That was our main job. A lot of times, if they were insurgents, the hospitals in Baghdad and Balad would send them to Abu Ghraib's hospital for convalescent-type care and finishing touches on their rehab and everything, and they'd throw them in the general population of the prison.

The prison was kind of a nasty place. I ended up there right around the time of the controversy. That was part of the reason why I went there, because they were thinking about tearing down Abu Ghraib and building a new prison to kind of exorcise the demons or whatever. And the Iraqis weren't having that. A lot of them didn't really want to see it torn down because they had relatives there and they wanted to visit them. So it never happened and that kind of cut my stay at Abu Ghraib short because I was going to take down the hospital there and set up a new one somewhere else. When that fell through my mission was over.

I spent three weeks there. It wasn't a fun place at all. It was dirty. It was just what you think it would be. It was dangerous. We'd get shot at. We'd get mortared. The convoys to and from there were not safe. And the prisoners, some were bad, some were good. It was very surreal to be there after reading about it and hearing about what took place. It was a very strange time when I was there. Actually, the day before I got there Rumsfeld was there. I don't know why. Giving a pep talk or something. But I missed him.

It was actually a very big complex. It's not like a prison here. It was a huge area with four or five different complexes in it. I think there were three actual prison areas in it. The rest were living quarters and other things. From where I stayed to the hospital was about a mile walk. It was pretty much in opposite corners. It was a big square. I lived right by the wall, and there is an actual town named Abu Ghraib, just outside the wall. There were apartments over there. They'd get up on the roof of the apartment and shoot at us from there. It was in plain sight. They'd mortar us nightly. Every day we'd get attacked or something from there. They can look in from bridges and minarets. It was not a very safe place, and it was obviously a target and a place to channel a lot of frustration and anger by the Iraqis.

I can't blame them. I don't blame them for a lot of what they do. I don't think a lot of the leadership of the insurgency are good people or anything. I think they are there for the same reasons Americans are there: power, oil, and money. But I don't feel the average Iraqi is a bad person or someone that is to blame for what's happening or what they were doing. They were protecting their family. They were upset because people they knew were dying and someone was in their yard. No one wants that.

After Abu Ghraib we got orders to go home. Of course we were a little skeptical. We left Abu Ghraib and convoyed to Baghdad Airport and while we were on the bus, on the tarmac, and the plane was right there, three mortars flew right over our heads, hit the hangar right behind us, and blew it up. We weren't too happy about that because our plane was delayed for about an hour. But we got out of there and flew back to Kuwait.

We spent about two weeks in Kuwait, just kind of sitting around waiting for a flight home. We had to wait for a flight because we were no longer coming home as a unit. We came home piece by piece whenever missions were up and whenever people didn't need us anymore. We caught a ride with a bunch of other people that had the same type of experience.

We landed in New Jersey, spent a night in New Jersey, flew back to Georgia and spent about a week in demobilization, and I came home. It was actually a little disheartening the way my homecoming was just because you see a lot of these things on the news with units coming home and everyone's there to greet them and everything. That's not how it was for me. I came back alone on a plane and that was the end of it. There wasn't a lot of pomp and circumstance to it. It just really shows how they feel about the soldier and how they value each and every soldier that's been deployed, how they feel about their service. They really don't care. You're just another guy. You're just another body. When we're done with you, we'll send you home. You're not in a unit. We'll use you at our discretion, and if you don't like it, too bad. That's pretty much how it is.

That really was kind of the final straw with how I felt about this war. It really put kind of the final insult on the whole thing. I was gone for a total of 17 months, and it was long enough.

I'm still in the Reserves, inactive ready Reserves, until December 9. I'm still hoping I don't get stop-lossed or anything like that.

That will be my eight years in the Reserves and there is no obligation past that. I'm glad it'll finally be over. It's changed my life and who I am probably in ways I don't understand. It's given me a whole new look on what's important to me and what's worth fighting for. I don't feel what I served for is worth it. I don't feel what I saw was worth what we're getting out of it.

We have accomplished nothing that has improved our way of life whatsoever. It hasn't improved anyone's way of life. It's just destroyed lives and made everyone a little more unsafe.

There isn't a day that goes by that I don't think about something that happened while I was there. That has changed me. I can't go a day without thinking about it or feeling like I should do something. It's on the news every day. There's still the chance I could end up back there. There are still people I know that are there. There's still … it never ends.

It was pretty rough when I got home just because people in my unit, people I worked with for a long time, people I worked with closely, were still there. It was still dangerous. There's a lot of guilt involved with being sent home. It was very hard for the first three months to do anything or go a day without thinking about it. Almost wanting to go back because you felt bad that you're home and people you know aren't. There are people that I felt deserved to go home a lot more than I did. It's not that I was rewarded for anything. It's not that I did a better job than them.

It just makes no sense. None of it does. That's the worst part. There's no real logic to it. It's like the entire war. It's illogical. It doesn't make sense. There's no organization. You don't know why. It was hard to get past that until I knew the people I was with were home and safe. It was hard to really get past that and move on and do things that I wanted to do with my life.

My mom and dad worry about it a lot still. It upsets them to see other kids dying, other kids younger than me. I know it's hard for them to see that and think that it could have been me, it could have been anyone. I don't think it's affected our relationship at all. If anything, I value my family a lot more. I value my time with them.

A lot of times I get a lot of resentment when I see a lot of apathy and lack of caring for what's happening over there. At work or at school it upsets me because I know what people have done. I know what people have given up, and it bothers me when I don't see any concern whatsoever about what's happening, any response. It bothers me when I see that to this day. I try and do what I can at school to make people aware. I've done a few talks in a few classes about my experience. I try and promote events and other things. I discussed the *Purple Hearts* presentation a lot before it happened. I feel it's important whether it's on the news that day or not, whether you know it, whether you see it on the news or in the paper, something bad is happening over there right now. Somewhere over there something bad is happening.

The only way this is going to change is through legislation and letting our legislators know that any support of this war is unacceptable. Unfortunately what happened is that people talk about how against this war they are and then vote for the same legislators. Incumbents win well over half the time in elections. We need to do something.

The popularity of this war is so low, it just boggles the mind that it's still continuing, that there's been no progress whatsoever in trying to bring troops home. I do not understand. I don't think polls are enough. Polling people doesn't mean anything. I don't think the White House or Congress really listen to that. If they get elected, that's fine. What happens in the two years in between, no one cares. They care for eight months of their election and that's about it.

I don't know what kind of solutions there are to make a government listen to the majority of the people that are against this war. It's hard to make someone go and demonstrate against the war. If they don't want to, they're not going to.

Unfortunately, with this war there isn't a draft. It's affecting the same families again and again. People that aren't in the military don't have to worry about it. They know there's not going to be a draft. I think it's hard for a lot of people. I'm not judging them, I'm not mad at them. I think it's hard for them to really empathize when this isn't affecting everyone. In Vietnam, everyone, every family in the country, was affected through the draft. That's part of the problem, that it's the same families over and over again.

I don't want to see a draft come back but I don't think it's fair for the same people to go back three, four, five times. I can't imagine what that would do to someone. To be in a combat situation for five years is unheard of. It really is. The lasting effects aren't going to be known for years. It probably will never be known what this has cost our country and Iraq and Afghanistan. We will never know because we're not counting bodies there. We're not doing anything to help them. We're not going to do anything to help them recover from this, or this administration won't. We're going to set them up and leave them there to kill each other.

We need to make sure the president can't do what he did and go to war without the voice of everyone, and if that's through Congress, then fine. If it's through a public vote, then fine. But what he did was not what was intended through the Constitution.

I don't believe it was meant for a president to go to war without asking Congress. I don't think it was meant to allow him to do what he wants without the approval of the American people. He's continuing to do that by not bringing the troops home, or drawing down the campaign because over half the people in this country are against this war, and he's not listening.

It's a tall order to change the political system and legislation in this country. More realistic and something I like to do is make people aware of everything that's happening over there. I like to tell my experience. It helps me personally to talk about it. If I can show one person something that happened there that they weren't aware of, if they can actually see someone that was there that experienced a lot of the bad things, a lot of the physical violence and the physical human cost of this, I think that'll help.

A lot of times people just don't know, and that's not their fault. It's not anyone's fault. It's just the way it is. This isn't World War II. There aren't millions of veterans coming home.

It's not a body count like Vietnam. It is a smaller war. There's less people fighting it. And Madison isn't a military town. I think a lot of people may not be totally aware of just what is happening over there.

The best thing I can do is tell my story and tell people about my experience. If that makes one person more aware and more sensitive to what's happening, then that's my job. That's what I want. That's why I wanted to join Veterans for Peace. I want to be able to be in a veteran's organization that reflected what

I believe in, and what I value. I wanted some way to show people that war isn't the answer for the problems we're having today. It's not going to help.

It's not going to lower gas prices. It's not going to make it safer. I wanted to be able to tell the story of this war in Veterans for Peace. As far as I know, I'm the only Iraq vet in our chapter. I wanted to even educate other veterans on what's happening there. Everyone's experience is different. I wanted to hear about other's experiences, and I wanted to share mine as well.

I was aware of Veterans for Peace when I got home. I wasn't sure about how active I wanted to be right away. I gave it some time. I went to the *Purple Hearts* program and I actually joined a few days later. I knew that's what I wanted to do. A lot of what I saw reminded me, seeing Robert Acosta and everyone else in that book, just really helped me personally because I saw a lot of that.

I saw people like him come through minute after minute, and I always would ask myself what are they going to do? Who are they? How are they going to deal with this? This may be one minute for me, but their lives are changed in ways I can't imagine. It really helped to see that and put a name with the face. For everyone who can't do that, I want to be able to tell my story. It's one of the stories that came out of it, and I consider myself lucky for the way I turned out afterward, compared to many others.

CONCLUSION

David Giffey

This book was three years in the making. Or it could be said, *Long Shadows* was 70 years in the making. Seven decades, 9 wars, and a collective decision reached separately by 19 veterans who tell their stories here: No more war. Aside from a growing passion for peace, these veterans shared little until coming together as activists. Each dealt with their memories personally, painfully, and often in secret. *Long Shadows* contains stories about war as preludes to quests for peace undertaken by each narrator.

Weeks before Joey Cammarano died, he took a deep breath and told me the third and truthful version of what happened in Vietnam, the version he couldn't tell his mother.

"He never talked about it," Jean Sweet said of husband Charlie's World War II recollections after they were put down on paper. Emotions were abundant as Robert Kimbrough recalled the 94 soldiers he commanded as a 23-year-old Marine Corps platoon leader in Korea.

Most of the stories describe people being used, but not used up. As they spoke, the veterans seemed to be sifting through remnants and memories in search of a method of working against the machinery of war. A universal aspect of veteranhood is wonder and guilt at having survived. That you will find in these stories. Some of the veterans in *Long Shadows* chose work as healers, some became teachers, husbands, wives, and parents.

Jim Allen was an ophthalmologist in a veteran's hospital for 33 years. Mike Boehm's life is a conciliatory bridge to Southeast Asia. Sid Podell sees war as expiating the victors of guilt, even though they committed war crimes. Will Williams struck words used in Vietnam from his vocabulary after realizing their similarity to Jim Crow racism he endured in Mississippi. Don McKeating left abuse at home only to face abuse in the Army. Joel Garb, philosopher-veteran, became immersed in a new culture during war. Paul McMahon was bemused at the charade he was ordered to play ... pretending to be an officer to balance a weird military bureaucracy.

Many of the stories begin with references to the militaristic traditions of American families and the pressure young men felt to join the service, generation after generation. Most of Dennis McQuade's Eastside buddies went to Vietnam. Tradition also called Esty Dinur, who accepted mandatory duty in the Israeli military even though she was a feisty activist before and after. Elton Tylenda was a reluctant draftee who later counseled veterans. An astonishing story is told about the mortal impact Jeffrey Knupp's deployment to Vietnam had on his father. Keith Daniels saw his Vietnam era duty as something to get through, and founded a bar called Harmony where alternative causes have a home.

Don Kliese is a Cold War veteran. If the Cold War wasn't a war, what was it? He patrolled a border a few feet from his young East German counterparts in the shadow of nuclear arsenals on both sides. Frances Wiedenhoeft's story is contemporary and ongoing. It includes September 11, 2001. Patrick

LONG SHADOWS

Wilcox's accounts of Abu Ghraib and the destruction of Iraq ends *Long Shadows* with harsh realism.

This isn't a book with a happy ending. The word "love" isn't used often in *Long Shadows*, but there is an obvious feeling of love and concern for comrades and innocent victims missing and lost. Clarence Kailin wrote a book about his dear friend John Cookson who died in the Spanish Civil War.

The tellers of these stories about wars past and present are actively involved with the future. Clarence Kailin summed it up: "We've got to understand that war is a part of the system that we live under. New wars should not catch us by surprise. We should be ready at all times to resist as much as we can and make it uncomfortable for the war makers."

Conclusion

About the

CONTRIBUTORS

JAMES C. ALLEN, M.D., was born July 25, 1928 in Janesville, Wisconsin, and grew up in Brodhead, Wisconsin. He served in the Army Signal Corps from 1952 to 1954. He attended Milton College, Platteville State College, and graduated from Marquette Medical School in 1959. He spent his career at the University of Wisconsin Medical School's Department of Ophthalmology and Veterans Affairs Hospital from 1960 to 2000. He has two sons,

John and David. He and his wife Kathryn are retired in Madison, Wisconsin.

MIKE BOEHM is a veteran of the American war in Vietnam and project director for the Madison Friends (Quakers) humanitarian projects in Vietnam. He first returned to Vietnam in 1992 to help build a medical clinic. While there, he began to come to terms with his own experiences there and to understand the tremendous capacity of people-to-people projects for building peace and reconciliation between our two societies. Boehm has traveled to Vietnam 14 times since then to facilitate these projects.

JOSEPH CAMMARANO was born in New Jersey in 1949. He joined the Marine Corps in order to avoid the draft, but was sent to Vietnam anyway. His time in Vietnam left him with the conviction that war must stop and that young people must not be sent into these inhuman situations. As a result, he became a member of the Vietnam Veterans Against the War, Veterans for Peace, and worked on rallies and educational programs. Joey was many things in his lifetime, including a welder, an activist, an artist, a carnival worker, and a chef. His talent for cooking combined with his Italian heritage to produce an Italian cookbook/calendar. He became an early catalyst for this volume. He said that telling his story here gave him some peace. Just weeks after conducting this interview, Joey died from complications of his Vietnam service.

KEITH DANIELS was born in Burlington, Wisconsin, in 1951. He graduated from high school, attended college, and joined the U.S. Navy during the Vietnam era, serving from 1973 to 1977. He lived and worked in Wisconsin and Southern California, spending a year traveling around the world in the mid-1980s. He moved back to Wisconsin and opened the Harmony Bar & Grill in Madison in 1990.

ESTY DINUR was born and raised in Israel, where she served in the military from 1973 to 1975. She had careers in modern dance and film making and spent two years on the road in Europe and the United States. She eventually settled down in Madison, Wisconsin, where she promotes performing arts, does a weekly political call-in radio show, and writes about political, social, and environmental issues for various publications. She is the mother of two young adults.

JOEL and Susan GARB, married for 35 years, attended the 2004 national conference of Veterans for Peace in Boston. A presentation by Cynthia Enloe and a walk through Boston Commons with a convention delegate, John S., were important for Joel. He recalled Enloe's presentation about the significance of women who help enable militarization by contributing to the reproduction of masculine domination in the lives of soldiers and veterans. Garb's conversation with John S. awoke a need for a spiritual path to peace.

DAVID GIFFEY grew up on a dairy farm in Fond du Lac County, Wisconsin. He was drafted into the U.S. Army while working as wire editor of a daily newspaper, and served as a combat journalist and assistant editor with the 1st Infantry Division based at Di An in 1965 and 1966 during the war in Vietnam. For the past 40 years, he worked as an artist, journalist, and photographer. Major visual art projects include mural installations in Eastern Orthodox Christian churches, community centers, schools, and public buildings in the Upper Midwest and Greece. His publications include chronicles of the migrant farm worker labor movement and the African American community. He designed the Mourning Dove Effigy Mound at the Highground Veterans' Memorial in Wisconsin, and was present at the dedication in 1995 of Vietnamese-American Peace Park north of Hanoi, Vietnam. A member of Veterans for Peace, Giffey continues working as a journalist and artist in Arena, Wisconsin, where he lives with his wife Nancy.

CLARENCE KAILIN was born August 20, 1914, in Madison, Wisconsin. The son of a Socialist father, Clarence was a volunteer with the Abraham Lincoln Brigade fighting Fascism during the Spanish Civil War in 1937 and 1938. After being wounded in Spain, he was a lifelong peace and justice activist. He was a founder of the Socialist Potluck, a monthly political forum. His writings include *The Black Chronicle* (1974) and *Remembering*

John Cookson (translated to Spanish and published in Spain), the story of his beloved comrade killed in Spain.

ROBERT KIMBROUGH is a retired professor of English literature, having taught at the University of Wisconsin–Madison from 1959 to 1991. He is the author or editor of 12 books, plus numerous articles and book reviews. In 1976, Kimbrough began acting in local theater, and after retirement added directing and producing to his repertoire, founding his own company, Honest Puck Productions. In 1994, he fulfilled a 35-year desire by visiting Cuba, and has since returned yearly. He is occupied in various solidarity activities with Cuba. Kimbrough is a member of the Socialist Party and is an advocate for peace, justice, and labor.

DON KLIESE is a native and current resident of Wisconsin. What hope he maintains he finds resides in the nonhuman inhabitants of our battered earth who live their lives with courage and wisdom in spite of the insanity of the humans around them.

JEFFREY KNUPP was born and raised in Warren, Pennsylvania, and earned a bachelor's degree in history and theater from St. Olaf College in Northfield, Minnesota. After graduation, he served as a combat infantryman with the First Infantry Division in the Vietnam War. He moved to Madison, Wisconsin in 1970 for graduate school and has lived there since. He recently retired after 28 years of employment with the Wisconsin Department of Transportation as a supervisor and program analyst. He worked on the staff of the Madison Scouts Drum and Bugle Corps for seven years as a marching and color guard instructor. During that time, the group won numerous national and international titles. He has been a marching band visual analysis judge for over 25 years. Jeff is also a well-known professional actor and director with many theater groups in the Madison area, including the Madison Repertory Theatre, Stroller's Theatre, Edgewood College Theatre, and the University of Wisconsin Theatre. He is currently appearing in a number of radio and television commercials in the Madison area.

DON MCKEATING was born in Chicago during the post-war baby boom. His mother was an artist. His father was an Army veteran from a wealthy family. Because of his father's gambling, Don experienced periods of homelessness and hunger. His family moved 27 times by the time he was drafted in 1967. He learned early in life to stand up to injustice, to question authority, and to be self-reliant. Don thought the Army was his chance for a better life. He was assigned to a missile battalion in West Germany, but volunteered for duty in Vietnam where he served with the Americal Division, and was honorably discharged in 1969. While working his way through college in hospital security, he decided on a career in police work. Unable to successfully deal with the corruption around him, he returned to college, earned a degree in Police Science, and spent the remainder of his career as a sheriff's deputy where he helped organize a union and was a union representative. Married since 1973, he and his wife Nancy, a former postmaster, enjoy early retirement. They moved to Madison, Wisconsin, where Nancy is an artist and Don is an activist in the cause of peace and justice. He organized and was president of the Madison Chapter of Veterans for Peace. (Note: Don has intentionally not named or identified certain persons, places, government agencies, because of privacy concerns.)

PAUL MCMAHON was born in Kingston-on-Thames, England in late 1945. His father, an American soldier stationed near London, met and married an English woman in 1943. In early 1946, his mother immigrated to the United States arriving in Doylestown, Wisconsin, with two small boys in tow. Later, two brothers and a sister were born in Wisconsin. All four boys eventually served in the military, including two in Vietnam. Always proud of his foreign birth and often feeling he was more English than American, McMahon grew up in a small Wisconsin village. His blue-collar, Irish–English parents imbued him with a firmly Roman Catholic outlook. Encouraged to be a scholar, he would have preferred a life of baseball, but no signing bonus was offered. Educated at UW–Platteville, he earned a full graduate fellowship to Georgetown University. Studies in international relations were interrupted when he was drafted in 1968. Enlisting in the Army, he was schooled in intelligence in Baltimore, Maryland, and the Vietnamese language in El Paso, Texas. His final military year was spent in and around Quang Tri, Vietnam, just south of the demilitarized zone. In 1995 he returned to Vietnam with a small group of veterans to dedicate a Peace Park near Hanoi. He lives in Madison with his wife of 36 years, Nancy, a teacher. He has three children and two grandchildren. He regrets not being able to speak Vietnamese, but still occasionally dreams of playing professional baseball.

DENNIS MCQUADE is a lifelong resident of Madison, Wisconsin. He was drafted into the Army in December of 1965, and was an infantryman in Vietnam from September 1966 to September 1967. After Vietnam, he received his bachelor's and master's degrees in social work from UW–Madison. He worked as an advisor to special students at UW–Madison and for the Dane County Department of Human Services as a residential living advocate and social worker for 26 years.

McQuade established the Dane County Elder Abuse Program and was a social worker in the field of child abuse. He is a community social worker for the Joining Forces for Families Program on the northeast side of Madison. Dennis was involved in the civil rights movement in Mississippi, Vets for Peace in Vietnam, and Vietnam Veterans Against the War (VVAW), as well as the Madison Newspaper strike in the 1970s. He was active in Community Action of Latin America, VVAW, and Medical Aid to Central America in the 1980s. Dennis is married to Carol McQuade, a nurse practitioner with the Madison Metropolitan School District. They have two children, Roberto, a freshman at UW–Madison, and Miguel, a senior at Madison East High School.

SIDNEY PODELL was born in Milwaukee in 1920, and his family struggled to survive the Great Depression. He attended the University of Wisconsin–Madison as a sociology major from 1938 to 1942. After military service during World War II, he returned to graduate with a law degree in 1949. Podell retired in 1983 after practicing as a self-employed attorney in Milwaukee. Now living in Madison, he owns and restored buildings on a nearby farm where he raises organic vegetables, plants trees, and cares for 60 acres of land in a Conservation Reserve Program. Sid and Mary have two children and two granddaughters.

CHARLES W. SWEET was born July 12, 1923 at home in rural southern Michigan. He attended country school through eighth grade and graduated from Adrian High School, Adrian, Michigan, in June of 1941. After attending Michigan State College, he enlisted in the Army and was called to active duty December 12, 1942. He was trained in conversational German at the University of Wisconsin's army specialized training after completing military basic training. Sweet then went to Military Intelligence Training at Camp Ritchie, Maryland, to be a prisoner of war interrogator—after which he was sent to New Guinea, then to the Philippines and the Battle of Leyte, and later to Okinawa from the invasion April 1, 1945 until September 18, 1945. After deployment to South Korea in the Army of Occupation, he was discharged at Camp McCoy, Wisconsin, on April 3, 1946. He married Jean M. Holzschuh on May 26, 1946 in Plymouth, Wisconsin, and enrolled at the University of Wisconsin–Madison, on the G.I. Bill. Sweet graduated in 1948 with a bachelor's degree in accounting, and worked for the State of Wisconsin Department of Agriculture as fiscal officer until retiring in 1988. The Sweets have two children, daughter Debra and son Jeffrey, and two grandchildren.

ELTON TYLENDA lives in Madison, Wisconsin, where he speaks and writes on issues of peace. His articles and presentations challenge beliefs and myths, both religious and secular, that unwittingly promote war and violence. He holds a Master of Divinity degree from Chicago Theological Seminary and a bachelor's degree in psychology and philosophy from Eastern Connecticut State University. Tylenda has developed a course titled "Embracing Sophia: The Pathway to Inner Disarmament and Real Peace," which presents the peacemaker's perspective common to all wisdom traditions.

FRANCES WIEDENHOEFT has enjoyed a 22-year nursing career, the last 12 years as a nurse anesthetist. Sixteen of those years have been spent in the Army Reserve, with whom she was deployed in Desert Storm and Afghanistan. When not called to active duty, she lives, works, enjoys her family, and is active in community affairs in Madison, Wisconsin.

PATRICK WILCOX is 25 years old and lives in the Madison area. He attends Edgewood College in the nursing program. He recently joined the board of directors of the Madison area chapter of Veterans for Peace. Patrick also works at a Madison area hospital. He is no longer in the Army Reserves, and stays in contact with some of those he was deployed with. Since being home, he has been attending school and visiting schools to educate others of his experience.

WILL WILLIAMS lives along U.S. Highway 51 in Wisconsin, 850 miles north of his birthplace along U.S. Highway 51 in Mississippi. A longtime union member, he worked as a miner, truck driver, mail carrier, Greyhound bus driver, Veterans Administration hospital employee, and counselor for juveniles in the Department of Corrections for the State of Illinois. Will and Dot have been married for 40 years. They are parents of a daughter and have four grandchildren and nine great grandchildren.